S0-CFI-394

OPENING DAY

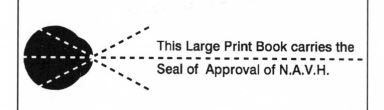

This Large Print Book carries the
Seal of Approval of N.A.V.H.

OPENING DAY

THE STORY OF JACKIE ROBINSON'S FIRST SEASON

JONATHAN EIG

THORNDIKE PRESS
An imprint of Thomson Gale, a part of The Thomson Corporation

THOMSON

GALE

Detroit • New York • San Francisco • New Haven, Conn. • Waterville, Maine • London

THOMSON
™
GALE

LIBRARY OF CONGRESS CATALOGING-IN-PUBLICATION DATA

Eig, Jonathan.
    Opening day : the story of Jackie Robinson's first season / by Jonathan Eig. — Large print ed.
        p. cm.
    Includes bibliographical references.
    ISBN-13: 978-0-7862-9674-3 (hardcover : alk. paper)
    ISBN-10: 0-7862-9674-7 (hardcover : alk. paper)
    1. Robinson, Jackie, 1919–1972. 2. Baseball players — United States — Biography. 3. African American baseball players — Biography. 4. Baseball — United States — History. 5. Discrimination in sports — United States. 6. Large type books. I. Title.
GV865.R6E35 2007
796.357092—dc22
[B]   2007014109

Published in 2007 by arrangement with Simon & Schuster, Inc.

Printed in the United States of America on permanent paper
10 9 8 7 6 5 4 3 2 1

For my parents, Phyllis and David Eig

Be the change you want to see
in the world.
— Mohandas Gandhi

A life is not important except in the impact
it has on other lives.
— Jackie Robinson

CONTENTS

9

PROLOGUE

April 10, 1947

The telephone rang like an alarm, waking Jackie Robinson from deep sleep.

"Hello," he mumbled.

It was early morning in Manhattan. Robinson was alone in room 1169 of the McAlpin Hotel, across the street from Macy's. He had been on edge all week, his stomach in knots. As he listened to the voice on the other end of the phone, he was poised to embark on a journey — one that would test his courage, shake the game of baseball to its roots, and forever change the face of the nation. Throughout history, heroic quests have often been launched on grand orders. "The object of your mission is to explore the Missouri River . . . ," wrote Thomas Jefferson to Meriwether Lewis. "The free men of the world are marching together to Victory!" General Dwight David Eisenhower exhorted his troops before the D-Day inva-

11

sion. But the commanding words that sent Robinson on his way this cool, gray morning were uttered by a humble secretary.

Come to Brooklyn, she said.

He showered and shaved and hurried out of the hotel. He was on his way to meet Branch Rickey, president and part owner of the Brooklyn Dodgers, and to learn whether Rickey was ready to end the segregation of the races in big-league baseball.

In 1947, some southern states still denied the vote to black Americans. Black children were not entitled to attend the same schools as white children. Lynch mobs executed their own bloodthirsty style of justice while local law enforcement officials looked the other way. "I'm sorry, but they done got him," one sheriff in North Carolina announced that year after a gang of white men made off with one of his prisoners. Black Americans were excluded not only from certain schools but also from parks, beaches, playgrounds, department stores, night clubs, swimming pools, roller-skating rinks, theaters, rest rooms, barber shops, railroad cars, bus seats, military units, libraries, factory floors, and hospitals. In the North, WHITES ONLY signs were far less evident than in the South, but the veiled message was often the same. Black men on business

12

in Chicago, Detroit, or Cleveland usually stayed in black-owned hotels, rode in black-owned taxis, and dined in black-owned restaurants. If a white man became acquainted with a black man, odds were good that the acquaintance stemmed from some service the black man performed for the white man — shining his shoes, for example, or mowing his lawn, or mixing his cocktails.

Segregation suffused the nation's culture, and yet profound changes were rippling across the country. Black workers moved from South to North in great waves, reshaping urban spaces and lending new muscle to organized labor. Black soldiers coming home from the war declared they would no longer tolerate second-class citizenship. Federal judges commanded southern states to stop obstructing the black vote. President Truman signed an order to end segregation in the military. And in major-league baseball, where there were sixteen teams and every player on every one of those teams was white, a single black man was presented an opportunity to change the equation: to make it one black man and 399 white.

The test case represented by Jackie Robinson was one of towering importance to the country. Here was a chance for one person to prove the bigots and white supremacists wrong, and to say to the nation's fourteen million black Americans that the time had come for them to compete as equals. But it would happen only if a long list of "ifs" worked out just so: *if* the Brooklyn Dodgers gave Robinson the opportunity to play; *if* he played well; *if* he won the acceptance of teammates and fans; *if* no race riots erupted; *if* no one put a bullet through his head. The "ifs" alone were enough to agitate a man's stomach. Then came the matter of Robinson himself. He perceived racism in every glare, every murmur, every called third strike. He was not the most talented black ballplayer in the country. He had a weak throwing arm and a creaky ankle. He had only one year of experience in the minor leagues, and, at twenty-eight, he was a little bit old for a first-year player. But he loved a fight. His greatest assets were tenacity and a knack for getting under an opponent's skin. He would slash a line drive to left field, run pigeon-toed down the line, take a big turn at first base, slam on the brakes, and skitter back to the bag. Then, as the pitcher prepared to go to work on the next batter, Robinson would take his lead from first base, bouncing on tiptoes like a dropped rubber ball, bouncing, bouncing, bouncing, taunting the pitcher, and daring everyone in

14

the park to guess when he would take off running again. While other men made it a point to avoid danger on the base paths, Robinson put himself in harm's way every chance he got. His speed and guile broke down the game's natural order and left opponents cursing and hurling their gloves. When chaos erupted, that's when he knew he was at his best.

On that April 10 morning, as he rode the subway from Manhattan to Brooklyn, Robinson understood exactly what he was getting into. One prominent black journalist had written that the ballplayer had more power than Congress to help break the chains that bound the descendants of slavery to lives lived in inequity and despair. Before he'd even swung a bat in the big leagues, Robinson was being compared to Frederick Douglass, George Washington Carver, and Joe Louis, with some writers concluding that this man would do more for his people than any of the others. The time had come, they said, for black Americans to stake their claim to the justice and equal rights they so richly deserved, and now a baseball player had arrived to show them the way. Robinson absorbed the newspaper articles. He felt the weight on his shoulders and decided there was nothing to do but carry it as fast

15

and as far as he could.

A cold wind met him as he climbed out of the subway onto the busy streets of Brooklyn. He walked to 215 Montague Street. Waiting for him there was Branch Rickey, a potato-shaped man in a wrinkled suit. The office was dark and cluttered. Rickey got straight to business, offering Robinson a standard contract for five-thousand dollars, the league's minimum annual salary.

"Simple, wasn't it?" Robinson recalled later. "It could have happened to you. The telephone rings. You answer it . . . and you're in the Big Leagues. . . . Just like a fairy tale. . . . I went to bed one night wearing pajamas and woke up wearing a Brooklyn Dodgers' uniform."

He knew it was no fairy tale, of course. He knew that a happy ending was far from assured. Most big-leaguers in 1947 had never been on the same field as a black man, had never shared a locker room, a shower, a taxi, a train car, or a dining-room table with one. Big-league culture was so thoroughly dominated by white southerners that even rough Italian kids from northern cities experienced shock and isolation upon arrival. There was no telling how Robinson would be received. He was not yet a member of the Brooklyn Dodgers, and already half a

16

dozen or more of his prospective teammates promised they would quit or demand a trade before they would play with him. Elsewhere, players spoke of a league-wide strike. They were willing to destroy the game they loved rather than see it stained by integration. Others said it would be simpler to take Robinson out with a well-aimed fastball to the head, or with a set of metal cleats driven through his Achilles tendon on a close play at first base — something that would look like an accident.

Rickey made only one demand of Robinson. He asked the ballplayer to promise that he would never respond to the racist attacks that would surely come his way. When Rickey quoted a passage from Giovanni Papini's *Life of Christ* — "But whosoever shall smite thee on thy right cheek, turn to him the other also" — Robinson sought clarification. Did Rickey want a player who didn't have the guts to fight back? No, the boss answered, "I want a ballplayer with guts enough *not* to fight back."

Rickey turned and walked away while Robinson thought about it for a moment. Though the request would require Robinson to subdue his most basic instincts, and though he had no idea, honestly, whether he could compete without an outlet for his

17

seething sense of indignation, he said he would try. With that, the season's storyline was set.

Robinson became baseball's biggest attraction in 1947. According to one survey, he was the second most famous man in America, trailing only Bing Crosby. Americans yearned for a sense of normalcy in the aftermath of the war, yet everything around them was in flux. Robinson, a human whirlwind, captured the spirit of the time better than anyone. When the Dodgers went on the road, thousands of black men and women traveled great distances to get a glimpse of him, as if to see for themselves that he was real, to share his dignity and glory, to watch this proud, defiant man, the grandson of slaves, stake a claim on their behalf to what Langston Hughes called "the dream deferred." Railroad companies scheduled special runs. Black parents named their children, boys and girls, after him. White kids from small towns in the Midwest sat surrounded by black men and women at the ballpark and wondered why their parents seemed anxious. Jewish families in Brooklyn gathered around their dining-room tables for Passover Seders and discussed what Moses had in common with a fleet-footed, right-hand-hitting infielder with the number

42 on his back. White business owners integrated their factory floors and wrote to Robinson to thank him for opening their eyes. Young ballplayers of every color imitated his style, wiping their hands on their trousers between pitches, swinging with arms outstretched, and running helter-skelter around makeshift bases.

Jackie Robinson showed that talent mattered more than skin color, supplying a blueprint for the integration of a nation. He led the Dodgers to the greatest season the team's fans had yet seen, to a World Series showdown with the New York Yankees, the outcome in doubt until the final inning of the seventh and final game.

But it was something else, something more personal, that captured the American imagination that summer.

It was the story of a man filled with fear and fury. It was Jackie Robinson, all alone, taking his lead from the base, bouncing, bouncing, bouncing . . . and a nation waiting to see what he would do next.

ONE:
JACK ROOSEVELT ROBINSON

His name was Jack Roosevelt Robinson, not Jackie. Mallie Robinson, his mother, chose the middle name in honor of former president Theodore Roosevelt, who had died a few weeks before her son's birth. "Speak softly and carry a big stick," Roosevelt had said. "You will go far." Mallie Robinson had no big stick. All she had was a sixth-grade education, a powerful faith in God, and a sense of determination that bordered on mulishness. She didn't expect to go very far, but she believed strongly that her children would.

Jack, the youngest of five, was born January 31, 1919. He lived with his family in a ramshackle cottage near the town of Cairo, Georgia, not far from the Florida state line. Jack's father, Jerry, could neither read nor write. He knew how to farm, but he preferred not to. Fortunately for the Robinsons, Mallie was big-boned, strong, and not one to back down from a challenge. It was Mallie who raised the children, Mallie who worked the soil, and Mallie who negotiated with the plantation owner for a share of the crop instead of straight wages. "You're about the sassiest nigger woman ever on this place," the plantation owner once told her. She took that as a compliment.

Yet for all her sass and strength, Mallie couldn't overcome the crushing poverty that afflicted so many black families in the Deep South. Nor could she control her husband, who wouldn't work, wouldn't stay home, and wouldn't confine his loving to one woman. "I always lived so close to God [that] He would tell me things," Mallie once said. So when God told her to take the children and get away, she did just that, ignoring Jerry's attempts to convince her that it was the devil talking to her. She packed her things, herded the kids out the door, and caught a train heading west. Jack was sixteen months old.

It was an enormous gamble — truly an act of faith. She had little money and no plan. All she had, really, was a half brother in Pasadena who had bragged to her once, "If you want to get closer to heaven, visit California." Whether it was closer to heaven or not, Mallie figured it couldn't be worse than Georgia, where an impudent black woman might get strung from a tree if she wasn't careful.

She and her children arrived in Los Angeles by night, the city lights aglow, brighter and more beautiful than anything she had ever seen. In almost no time she found a job working as a maid in a wealthy white man's household. When the boss sent her home at four in the afternoon, she didn't know what to do. In Georgia, plantation work had been her mornings, afternoons, and nights. To quit so early seemed unnatural. So she found jobs cooking and cleaning in other homes to fill her hours and her cupboard. She worked so much in those first few years that her children seldom saw her. "She was hands caressing us or a voice in our sleep," her youngest son recalled. It was a voice that would speak to him for years to come.

Pasadena in the 1920s was one of the richest small cities in the United States. It was a winter getaway for tourists, a place of wealth and culture and fine architecture, a boom town with little reason to fear a bust. The Robinsons arrived at an opportune moment, as the rich got richer and the poor got jobs. Pasadena had a few working-class

23

neighborhoods, but nothing that qualified as a ghetto. By 1922, to the astonishment and dismay of her white neighbors, Mallie and her relatives saved enough money to buy two small houses that occupied a single plot of land at 121 Pepper Street, a predominantly white block in a working-class part of town. One exasperated Pepper Street homeowner called the police whenever the Robinson children ran or roller-skated past his house, explaining that his wife was afraid of Negroes, using the polite term of the day. Others drew up a petition to get rid of the new family. By 1930, the U.S. Census showed ten people crammed into Mallie's little house — six children and four adults — a condition that probably didn't help win friends among the neighbors. Not for a minute did the family feel welcome.

Mallie, a devout Methodist, fought back with kindness. She performed chores at no charge for the richest white woman on their block, hoping to gain her loyalty and affection. She never quit trying and she never made much real progress, a fact not lost on her youngest son, who had plenty of his mother's strength but little of her patience. That same year, 1922, the city of Pasadena built the Rose Bowl. It was of no small importance that Jack lived in a town enam-

24

ored of sports, where blacks and whites often competed on the same ball fields, and where the weather let children play outdoors twelve months of the year. Jack's schools were filled mostly with white students. In Pasadena, a black person never forgot he was part of a minority group and that the group was treated far differently from the majority. Jack saw movies seated in segregated balconies, swam in city-owned pools only on Tuesdays, and gained entry to the local YMCA only one night a week. Such humiliations taught many black boys and girls to expect little from the world, but Mallie's children were different. They grew up surrounded by wealth and privilege and, while they were not naive enough to expect equality, they were at least encouraged to fight for whatever they could get.

As a boy, Jack was quick-witted and quick to anger. When he was eight years old, a white girl on his block taunted him one day with cries of "Nigger! Nigger! Nigger!" He responded by calling her a cracker. Soon the girl's father stormed out of the house and started shouting. Before long, the boy and the grown man were hurling rocks at each other. Mallie Robinson never said who threw the first stone, but she did remark

25

that her son had the better aim.

Mallie always bragged that she instilled in her young Jack a sense of racial pride. She claimed no responsibility for her boy's rage, however. While Mallie never bowed to white people, she seldom lost her temper. Perhaps Jack was angry because he grew up without a father in a home in which everyone tried to pretend the old man had never existed. Perhaps the rage sprouted from the rich soil of Pasadena, where he was removed from the overt racism of the South but still surrounded by razor-sharp inequities. There were no lynchings, no police roundups, no Ku Klux Klan rallies in his world. Here in Southern California, he had just enough opportunity and just enough freedom to flash his anger without fear of severe reprisal. He was smart, loquacious, and supremely confident, with a competitive streak as wide as a Pacific sunset. A white boy with such qualities might have been marked by his teachers as a future leader, but Jack's instructors in grade school did little to encourage his ambition. He didn't seem to care much about his grades, and he ran with a troublemaking group called the Pepper Street Gang. He treated school the way a cab driver treats traffic, as something to be endured, and not without seeking shortcuts.

26

His teachers recommended a career in gardening. Years later, Mallie said she had the feeling that Jack never forgave the people of Pasadena.

Even in his youth, Robinson was smart enough to notice that the jobs available to him as a boy — shining shoes and selling newspapers, to name but a couple — were not much worse than the jobs held by many black adults. Yet when he played sports, magical things happened. White kids wanted him on their teams. Coaches gushed. Teachers paid attention.

Games provided the closest thing to equal opportunity he had found in his young life. So he played as if sports were the whole world, a world more fair and open-minded than the one in which those who lacked his grace, speed, and strength lived. "If I was good enough, I played," he once said. "If not, I had to give way to some other kid."

As if to prove his theory of the superiority of the sporting universe, he watched the career of his older brother Mack, a track and field star whose swift feet and powerful legs earned him a scholarship to the University of Oregon. In 1936, when Jack was seventeen, Mack competed in the two-hundred-meter dash at the Berlin Olympics and finished second to Jesse Owens. Black

27

Americans became heroes back home for running over Hitler's notions of Aryan supremacy. Jack heard the cheers. He saw the silver medal his brother brought back. Yet while many of the white members of the Olympic track team went on to careers as coaches and teachers and radio broadcasters, Jesse Owens, the biggest hero of them all, found himself racing against horses at county fairs and minor-league baseball parks, one small step removed from a circus act. Mack settled for work as a street sweeper on the night shift. In what was an act of either remarkable provocation or extreme self-pity, Mack wore his Olympic jacket while he swept trash.

The lesson was as clear to little brother as the "USA" on Mack's jacket: Sports were a great equalizer, but games could only do so much. When the competition ended, the universe reverted to its original form. The only thing to do was keep playing.

He remained Jack, not Jackie, at John Muir Technical High School. "Dusky Jack Robinson," the *Los Angeles Times* called him, the adjective serving as a signal to readers who might not have been aware of his race. From Muir Tech, he went on to Pasadena Junior College, where he achieved a small measure of celebrity as an outstanding football player, and where newspaper writers began referring to him as Jackie. At about this time, he also came under the influence of the Reverend Karl Downs, a young and energetic pastor from Scott's Chapel Church, who persuaded Robinson to quit the Pepper Street Gang and start teaching Sunday school.

In 1939, Robinson stepped up to the University of California at Los Angeles. It was here, starting at halfback for one of the nation's best college football teams, that he emerged as a full-blown star. "All Jackie did at Pasadena," wrote the *Los Angeles Times,* in welcoming him to UCLA, "was throw with ease and accuracy, punt efficiently and run with that ball like it was a watermelon and the guy who owned it was after him with a shotgun." All he did at UCLA from that moment on was play baseball, basketball, and football, compete in the long jump and broad jump with the track team, and dabble a bit in tennis. No matter the game, his reputation as a ferocious competitor preceded. "I was aggressive . . ." Robinson recalled years later. "Often I found myself being singled out by the other players. . . . I enjoyed having that kind of reputation."

Robinson on the run looked like a funnel

cloud. If you were an infielder watching him spin your way, or a linebacker contemplating a tackle, or a basketball player trying to keep him from the hoop, you could never tell which direction he would go or when he might hit. You only knew there would be damage. He was big, just under six feet tall and a bit less than two hundred pounds, solid from head to toe, yet with the agility of a much smaller man. He ran with his toes pointed slightly inward, and with his arms lashing wildly, so that even when he was moving in a straight line he appeared to be going this way and that. But it wasn't his size, his speed, or his agility that impressed people most. It wasn't the blue-black darkness of his skin. Nor was it his high-pitched voice. The thing that struck people most strongly was something subtle, something that became obvious only after they'd come to know him. It was the fire. It seemed to burn constantly, just below the surface. It fueled his competitive spirit even as it threatened at times to undermine his accomplishments.

At UCLA, as in Pasadena, Robinson enjoyed a relatively friendly environment. Racism was unavoidable, but it was much more subtle than in the South. It was the kind of racism white people often failed to

30

notice, which no doubt made it all the more hurtful at times to men like Robinson. The university had no black professors. Black students could not live in the village of Westwood. Nor could they work in the college bookstore. But UCLA, eager to compete athletically with powerhouse schools such as Oregon, Stanford, and USC, had nonetheless decided to bring more black students to campus. That left Robinson surrounded by a student body that was for the most part happy to have him around. On the football team, he was joined by the great halfback Kenny Washington and the gifted receiver Woody Strode, both of whom were black. The press called them "The Gold Dust Trio." Robinson became famous, not just in Southern California, but nationwide, with a reputation as one of the country's finest all-around athletes. He never acquired a nickname at UCLA. Every so often a reporter would label him "the Brown Comet," "the Black Meteor," or "the Sepia Flash," but none of the names stayed with him.

As a part of the Gold Dust Trio, his life at times did seem to be dusted in gold. He was living in Southern California, cooled by the sweet Pacific breeze. When he got into a jam with the police (not for the first time), a jam Robinson attributed (not for the first time) to the bigotry of a white police officer, there were powerful people at UCLA on hand to extricate him. Still, to his friends and teammates, he seemed easily and often perturbed. Strode recalled Robinson as a loner with "steely hard eyes that would flash angry in a heartbeat." He was not the sort of athlete who performed with a smile on his face, whose physical ease went hand-in-hand with emotional delight at play. No one would ever compare him to Babe Ruth or Satchel Paige, or Willie Mays, or any of the other great athletes who retained their child-like joy into adulthood. If he did experience pure pleasure at play, he seemed determined to make sure no one saw it.

Late in the summer of 1940, when he met a young woman named Rachel Isum, Robinson showed signs of mellowing ever so slightly. Rachel was tall and beautiful, and looked taller and more beautiful for the way she carried herself. She was just seventeen, slender and serene, with soft brown curls stacked cloudlike atop her head. She studied nursing at UCLA and took her school work seriously. She took most things seriously. Like Jack, she neither drank nor smoked. When her father became too sick to work, her mother found a position as a caterer,

32

and Rachel took on two jobs: assistant to the caterer and nurse to her father. She had developed excellent skills for taking care of a family but had not yet abandoned hope of becoming a doctor or a nurse. The first time she saw Jackie Robinson on campus, she was intrigued. She admired his preference for crisp white shirts, which accentuated the dark hue of his skin. She took the fashion choice as a token of his pride. He seemed confident, strong, and yet very shy, with a smile that made her melt. While the campus knew him as Jackie, she preferred to call him Jack. He called her Rae.

On their first date, Rachel and Jack went to the UCLA homecoming dance at the Biltmore, one of the ritziest hotels in Los Angeles. She wore a new black dress and a matching black hat with fox trim. He wore a blue suit, the only one he owned. The orchestra played "Stardust" and "Mood Indigo." They danced awkwardly. At the end of the evening, he gave her a disappointing peck on the cheek and said goodnight. Both said later that they knew right away they were destined to be married. Robinson played only two years at UCLA, using up his football eligibility. By the end of his second season he was falling behind on class work, and none too upset about it. He stuck

33

around for one more basketball season and then dropped out.

Suddenly, the future seemed unclear. There were no black players in the National Football League, and none in the National Basketball League, either, or his path would have been more obvious. Instead, he went to work as an assistant athletic director at the National Youth Administration, a Depression-era job-training agency on the campus of the California Polytechnic Institute, making $150 a month. He was still living with his mother and still contemplating marriage in December 1941 when the Japanese bombed Pearl Harbor and President Roosevelt called the nation to war. His draft notice arrived a few months later.

Late one night, on July 6, 1944, Lieutenant Jack Roosevelt Robinson stepped aboard a bus at Camp Hood, the army base in Texas where he was stationed. He took a seat in the middle of the bus as it bounced toward the nearby town of Temple. He was twenty-five years old, with a bum ankle that was threatening to keep him from shipping out to Europe with the rest of his battalion.

Robinson had quickly established a reputation as a hothead at Camp Hood. As a morale officer, he often heard complaints

34

from black soldiers, and he rarely hesitated to take those complaints to his white superiors. When some of his peers complained that there were not enough seats for black soldiers in the post exchange, where they went for snacks, Robinson telephoned the provost marshal to bring the issue to his attention. The provost marshal, not alerted by the sound of Robinson's voice that he was black, asked how the lieutenant would feel if his own wife wound up "sitting next to a nigger." With that, Robinson blew. "Pure rage took over," he recalled. "I was shouting at the top of my voice. Every typewriter in headquarters stopped." The provost marshal hung up. Another time, when a captain refused to let him play on the Camp Riley baseball team, Robinson and the captain argued. The captain threatened to beat Robinson with a baseball bat. Robinson stepped in close and urged the captain to repeat his threat. "What did you say you were going to do?" he asked. Just then a colonel got between the men and forced them to separate.

But it was the incident on the bus that nearly ruined him.

The bus had gone only five or six blocks when the driver looked in the rearview mirror and spotted Robinson talking to a light-skinned black woman. The driver, mistaking the woman for white, stopped, got up, and ordered the lieutenant to take a seat in the rear. "I didn't even stop talking," Robinson recalled in *I Never Had It Made,* one of his autobiographies, "didn't even look at him. . . . I had no intention of being intimidated into moving to the back of the bus."

Robinson knew there was considerable risk in provoking a white man, even a lower-ranking one. Throughout the war, black soldiers had been beaten and killed for less. In some cases, the mere sight of a black man in uniform had been enough to inspire brutal attacks. The sense among many whites, particularly in the South, was that black men serving in the military were beginning to think too much of themselves. Later, Rosa Parks would take the same stand as Robinson, refusing to move to the back of a bus in Montgomery, Alabama. Her brave decision touched off widespread protest and earned her a place in history as the so-called mother of the civil rights movement. Robinson's ride came eleven years earlier. It inspired few news stories, and no protests or marches.

The bus driver shouted at Robinson. At some point he used the word "nigger," which sent Robinson into a rage.

The driver warned that Robinson would be in trouble if he didn't shut up and obey.

Robinson said he didn't care, that he'd been in trouble his whole life.

"I walked up and put my finger right in his face," Robinson recalled. "I figured the best thing to do was not to shrink in a case like this, but get more bold, you know?" This was becoming a recurring theme in his life. "I put my finger right in his face and told him to leave me alone — that I didn't want to be bothered with him and I was sick and tired of being pestered."

The driver went for help. Soon a couple of military police officers arrived and took Robinson to meet their captain. In the meeting, Robinson not only complained about the bus driver but went a step further, accusing his interrogator of being a racist. "Captain, tell me," Robinson said, seeking to provoke, "where are you from anyway?" Now it was the captain's turn to get angry. Robinson soon found himself under arrest.

At the military trial, he took the stand in his own defense, and while he admitted using obscenity in his argument with the driver, he justified his behavior. He told the jury about his grandmother, Edna Sims McGriff, his mother's mother, who had been born a slave in Georgia in 1858 and who had come to live with Mallie and the kids in Pasadena in the 1920s, a reminder of his family's bitter legacy right under his roof. He discussed the definition of the word nigger, and how it felt to be called by the name: "I looked it up once, but my grandmother gave me a good definition, she was a slave, and she said the definition was a low, uncouth person, and pertains to the negroid or negro. . . . I objected to being called a nigger by this private or by anybody else. . . . I told the captain, I said, '. . . I do not consider myself a nigger at all. I am a Negro, but not a nigger.' "

Robinson's lawyers presented character witnesses, and then wrapped up their defense by arguing their client had been accused not because he'd committed any real crime but because a group of white men didn't like getting lip from an "uppity" black man. After a four-hour trial, he was found not guilty of all charges.

So it always seemed to go for Robinson, as he dashed in and out of trouble. Later in life, he would establish a reputation as the most cunning base-runner in the major leagues. For almost all other ballplayers, getting caught in a rundown on the base paths was considered a grave error, and an almost certain out. For Robinson, it was often an opportunity. Sometimes after a hit, he would pretend to have taken too big a turn off first base, hoping to draw a throw. And then, when the toss came in behind him, he would bolt for second. It was remarkable how often he fooled opponents. It was as if it had never occurred to the outfielders that he might outsmart them. Like the black men and women who sang the blues, he made an art form out of hardship and trouble.

After the army, it was time for Robinson to decide what he intended to do with his life. A job offer came from his former pastor, Karl Downs, who had moved from Pasadena to Austin, Texas, and now served as president of Samuel Houston College. Downs recruited Robinson to teach physical education and coach basketball at the all-black school. Not surprisingly, Robinson proved a tough coach, punishing players who missed practices or skipped classes. He grew frustrated at times, though, because his players were neither as determined nor as talented as he. In exhibition games, when his team fell behind, he would insert himself in the lineup, teaching his young athletes the absolute wrong lesson: that it was winning that mattered more than how you played the game. "He liked to play around the basket, rebounding and all that. He was tough around the basket," said Harold "Pea Vine" Adanandus, who was then the team's trainer. "He was just an exceptional athlete, and you could tell he still wanted to play."

Before the season's end, Robinson got a job offer from the Kansas City Monarchs, one of the top teams in baseball's Negro leagues. He considered himself a mere dabbler in baseball, and not even much of a fan. If he'd collected baseball cards as a kid, he never mentioned it. Still, he longed for real competition, and he knew he lacked the patience for coaching. The Monarchs were one of the most successful squads on the Negro baseball circuit, and their offer of four hundred dollars a month in salary looked much better than any of his other options. Yet he soon came to despise his first foray into professional baseball. A "pretty miserable way to make a buck," he called it. For a perfectionist such as Robinson, the Negro leagues were torture. Sometimes the ballplayers were permitted only on the diamonds and not in the locker rooms, because the white men who controlled the facilities didn't want their showers used by black men. Sometimes there were no hotels willing to take them, sometimes no restaurants. The men considered themselves lucky if they were permitted to go in through the back door of a putrid roadside rest stop, pay for some hamburgers, and walk back to the bus with grease-stained brown bags in hand. Every day offered new lessons in humiliation. Most of the Monarchs were accustomed to the indignities, but Robinson would never get used to them.

"We . . . pulled up in service stations in Mississippi where drinking fountains said black and white, and a couple of times we had to leave without our change, he'd get so mad," teammate Othello Renfroe recalled of Robinson. Once, when the white owner of a gas station refused to let the men use the rest room, Robinson ordered the driver of the team bus to stop filling the bus's enormous twin tanks. They'd buy their gas elsewhere, he announced. The station's owner relented. The Monarchs had faced similar indignities in their travels, but never had one of them responded so forcefully.

Even the ballgames frustrated Robinson. The action was sloppy. Some games were never completed. If teams were in a rush to get back on the road, they might knock off after six or seven innings. The Monarchs played hard at times, but only at times.

Robinson fit in like a schoolmarm in a brothel.

The Negro leagues were not exactly a business juggernaut, but they were mostly profitable in the years after the war, one of the few black-owned and black-operated institutions with national recognition and a widespread support. The best-known black player in the country was Leroy "Satchel" Paige, one of Robinson's teammates, and a celebrity of the brightest wattage. Paige, long-legged and long-armed, spoke as cunningly as he threw. He bragged that his aim was so precise that he could "nip frosting off a cake with my fastball." But he had much more than a fastball. "I use my single windup, my double windup, my triple windup, my hesitation windup, my no windup," he once said. "I also use my step-'n-pitch-it, my submariner, my sidearmer, and my bat dodger. Man's got to do what he's got to do." Which might well have become the motto for Negro-league baseball. Paige and the slugger Josh Gibson were the two greatest black ballplayers in the country. Either one of them could have been a star in the major leagues. Paige had proved on the barnstorming circuit that his pitches worked as effectively on white hitters as they did on black, but he still doubted the major

42

leagues would give him a chance. Even if they did, he was fond of saying, they would never pay him anywhere near what he made in the Negro baseball business.

In one interview, Paige blasted black journalists for pushing integration, warning that it would only bring trouble. "You keep on blowing off about getting us players in the league without thinking about our end of it . . . ," he said, "without thinking how tough it's going to be for a colored ball-player to come out of the clubhouse and have all the white guys calling him nigger and black so-and-so. . . . What I want to know is what the hell's gonna happen to good will when one of those colored play-ers, goaded out of his senses by repeated insults, takes a bat and busts fellowship in his damned head?"

Robinson's career with the Monarchs was brief. Researchers have recovered box scores from only fourteen league-sanctioned games in which he played. He almost certainly played more than that, but there's no telling how many. In those fourteen outings, Robin-son hit .434, with one home run and one stolen base, which is astounding given how little experience he had in baseball.

Traveling with the team, Robinson longed for a reunion with Rachel. He wrote to her several times a week. But he didn't know what to do next. There seemed no future in the game, and as long as he kept kicking around with the Monarchs, his future with Rachel remained on hold, too. "I never expected the walls [of segregation] to come tumbling down in my lifetime," he wrote years later. "I began to wonder why I should dedicate my life to a career where the boundaries for progress were set by racial discrimination." He was not one of those ballplayers who loved the game so deeply that he would find a way to play no matter the pay and no matter the conditions. If baseball didn't need him, then he didn't need baseball.

Two:
"Some Good
Colored Players"

On August 24, 1945, the Kansas City Monarchs visited Comiskey Park to play a double-header against the Chicago American Giants. Robinson was nursing a sore shoulder. Between games, columnist Fay Young of the *Chicago Defender* cornered the young ballplayer and asked if he planned to go east to meet with Branch Rickey, owner of the Brooklyn Dodgers. Rickey was scouting players for a new Negro league, according to news reports, and promising that his organization would be more stable and more professionally managed than the other Negro leagues.

Rickey was known throughout the land of baseball as a careful calculator, but something about his plan didn't add up, and Fay Young sensed it. Negro-league baseball was a tricky business, full of hustlers and fly-by-nighters. Like the used-car trade, it was lucrative and professionally run in some locations, and a complete mess in others. Young couldn't understand why Rickey, a man of famously high standards, would want to slop around in such muck. The writer wondered if the Brooklyn boss had an ulterior motive, and he pressed Robinson for whatever information he had.

Was he going to Brooklyn? Was he meeting Rickey?

"Just rumors," the ballplayer insisted.

Robinson was a newcomer to Negro-league ball, and far from the best player around. But his football heroics at UCLA had made him famous, which meant he might be a nice catch for a white businessman trying to bring attention to a new league. If Robinson planned to cut a deal with Rickey, the athlete had a duty to inform readers of the African-American *Defender,* Young argued.

"Well, it's a rumor," Robinson said, smiling. "If you don't see me here tomorrow, then there's something to it."

The next day, Robinson was gone.

During the war years, when other teams had scaled back their scouting operations to save money, Branch Rickey, sensing opportunity, doubled the budget for Dodger scouts. He was a staunch patriot and never doubted

46

that the United States would win the war quickly. At the same time, he addressed a secret meeting of the Dodgers' board of directors and asked their approval to pursue black ballplayers. In the meeting, which was held before the start of the 1943 season at the exclusive New York Athletic Club, the directors granted their permission, although they warned Rickey that it was one thing to seek a competitive advantage on the ball field and another thing to set out to change the world. Rickey declared his priorities: "First, to win a pennant. I think there's some good colored players. The second reason is . . . it's right!" So he sent his scouts to look for black ballplayers as well as white — and to keep quiet about it.

The pressures facing Rickey in 1945 were not like those facing baseball executives in Pittsburgh, Boston, and Cincinnati. New York City was a political powder keg. Black activists, trade unionists, integrationists, communists, pacifists, and religious leaders in New York were exceedingly well organized and highly combative, and they had decided to make the integration of baseball one of their core goals. It seemed to them a relatively easy target. How could any game calling itself the national pastime, they asked, get away with excluding 10 percent of the population? The hypocrisy was so jolting that even the Japanese had picked up on it during the war, showering black troops with leaflets intended to sap their morale. "If Americans are fighting for the freedom and equality of all people," the propaganda read, "why aren't Negro Americans allowed to play baseball?"

In New York after the war, Ben Davis, a black communist running for city council, printed his own pamphlet saying the Japanese had been right. He vowed to make integration of the major leagues one of his top priorities in office. Davis was elected — with the endorsement of Tammany Hall *and* the Communist Party — and he told his cheering supporters in 1945 that he intended to make New York "the most liberal city in America," entirely free of racism, with equal rights for everyone, from busboys to ballplayers.

Indeed, New York did become the most liberal city in America. And the liberal factions were not the only ones pushing for baseball's integration. Many mainstream writers and hardcore baseball fans believed integration would prove good for the game. The principles soldiers fought for in World War II remained vivid in people's minds, and Americans were eager to continue the fight on the home front.

"If baseball belonged to all the people and the people had a vote in its conduct," the popular sportswriter Damon Runyon wrote in 1945, "Negroes would be permitted to play in organized ball if they could make good by the same standards set for the whites." Dan Parker of the *New York Daily Mirror* wrote, "There is no good reason why, in a country that calls itself a democracy, intolerance should exist on the sports field, most democratic of all meeting places." Others in the press tried to explain why the integration of the national pastime would never work. Jimmy Powers of the *Daily News* said black ballplayers weren't talented enough to crack a big-league team, while Stanley Frank of the same paper worried about the black ballplayer's safety. "I know Southern ballplayers will brandish sharp spikes with intent to cut and maim Negro infielders," Frank wrote, "that there will be an unprecedented wave of murderous beanballs thrown at Negro batters; that jockeying from the benches will descend to subhuman levels of viciousness."

But the issue at hand was nevertheless straightforward, which made it popular among activists. One was either for the integration of the game or against it. So the

49

black newspapermen buttonholed big-league players, coaches, and owners at every opportunity, asking them to vote yea or nay. Although they might have spoken differently in the privacy of their all-white clubhouses, most of them voted yea: "It's too bad those colored boys don't play in the big leagues," the legendary pitcher Dizzy Dean once said, "because they sure got some great players."

In 1945, the New York state legislature passed the Quinn-Ives Act, a ban on discrimination in hiring. The same year, New York City's mayor, Fiorello H. LaGuardia, appointed a commission to investigate discrimination in hiring and appointed the sociologist Dan Dodson chairman. When Dodson turned his investigation to baseball and interviewed Branch Rickey, the Dodger boss was thrilled. He believed the public pressure and the commission's investigation would make it easier for him to integrate his team, and he quickly shared the details of his secret plan with Dodson. What's more, he asked Dodson for his help. Rickey told the sociologist he wanted to learn the politics and psychology of integration. He wanted to study the track records of institutions that had already integrated. He also wanted Dodson to help him stall. With a little more time, Rickey knew, he would

50

have the chance to corner the market on black players, select just the right black man to break the color line, and prepare his white players for the new man's arrival. Dodson, thoroughly charmed, agreed to do whatever Rickey asked of him.

Rickey thought of everything, and then he thought of more. He was a lawyer by training and believed that baseball, like the law, required careful analysis as well as bold action, but more of the former than the latter. Reporters said he was the smartest man ever associated with the game, and Rickey tended to believe his press clippings. Rickey was famous for his long-winded sermons. The writers who covered the Dodgers sometimes rolled their eyes, but they nevertheless cherished him. He was nothing if not good copy. "Things worthwhile generally don't just happen," he once said, just warming up. "Luck is a fact, but should not be a factor. Good luck is what is left over after intelligence and effort have combined at their best. Negligence or indifference or inattention are usually reviewed from an unlucky seat. The law of cause and effect and causality both work the same with inexorable exactitudes. Luck is the residue of design." He uttered the concluding sentence of that refrain — *Luck is the residue of design* — so

51

often that it would become his credo. He hung a sign with that maxim in his office. The other epigram hanging in his office, attributed to the Scottish philosopher William Drummond, read: "He who will not reason is a bigot; he who cannot reason is a fool; he who dares not reason is a slave."

Reporters tended to leave Rickey's wood-paneled office ("the Cave of the Winds," they called it) in a terrific hurry, exuberant, convinced that they had filled their notebooks with pure gold, only to start typing and realize that they had nothing but blabber. He was a heavy man, five-foot-nine, 215 pounds, "massive, benign, and bucolic," in the eyes of one correspondent. A cowlick poked from the top of his head. Bushy eyebrows climbed up and over his glasses, threatening to take over the whole face. He sucked fat cigars at all times of day. Though his extra-wide bowties were custom-made at Lord & Taylor and Brooks Brothers, one sartorial splash was not enough to fool anybody. He was a mess. Even his shoes looked rumpled.

Rickey was a deeply religious man, the son of a Methodist preacher, calm and careful, as tight with money as he was loose with lips. Though he didn't finish high school, he nevertheless earned baccalaureate degrees in art and literature and a doctorate in law. He coached the University of Michigan's baseball team while pursuing his degree in law. Later, he claimed to own every book published on the life of Abraham Lincoln, and he always kept Shakespeare, Plutarch, Boswell's Johnson, and the Bible close at hand in his office. He preferred reading to sleeping. "Who wants to sleep anyhow?" he once asked, and then tossed in a little Shakespeare to make his point. "What's it good for outside of 'knitting up the ravell'd sleaves of care'?"

Multitasking was not in the lexicon of the day, but Rickey certainly took to the concept. He sometimes summoned his secretary to join him in the bathroom so he could dictate letters. He shaved in the bathtub, without benefit of mirror or cream, in order to save a few precious minutes, a process that left his face as rough as an avocado skin. He may indeed have been the most brilliant man ever to wrap his mind around the game of baseball. On the other hand, with his bloated rhetoric and moralistic sermons, he may have been the game's all-time greatest swindler, too. Like a great revival preacher, he made the pursuit of profits seem somehow holy. He wouldn't go to the ballpark on Sundays, keeping a promise he'd made to his parents as a young man ("Dear Ones at Home," he addressed the 1904 letter containing his oath), but he had no trouble keeping his share of the receipts collected on the Lord's day.

Rickey loved baseball (as a catcher, he played four seasons in the majors, hitting a feeble .239). He also loved money, and wanted loads of it. But he didn't want any overpaid players on his club, in part because he thought the men would be corrupted by their wealth. Rickey believed firmly that it was better to unload an aging player a year too soon than a year too late. When he arrived in Brooklyn and dealt the beloved Dolph Camilli to the hated Giants, it was indisputably the right move, but it infuriated fans, who hung Rickey in effigy from Brooklyn's Borough Hall. "El Cheapo," the columnist Jimmy Powers dubbed him, a nickname that infuriated Rickey, in no small part because it stuck. But so did "The Mahatma" and "The Deacon," nicknames coined by the more affectionate sportswriters. Red Smith, no sycophant, called him "the finest man ever brought to the game of baseball" and said he would have made a giant of a Supreme Court justice. Whether Rickey's motives were pure or not — and even the most astute reporters were taken

54

by his razzmatazz — there was never any doubting his complexity. "A man of many facets — all turned on," as they used to say in Brooklyn.

Long before integration became an issue, Rickey had already assured his reputation as one of baseball's great innovators. While running the St. Louis Cardinals, he had created a system of minor-league farm clubs to supply his big-league team with young players. He amassed so much talent that the Cards dominated the National League for years, until the rest of the league caught on. Now he was after something bigger. And the careful notes he made — scribbled on whatever pieces of paper he had stuffed in his pockets, and preserved so that future generations might attest to his brilliance — show that he understood long before most of his peers that the first team to break baseball's color line would win a huge advantage. His design was to sign the most talented black players available, pay the men as little as possible for as long as possible, to make the Dodgers winners, to increase ticket sales, to live up to his religious values, and to make baseball a more democratic game. In what order did he rank those priorities? He never said. He didn't have to. He knew he was doing the right thing.

At the start of the 1945 season, when Robinson was starting his season with the Monarchs, Rickey announced that his scouts were looking for players for the Brooklyn Brown Dodgers, a new team that would become part of a new Negro league called the United States League. Rickey told one writer there was "not a single Negro player in this country who could qualify for the National or American leagues." But if one of the players in his new Negro league eventually developed the necessary skills, he would be open to promoting that players to the majors.

Rickey managed to offend everyone at the same time, but his plan was not so crazy as it sounded. With Ebbets Field empty half the summer and Brooklyn's black population growing, a black team could have helped fill the ballpark when the white Dodgers were out of town. Even so, many people suspected that Rickey had no intention of creating a new black baseball league and no intention of bringing black men to the majors. They figured he was buying time, trying to keep the integrationists off his back.

By 1945, Rickey and his scouts had narrowed their attention to a handful of black ballplayers, including Robinson, Roy Campanella, Don Newcombe, Larry Doby, and Monte Irvin. The scouts applied their usual standards, looking for a man who could hit, run, and throw. Campanella, a slugging catcher, and Newcombe, a flame-throwing pitcher, both impressed Rickey's men. Yet Campanella seemed to the scouts too easygoing, and Newcombe too immature. The more his scouts scoured the marketplace, the more they focused on Robinson. He had been to college and played alongside whites. He didn't drink or smoke. He'd served in the military and taken a stand against Jim Crow during his military trial. The scouts recognized that the young ballplayer's temper posed a threat, but if the boss wanted someone smart and tough, they said, Robinson was the man.

Robinson and Rickey met for the first time on August 28, 1945, in Rickey's office on Montague Street in Brooklyn. On one wall hung portraits of Abraham Lincoln and Leo Durocher, manager of the Brooklyn Dodgers. On another wall hung a blackboard listing the names of every baseball player at every level of the team's organization, every member of Rickey's dominion. Goldfish swam in a lighted tank in a corner of the room. Rickey's desk was probably cluttered.

It almost always was. He kept a dictionary the size of a cinderblock nearby, as well as a somewhat more slender edition of *Bartlett's Quotations.*

Robinson and Rickey stared at each other in silence. Fifteen seconds, thirty, a minute went by, and, still, neither man said a word. Rickey gazed out from his wire-rimmed glasses, his doughy face offering no hint of his mood. He wore a jacket and bowtie. He twirled an unlit cigar in his hand. Rickey had a high estimation of all his abilities, not the least his ability to judge a man's character. Now, he peered at Robinson as if he were looking through the young man's dark brown skin and into the depths of his soul, as if he could foretell his future. "He stared and stared," recalled Clyde Sukeforth, the scout who had brought Robinson back from Chicago and sat in on the interview. Robinson stared back. Sukeforth waited to see which of these stubborn men would speak first.

Rickey finally broke the silence.

"Do you have a girl?" he asked.

Yes, Robinson said, he had a girlfriend. In fact, he had been engaged for more than a year, and his fiancée was pressuring him to set a wedding date. Rickey advised Robinson to get married.

Rickey loved to ask ballplayers the girl question, because he learned something about their character, and he liked employees who had families relying on them to work hard and behave responsibly. After the girl question, he usually turned the interview to baseball technique, asking pitchers how they gripped their curves, or asking first basemen about the best way to hold runners close to the bag. In Robinson's case, though, he didn't spend much time on baseball. By now, Robinson knew he hadn't been summoned to talk about playing for the Brown Dodgers. He had figured out from the clues dropped by Sukeforth that a bigger opportunity was at hand. Rickey explained that he wanted to start Robinson in the minors, but with the hope that he would quickly receive a promotion to the major leagues.

Rickey and Robinson chatted, intensely at times, although they were interrupted more than once by telephone calls. Rickey could never keep his mind on one thing for long, even when the one thing was as important as this. Eventually, though, the Dodger president found himself fully engaged with Robinson, ready to test his mettle. He began to get emotional. He stood up from his chair and began shouting, firing a series of questions designed to measure the young man's temper. "What will you do? What will you do when they call you a black son of a bitch? When they not only turn you down for a hotel room but also curse you out?" As he went on talking about supercilious waiters, rude railroad conductors, vicious base-runners, and beanball-hurling pitchers, he stood up and walked over to Robinson, who found Rickey's speech so compelling that his hands were clenched now behind his back. Rickey stepped up to Robinson and pretended to throw a punch at his face. "What would you do?" he shouted.

Robinson calmed himself. That's when he asked if Rickey wanted a man who was afraid to fight back, and Rickey responded by saying he wanted a man with the courage not to. That's when these two faithful Methodists began discussing Christ. And that's when Robinson said he would do it — for his fiancée, for Mr. Rickey, and for black people all over the country.

Thus was born one of baseball's favorite legends. The story of the meeting between Rickey and Robinson has been told in countless media, passed down through the generations, shined up and smoothed over so that it has become one of America's great fables. But in one important way, the accounts are often misleading. Rickey didn't choose Robinson for his ability to turn the other cheek. Had Rickey wanted a pacifist, he might have selected any one of half a dozen men with milder constitutions than Jack Roosevelt Robinson's.

Rickey wanted an angry black man. He wanted someone big enough and strong enough to intimidate, and someone intelligent enough to understand the historic nature of his role. Perhaps he even wanted a dark-skinned man whose presence would be more strongly felt, more plainly obvious, although on this point Rickey was uncharacteristically silent. Clearly, the Dodger boss sought a man who would not just raise the issue of equal rights but would press it.

It is testament to Rickey's sophistication and foresight that he chose a ballplayer who would become a symbol of strength rather than assimilation. It is testament to Robinson's intelligence and ambition that he recognized the importance of turning the other cheek and yet found a way to do it without appearing the least bit weak. So long as he showed restraint when fans and players baited him, he could fight like hell on the ball field. No one could fault him for playing too hard.

Shortly after agreeing to a minor-league

contract with Rickey, Robinson was asked to return a questionnaire to the American Baseball Bureau, a public relations group. He filled it out by hand:

Name: Jack Roosevelt Robinson
Nicknames: Jackie
Nationality: American Negro
Hobbies: Boys Club work
Ambition in Baseball: To open door for Negroes in Organized Ball.

Technically speaking, professional baseball had been integrated long before Robinson. The man most often credited with breaking the color barrier is John "Bud" Fowler, who learned to play baseball as a boy in Cooperstown, New York, and later hopped from one small-town team to another in the 1870s and 1880s, first in New Castle, Pennsylvania, later in Stillwater, Minnesota, and later still in Keokuk, Iowa, trying to make a living wherever the game he loved would take him. Fowler was a gifted hitter with great speed and a knack for self-promotion. Some opponents reacted so violently to Fowler's presence that he sometimes wore wooden shin protectors to protect himself from slashing spikes. "If I had not been so black, I might have caught on as a Spaniard or something of that kind," he wrote in 1895, as his opportunities began to fade. "My skin is against me."

Other black ballplayers joined white teams after Fowler, but not many, and not for long. Brothers Moses and Weldy Walker played briefly in the majors in 1884 with Toledo of the American Association, which was one of the three recognized major leagues at the time. But the doors began to swing shut in 1887 when future Hall of Famer Cap Anson announced that he would not let his Chicago White Stockings take the field for an exhibition game against Newark if Newark's star pitcher, a black man named George Stovey, was allowed to play. Stovey's manager backed down, saying the pitcher was sick. Other managers soon followed Anson's lead, no doubt fearing that black men would take jobs from white players. Before long, Newark dropped Stovey from its roster, and by the mid-1890s, the color line was clearly set. Black athletes began forming their own teams. By the turn of the century, if you wanted to be a big-leaguer, you needed more than talent. You needed white skin.

And so it remained over the course of the next half century. There were any number of black ballplayers talented enough to crash the party, from Oscar Charleston to Cool Papa Bell, but they didn't have a chance. Whenever someone confronted Kenesaw Mountain Landis, the commissioner who presided over major-league baseball from 1920 to 1944, he noted calmly that no written rule excluded black men from America's pastime. He was right, but he also knew that baseball needed no written rule. Black ballplayers weren't fighting to get in, black fans weren't complaining, owners of white teams showed no interest in challenging the status quo, and white fans either didn't care or didn't know what they were missing.

"He is not now major league stuff," Rickey said of Robinson in 1945, so he sent him to the Montreal Royals in the International League, where he would be the first black minor-leaguer. Rickey's intention was to give fans and players more time to get used to the idea of integration, and to give Robinson more time to polish his skills. And if problems arose, better to have them arise in Montreal than in Brooklyn.

A few months after his meeting with Rickey, Robinson carried a shoebox full of fried chicken and boiled eggs as he boarded his plane in Los Angeles, bound for spring training in Daytona Beach. He wore his best blue suit, a double-breasted number with wide lapels and baggy pants. His wife, Rachel, had on a dyed, three-quarter-length ermine coat (her "certificate of respectability," she called it) and a carefully slanted hat, with an alligator-skin purse and matching shoes. The Robinsons had been married only eighteen days. They entertained an extravagant vision of their future as their plane took off for Florida. They were young and somewhat naive, but they believed they would look back on this trip as the start of the biggest and best thing they'd ever done, a defining moment of their lives. Only the powerful aroma emanating from the shoebox spoiled the mood. They were embarrassed to be toting the food, worried what their fellow passengers would think, and afraid a newspaper photographer might take a picture of them eating lunch from a shoebox like a couple of country bumpkins. But they'd been unable to refuse when Jackie's mother had pressed it on them at the airport.

From Los Angeles, they flew to New Orleans, where they faced a delay before the next leg of their flight. The weather was fine, the cause of the delay unclear. They searched for a place to eat while they waited, but none of the restaurants in the

65

New Orleans airport served black customers. Though they were told they could buy sandwiches and eat them outside, the Robinsons refused. Neither of them had spent much time in the South. Now, as they tore into the shoebox full of chicken, they realized why Jackie's mother had insisted they take it.

After New Orleans, the plane stopped again, this time in Pensacola. The flight to Daytona Beach had been oversold, an airline worker informed them. The Robinsons and a Mexican man were told they would have to wait until the next day to fly. Rachel, glancing over at her husband, was pleased to see he was staying calm. He explained to the airline worker that he was on his way to a tryout with the Brooklyn Dodgers, and that it was important that he be there on time. The best the airline agent could do was offer a limousine to take them to a hotel.

Off they went, lugging a big suitcase wrapped with heavy cord, two duffels, and a big, black hat box. The only trouble was that the limo driver didn't know of any black hotels in Pensacola, so he pulled up at a white one and asked a bellboy if he had any recommendations. The bellboy said he knew a Negro family that might have a room for rent. It was eleven at night when they reached the house, a tiny place with only one bedroom. The family offered to let the Robinsons have the bedroom, but Jackie and Rachel declined. They decided to head for the bus station instead.

Rattled and exhausted, the couple settled into the last row of reclining seats, one row from the very back, for the 360-mile haul to Jacksonville. From Jacksonville, a friend would drive them to the Dodgers' spring-training facilities in Sanford, near Daytona Beach. A handful of white passengers sat up front as the bus rumbled out of Pensacola. Jackie dozed off, but Rachel couldn't sleep, or not much anyway. She buried her face and cried. After a few stops, she noticed the bus driver standing over them. Silently, he motioned with his hand for them to move all the way to the back. The bus was largely empty, but the driver insisted that "back of the bus" meant the last row. They got up and moved.

They were still on the bus, still in the last row, when the gray-black sky revealed its first traces of orange. Dark-skinned men in work clothes began climbing aboard. The driver herded all of them to the back, as far as they could go. The Robinsons, still dressed in their finest attire, stood at times so that some of the men in their stained work clothes might sit. Fourteen hours later, they arrived in Jacksonville, where they looked around and spotted some of the signs that southerners saw all too often: "WE WASH WHITE FOLKS' CLOTHES ONLY," one of them read. For Rachel, never before exposed to such things, a "hot feeling close to sickness" rose within. But the signs were not as distressing as something else she'd seen on the trip. Jack was the strongest and proudest man she'd ever met, and yet he'd been reduced to a position of helplessness at what should have been the greatest moment of his life. When the bus driver had waved his hand and signaled them to the back of the bus, her husband hadn't said a word. Rachel wept, not for their misfortune but for their dignity. As she would write years later, "My man had become the white South's 'boy.'"

Robinson was two days late by the time he arrived in Sanford, where the Dodgers were practicing in a small park at the corner of South Mellonville and Celery avenues. Some two hundred baseball players fanned out across the grass, hitting fungoes, running sprints, and tossing baseballs. The Dodgers had chosen this remote spot to make things easier for Robinson as he tried to become the first black man in the twentieth century to play organized baseball in the United States. Rickey knew the nation would be watching. He knew dozens of reporters would dog Robinson's every step. In the few months since the Dodgers had announced their intention to give the ballplayer a chance to break baseball's color line, Robinson had quickly become one of the most famous black people in America, his name appearing in gossip columns almost as frequently as those of heavyweight champ Joe Louis and the singer and actress Lena Horne.

He carried nothing but his shoes and glove to the field. After slipping on a plain gray uniform with no team name across the front, he stepped onto the field and saw the army of white men out there, already engaged in drills. Robinson had to get through a curtain of reporters before he could join them.

"What are you going to do if the pitchers start throwing at you?" one reporter asked.

"Duck!" said Robinson with a smile.

While the rest of the team stayed at the Mayfair Hotel in Sanford, the Robinsons were guests of Mr. and Mrs. David Brock, a well-to-do black couple. Rickey had inspected the Brock home himself. The accommodations were fine, but on the second night of the Robinsons' stay there, the telephone rang. It was Rickey, telling them to leave at once. People in town were complaining, he said, and there might be trouble. The Robinsons fled to Daytona Beach, to the home of yet another black benefactor.

Robinson found himself wishing at times that he'd never come to Florida, never agreed to be a part of Rickey's experiment. He was afraid he'd be run out of Daytona, too, and wherever else the Dodgers tried to hide him. Some cities canceled games and padlocked their ballparks rather than allow a black man to play among whites. "Suddenly I hated everybody and everything," he recalled. "I didn't care about the team or baseball or making good. All I wanted to do was get back home."

But he stuck it out through spring training and went north with the team to Montreal, where circumstances improved. He won the admiration of his skeptical manager, Clay Hopper, a cotton farmer from Mississippi. Robinson stole forty bases and finished with a league-leading .349 average and 113 runs scored. At one point late in the summer of 1946, Rickey thought about bringing Robinson up to the majors to help the Dodgers in their drive for the pennant. It was a powerful temptation. The Dodgers and the Cardinals were running neck-and-neck, and the Dodgers could have used Robinson at first base or third, where they were sorrowfully weak. Robinson was a fine enough athlete to have handled the transition, though he'd been playing second base all year at Montreal. Even as a pinch hitter and pinch runner, Robinson might have made the difference. Rickey consulted some of his lieutenants, although the lieutenants knew that he would make up his mind alone. In the end, he didn't want to take a chance by bringing Robinson up too soon, especially under such pressure-packed conditions. Even for a pennant, he decided, it wasn't worth it. The Dodgers wound up tied with the Cardinals for first place. In a best-of-three-games series to break the tie, the Dodgers lost in two straight.

Robinson remained with the Royals, leading his team to victory in the Little World Series, as the championship contest was known. That same summer and fall, after more than a decade of segregation, professional football welcomed its first black players: Marion Motley, Bill Willis, Woody

Strode, and Kenny Washington. The latter two had been Robinson's teammates at UCLA, part of the Gold Dust Trio. Had he stuck with football, Robinson, too, might have been among professional football's first class of black athletes. He was certainly more experienced at football than baseball, and his physical gifts were perhaps better suited for the gridiron. But football had nowhere near the broad fan support that baseball had in the 1940s. On the gridiron, his impact on America's culture would have been negligible. As Motley, Willis, Strode, and Washington joined the game, making only small headlines along the way, their emergence served to remind fans of how far Robinson already had come. With almost no experience playing baseball, learning the game as he went along, he was competing at the highest level of the minor leagues. And he was doing it not as part of a pioneering quartet. He was doing it alone. In one startling summer, he emerged as the best player on the best team in his league — and he was accepted almost universally by his teammates.

"Those who had no prejudices acted toward me the same as they acted toward other fellows they were meeting for the first time," Robinson wrote a few months later

72

in a newspaper column. "And those who, because of Southern descendancy, had certain feelings about race, quickly set those feelings aside. There were some recalcitrants, of course, but they were in such a minority that they were inconsequential." Black sportswriters were convinced that if Robinson got the chance, he would do just as well in the big leagues. White sportswriters remained divided. But almost everyone in America by now knew Robinson's name and saw what was at stake.

After the last game of Montreal's championship season, a mob of about five hundred white fans chased him, tearing at his clothes, smothering him with hugs and kisses. One wag, Sam Maltin, noted that it was probably the first time a black man had ever been forced to flee a white mob intent on showing its love.

To escape the crowd, Robinson leaped into the car of a stranger. A white woman was behind the wheel. He smiled at her. She smiled at him. And so the great ballplayer rolled away from the stadium, out of Montreal, and on to the big leagues.

THREE:
THE UPRISING

Branch Rickey believed that Robinson would earn the respect and even the admiration of his teammates once they saw he could help the Dodgers win. He knew some players would be more open to playing with Robinson than others, but he believed that all of them would quickly come to put Dodger blue before black and white.

He was wrong.

The Dodgers in 1947 were distinctly southern in character. Their unofficial captain, Pee Wee Reese, was a Kentuckian, the son of a railroad detective. Their best hitter and the team's most popular player, Dixie Walker, grew up in Alabama and ran a small hardware store there in the off-season. Their hard-as-nails second baseman, Eddie "The Brat" Stanky, also spent his off-seasons in Alabama. The team's best pitcher, Kirby Higbe, was a hard-drinking, loud-mouthed South Carolinian. The backup catcher, Bobby Bragan, one of the most popular men in the clubhouse, grew up in Birmingham and spoke openly of his belief in white supremacy. Their top relief pitcher, Hugh Casey, hailed from Atlanta and owned a southern-style restaurant in Brooklyn that served as the team's favorite postgame gathering place.

Almost every big-league clubhouse at the time felt southern to the core, whether southerners were the majority or not. Conversation revolved around hunting and fishing. Packets of chewing tobacco passed from locker to locker. When Phil Rizzuto joined the Yankees in 1941, the Brooklyn-born Italian kid was struck by the dominance of southern players. They had their own dialects and customs, and they behaved as if those were the official dialects and customs of major-league baseball. Rizzuto was playing in his hometown for a team led by Joe DiMaggio, a fellow Italian-American, and yet he was the one made to feel out of place.

Rickey couldn't take the South out of the Dodgers, but he made up his mind to take the Dodgers out of the South, moving spring training in 1947 from Florida to Havana. In Cuba, the Dodgers rented a set of rooms at the Hotel Nacional, the country's most elegant resort, at the considerable cost of twenty dollars per player per day. For some of the men, it was the fanciest place they'd ever stayed. They drank beer, smoked cigars, and splashed like children in the hotel's enormous pool. But only the big-leaguers were extended deluxe accommodations. Minor-leaguers were assigned to dormitories at the newly built National Military Academy, near the team's practice fields, at a rate of eleven dollars per player per day. Black minor-league players, including Robinson, were exiled to yet a third tier of housing: the Hotel Los Angeles, a low-rent dive in downtown Havana. Reporters covering spring training didn't mention the cost of rooms at the Los Angeles, although they did observe that it was "near the slum district."

Robinson had three other black ballplayers to keep him company at the Los Angeles. They were Roy Campanella, the hardhitting catcher, with whom Robinson roomed; Don Newcombe, the lanky young pitcher; and Roy Partlow, another pitcher. All of them hated the Los Angeles. Newcombe described it as a place only a cockroach could love. But what irked the men most was the discovery that the segregated lodging had been imposed not by Cuban officials but by Rickey, who hoped to avoid conflict between black and white players. Campanella decided not to complain, to keep his mind on baseball. But Robinson was too angry to stay quiet. Until that moment, he had thought he could trust Rickey to do the right thing. Now some doubt crept in.

The Los Angeles had no restaurant. So while the men at the Nacional could order room service and the men at the Academy could eat in the dining hall, Robinson, Campanella, Newcombe, and Partlow had to fend for themselves. Campy, who spoke some Spanish, would lead them around downtown Havana, searching for anything that resembled American food. They ate in some of the cheapest, greasiest, dirtiest restaurants they'd ever seen — which, for ballplayers, was saying a lot. The *People's Voice,* a left-wing Harlem newspaper, said Robinson had been reduced to eating "Jimcro" food. The black newspapers made daily references to Jimcro — or Jim Crow, as it was usually written — to describe laws or customs of segregation. There were Jim Crow neighborhoods, Jim Crow schools, Jim Crow military units, Jim Crow hospitals, and Jim Crow restaurants. Before long, Robinson was suffering Jim Crow stomachaches.

For the first week or so of training camp, Robinson attracted scant attention. He was the only one of the four black men with a shot at making the big-league team, but expectations nevertheless remained low. "For what it is worth," the Associated Press reported on March 5, "not one of the numerous sports writers covering the Brooklyn camp thinks Jackie will be in the Dodgers line-up." The most obvious reason, beyond race, was that the team had no position for him to play. Robinson had been a shortstop in college and with the Monarchs, but the Dodgers had Reese at short, and there was no chance he would be displaced. Robinson had played second base in Montreal, but Stanky was firmly entrenched at that position. The assumption all winter long had been that Robinson, despite his weak arm, would play third. But during the off-season, the popular Arky Vaughan, a .319 lifetime hitter, announced his intention to come out of retirement and signed a rich contract. He was nearly thirty-five and hadn't played in three years. Still, he became the instant front-runner for the job, with John "Spider" Jorgensen, formerly of Montreal, also in contention.

All along, Robinson had tried to stay calm. The dingy hotel felt like an insult. His

78

back was aching, probably from a golf injury he'd suffered that winter. He had a nasty callus on his right foot. He had no idea what he was eating much of the time. (*Arroz con pollo* is chicken and rice? It came as news to him.) And now his stomach was killing him. Worst of all, he was beginning to wonder if Rickey truly intended to give him a chance to make the Dodgers. Then, as the Dodgers and Royals were preparing to fly to Panama for a series of games, one of Rickey's assistants handed Robinson a first-baseman's mitt and told him he'd been assigned a new position — one he had never played. First base is a busy place, he thought. And he began to worry that Rickey was stalling. Now the boss would have an excuse; he could say Robinson looked shabby at his new position and needed more time in Montreal. "I was a disgruntled ballplayer," he later recalled.

But Howie Schultz, one of the team's two first basemen in 1946, knew right away that Robinson would have no trouble mastering the new position. The two men began working out together for hours on end. Schultz, referred to as "Stretch" because he was six-feet-six and thin as pulled taffy, grew up in Minnesota. Schultz figured out quickly that he would soon lose his job, yet it didn't matter at all to him that he would lose it to a black man. He could see that Robinson was too great an athlete to be kept out of the lineup for long. He was impressed by the newcomer's quiet, patient approach. Many athletes with extraordinary gifts carry themselves with an air of superiority, Schultz had noticed, but not Robinson. Schultz heard that some players weren't happy about the arrival of a black player, but from what he saw in those workouts on the infield in Havana, he had a feeling that would change once Robinson started helping the Dodgers win. "You couldn't possibly dislike him," he recalled.

At times, Robinson's stomach hurt so badly he had difficulty bending. Doctors in Havana said he probably had colitis. But there was little time and much to learn at first base — when to go toward the hole for a ground ball and when to let the second baseman get it; where to stand for cut-off throws; how to field a bunt — so he played through the pain and made quick progress at his new location. And he kept saying all the right things. In a column for the *Baltimore Afro-American* and other papers in its national chain, written with the help of the black journalist Sam Lacy, Robinson told readers that "the experience is a nerve-wracking one, yet something I would not have wanted to miss for all the gold in the world." He told white reporters he wanted to be a Dodger only if the Dodger players wanted him. "I wouldn't want to feel that I was doing anything that would keep them from winning," he said. And in what may have been his slickest bit of public relations, he said his desire to make the team was not driven by politics or righteousness but by finance. "They've got a minimum salary in the majors which is more than I'm getting now," he explained.

Writers covering the team remained uncertain about his chances. "The only thing keeping Robinson off the Dodgers now, plainly, is the attitude of the players," Herb Goren wrote in the *New York Sun.* "If it softens at the sight of Jackie's skills, he'll join the club some time between April 10 and April 15. Otherwise, Robinson will spend the year playing first base for Montreal." Leonard Cohen, writing in the *Post,* noted that "among the majority of Dodgers there is a positive feeling of antipathy towards Robinson as a possible teammate."

Had the 1946 Dodgers been a fluke? That was the other question facing the team as it came together in Cuba for the start of the

81

1947 season. The answer was not clear. The entire team had hit a paltry fifty-five home runs in 1946, and only one pitcher had won more than fourteen games. Yet, almost as if by magic, the Dodgers had piled up ninety-six wins against sixty losses. How? Where had the runs come from? The consensus seemed to be that Leo Durocher, their manager, had pulled off some sort of managerial magic, that he had willed his team to score, or else scared them so terribly that they were afraid to lose. The Dodgers in '46 led the league in walks, stolen bases, and triples. In other words, they were burglars, taking bases that didn't belong to them, and making off with victories before their opponents knew what had happened.

Leo Ernest Durocher built the Dodgers in his own image. As a player, he had used cleverness and lip to make up for a lack of size (he was five-feet-nine, 160 pounds) and talent (his lifetime batting average was .247). He began his career with the Yankees of Ruth and Gehrig and yet displayed little appreciation for the respectability of Yankee pinstripes. From shortstop, he would urge Yankee pitchers to throw at the heads of opposing batters. "Stick it in his fucking ear!" he would cry. If Durocher spoke a sentence without curses, it was probably an accident, soon to be corrected. The Yanks shipped him to Cincinnati, Cincinnati sent him to St. Louis, and though he was the centerpiece of a brilliant Cardinal infield for five seasons, St. Louis sent him to Brooklyn. Nowhere did he stay out of trouble, and never did he shut up. But he found his calling as a manager. Branch Rickey must have been troubled by his manager's love affairs, his divorce, and his rumored gambling. Some of Durocher's own players were said to be mired in deep financial debt to their manager from their losses at cards. While Durocher thrived on animosity, not all his players did, and some Dodgers despised their skipper. But Rickey looked past all of that because he loved Durocher's winning percentage, which was .570 in his eight years with the Dodgers.

In 1947, Durocher would have roughly the same unimposing roster he had managed in 1946. Reese was his most important all-around player. The diminutive shortstop had a face like a basset hound, and a personality to match. His quiet affability, a perfect narcotic to Durocher's mania, helped ease the tension in the Dodger clubhouse. After three years with the Third Marine Division during the war, Reese had come back to baseball in 1946, and, at the age of twenty-eight, quickly rediscovered his winning form. Though his batting average in 1946, at .284, was merely respectable, Reese gave the Dodgers what DiMaggio gave the Yankees: poise. He did all the little things and many of the big things. He made it known by the way he played that he expected others to match his intensity.

His double-play partner, the second baseman Eddie Stanky, needed no reminders. Stanky, another man of modest size, was as tough as the leather palm of an old infielder's glove. Like Durocher, he was not a gifted athlete, and, like Durocher, he was foul-mouthed and stiff-necked. He didn't hit much, so he would foul off pitch after pitch, often hoping for a walk. And though no one was afraid to throw him strikes, he still ranked among the league leaders in walks, year in and year out. "He can't hit, he can't run, he can't field, and he can't throw," Rickey once said. "But if there's a way to beat the other team, he'll find it."

With Stanky and Reese at the center of the infield, and with the speedy Pete Reiser in center field, the team was strong on defense up the middle. But the Dodgers' best hitter — the only player to hit better than .300 and drive in more than 100 runs in 1946 — was Dixie Walker, the right fielder. With a lineup full of scrapers, scratchers, and scrap-heap reclamations, the Dodgers needed at least one man who could be counted on to hit the ball hard. Walker was the man.

It was no accident that the right fielder had become the most popular ballplayer in Brooklyn. Walker was built like a Louisville Slugger, long, lean, and strong. He was a humble, blue-collar southerner, the sort of aw-shucks fellow who had been gracing outfields since the game began. His jaw curved slightly one way, his nose the other, twisting his face into the approximate shape of a question mark. At thirty-six, his features were softening, crow's nests spreading at the corners of his eyes, giving him the perpetual appearance of calm. He looked like the sort of man with whom one might pull up a chair, knock back a couple of beers, and not say a word for the first twenty minutes or so. Walker was a second-generation big-leaguer, following in the steps of his father, Ewart Walker, who pitched briefly for the Washington Senators. Dixie's younger brother, Harry, was also a big-leaguer, and would lead the National League in hitting in 1947.

When he came up with the New York Yankees in 1931, Dixie Walker was pegged as the likely heir to Babe Ruth in right field. He hit for high average, reasonable power, and had a shotgun for an arm. After a fine rookie year, however, Walker was beset by injuries. Before long the Yankees gave up on him. After stops with the White Sox and Tigers, he wound up in Brooklyn in 1939. The Dodgers were one of baseball's bottom feeders at the time, and the eternally optimistic fans of Brooklyn embraced Walker as a potential star. For once, their optimism was rewarded. Walker shone, and, more shockingly, the Bums started winning. They finished second in 1940, and won the pennant in 1941. Walker hit .300 or better in all but one of his full seasons in Brooklyn, and he handled the caroms off the tricky right-field wall as if he'd been born to play at Ebbets Field. "The People's Cherce," they called him, conferring upon the Alabaman an honorary Brooklyn accent. Off the field, he was never quite so at ease as he appeared on the field. He was aloof, a bit of a loner. He'd taken a Dale Carnegie course to boost his charisma, and at times he did manage to convey the charm of a southern gentleman, but he was still a little rough around the edges. Dale Carnegie could do only so much.

Just as Durocher counted on Walker the

ballplayer to drive in runs, Rickey counted on Walker the fan favorite and veteran player to ease Robinson's assimilation. The boss knew Walker's passion for the game. He believed the outfielder would in good time come to judge the ballplayer on his abilities instead of his color. But Rickey failed to factor in one thing: For Walker, and for others in baseball, the connection to the South and the southern way of life counted for more than his connection to the team. Only two Dodgers had reason to worry about losing their jobs to Robinson: the first basemen, Schultz and Ed Stevens. Yet it was Walker who was most upset about the possibility of playing beside a black man, and it was Walker who apparently decided he would try to do something about it. Some teammates said he circulated a petition among his fellow players. Others said he organized by word-of-mouth.

Walker's protest was joined by most of the team's southern contingent: Bragan, the likable third-string catcher; Higbe, who claimed to have developed his strong arm as a child by throwing rocks at black children in South Carolina; Casey, who had begun his pitching career with the Atlanta Crackers of the Southern Association; and Carl Furillo, the young outfielder from near

Reading, Pennsylvania, the only northerner in the bunch. Some reports have suggested that Stanky, too, expressed support for the rebellion. Others have placed Ed Head, the Louisiana-born pitcher, in the cabal. Cookie Lavagetto, a Californian, has been mentioned in some accounts, as well. Higbe always maintained that Reese joined ranks with the malcontents, although many of the men who knew Reese best said they doubted it.

Years later, Reese said he saw the petition but declined to sign it. In at least one interview, however, he said he could relate to Walker's feelings and respected him for speaking his mind. Reese hadn't met Robinson at that point. He'd never shaken hands with a black person, and he was under the impression, fed by a common stereotype, that black ballplayers didn't perform well under pressure, that they lacked what athletes called mental toughness. He assumed Robinson wouldn't last. Still, he felt ambivalent about the protest.

Though he was a marginal player, Bragan played an important part in the movement. "Dixie Walker was my roommate, and he was more established than I, and I guess he influenced me some," Bragan recalled recently. When he was playing in the minor leagues, back in the late 1930s, some of Bragan's teammates had stuck him with the nickname "Nig" for his olive-complexioned skin. Bragan liked the nickname well enough that when he ordered his first batch of Louisville Slugger bats he had "Robert 'Nig' Bragan" etched into the barrels. Only when he reached the big leagues, breaking in with Philadelphia, did someone point out to him that some might find the nickname offensive, at which point he dropped it.

Facing the prospect of playing alongside Robinson, Bragan's biggest worry was how he would explain the circumstance to his friends and family back in Alabama. It wasn't that he had never been around black people before. His father was in the construction business, and the old man sometimes had twenty black men working for him. On occasion, one of the men would come around the house to borrow a dollar against his salary. A black man had cut the family's lawn, and when he came inside to cool off, the family invited him to play their piano. A black woman had served as the family's housekeeper, too. She was well liked by all. But the servants and workingmen had always used the back door and referred to the whites, even the children, as Mister and Miss. "We just grew up segregated," he said. "People thought whites were supreme."

Robinson posed a threat to that notion. Though he was a .241 hitter and running out of gas at age twenty-nine, Bragan decided it was worth risking his career to make a stand.

Kirby Higbe also stood firm. Higbe was the grandson of a Confederate soldier. As a boy, he was big and tough, with little interest in school. "Back then," he recalled, "it seemed like a husky, willing kid could get along all right, the way people always had, without much more than a grade-school education." When he did go to school, he would walk around or through the Bottoms. "The Bottoms was a colored neighborhood. . . ." he said. "We knew if we went across the Bottoms we would have to fight our way through with rocks. The colored kids were waiting for us with rocks. It was their Bottoms. So we would always fill our pockets with rocks when we left home because there wasn't time to look for rocks when we got there. When we hit the Bottoms, the rocking started. We would have to throw rocks from the time we entered until the time we got to the top of that steep clay bank."

Higbe was brash and difficult to control, but he was also the team's best pitcher in

90

1946, with seventeen wins against eight losses and an earned run average of 3.03. Once, during a radio interview in New York City, he was asked how he had developed such a strong throwing arm. He didn't hesitate: "Throwing rocks at Negroes," he said, matter-of-factly. The interviewer cut off his microphone. But Higbe protested, saying he was serious, and not seeing why the interviewer was so upset. It was a game, he said, and besides, "they threw as many rocks as we did." Higbe said many years later that he believed southerners were unfairly characterized as racists, and he insisted he had never mistreated a black person. But just the same, in 1947 he was not inclined to play with one.

The Dodgers hopped around Central America for exhibition games throughout spring training, and they were in Panama when Leo Durocher heard about the players' uprising. He roused the team from bed one night for a meeting in the team's dining room. The players came in various states of undress. Durocher wore a yellow bathrobe atop his pajamas. No one writing of the meeting bothered to mention the color of the pajamas, but even if they had been pink with purple bunnies Durocher's authority would have been undiminished and unquestioned. The manager had a cinderblock jaw and a piercing stare, which he likely used to full effect in this instance. "I don't care if a guy is yellow or black, or if he has stripes like a fuckin' zebra," he told the team, according to one eyewitness account. "I'm the manager of this team, and I say he plays." Robinson was going to put money in all their pockets by helping to get the team to the World Series, Durocher said, and anyone who didn't like it would be traded or released as soon as the details could be arranged. As for the petition, he concluded: "Wipe your ass with it!"

There were no questions.

The next day, Rickey arrived in Panama. No doubt he recalled the advice of Dan Dodson, the sociologist he had consulted in advance of this undertaking. Dodson preached that white people confronting integration should never be asked if they want to make change. They should be told that change is coming and that nothing they say or do will stop it. Dodson told Rickey to describe the experiment in terms having nothing to do with race. The goal should be winning a pennant. The professor also urged Rickey to be firm, never to back down, but to step aside at some point and let the players work out matters on their own. That's precisely what he did.

Rickey summoned the rebels to his hotel room, one at a time, asking each if he was prepared to play on an integrated team. He told them that Robinson was a great player who would help the team win. He also said Robinson was quiet, and that they wouldn't have to associate with him off the field. Furillo gave in at once and apologized, saying he'd made a mistake. Bragan waffled, saying he'd play, although not happily. Higbe continued to object. Walker, stricken with "an acute attack of indigestion," according to one reporter, had already left Panama and returned to the hotel in Cuba to get some rest. Another account said he had gone home to handle a family emergency. He left behind a note for his boss, dated March 26. It read:

Dear Mr. Rickey

Recently the thought has occured *(cq)* to me that a change of Ball clubs would benefit both the Brooklyn Baseball club and myself. Therefore I would like to be traded as soon as a deal can be arranged.

My association with you, the people of Brooklyn, the press and Radio has been very pleasant and one I can truthfully

93

say I am sorry has to end. For reasons I don't care to go into I feel my decision is best for all concerned.

Very Sincerely yours,
Dixie Walker

Years later, Walker said the letter had been misinterpreted. He said the request for a trade was a response to Rickey's allegation that he was responsible for the petition drive. Walker insisted he had never seen a petition, and that he had never tried to organize his teammates. If Rickey didn't believe him, he said, then a trade would be the best thing for everyone. He admitted, however, even many years later, that he was unhappy about the possibility that Robinson might join the team. He also admitted talking to other players about his unhappiness. Most of all, he said, he worried about the reaction he would get back home if he consented to play with a black man. "I didn't know if they would spit on me or not," he said. "And it was no secret I was worried about my business. I had a hardware and sporting goods store back home." He continued: "I grew up in the South, and in those days you grew up in a different manner. . . . We thought that blacks didn't have ice water in their veins and so couldn't

94

take the pressure of playing big league baseball."

The Dodger right fielder mentioned the hardware store often in explaining his opposition to Robinson. Dixie Walker Hardware was in a white building on the main street in Hueytown, Alabama, next to the Hueytown Café, where the sign out front advertised hamburgers, malts, and "HO-MADE PIES." Kids used to come into the hardware store to buy pearl-handled Lone Ranger cap guns and marvel at the stuffed bobcat atop the shelf behind the register, while Walker and some of his friends liked to sit around the potbelly stove in back, telling tales and drinking bottled Cokes from the five-cent Coke machine. In 1944, when Gunnar Myrdal published his groundbreaking book on segregation, *An American Dilemma,* he had surveyed white southerners, asking them to rank the most important forms of segregation. The results, Myrdal noted, were remarkable for their consistency. The southerners worried most about black and white people getting married and having sex. They feared that any breakdown in the social codes of segregation — even a small one — would lead to the amalgamation of the races. Sharing a lunch counter, a bus seat, or a water fountain was the first step down a slippery slope, and the slope led to sex between blacks and whites and the mixing of the races. Though the southerners' fears were misplaced, they were genuine. And though Branch Rickey, as a northerner, could not relate, Walker had good reason to worry what the men seated around the potbelly stove would say about him when he wasn't there.

Rickey had made up his mind on two counts: First, though he had not yet told anyone — not even Robinson — the Dodgers would open the season with a black man at first base. Second, the Dodgers would have to trade Dixie Walker.

Quickly, Rickey tried to work out a deal. Walker would go to the Pittsburgh Pirates for two part-time players and cash. Yet something about the transaction gnawed at the Brooklyn boss. Something made him hesitate. He could see that Walker and Robinson might clash spectacularly, that Walker's bitterness might spread like typhoid through the clubhouse, destroying the great experiment that he had nurtured so carefully. But he also sensed that Walker was under great stress. He was suffering. He was frightened more than angry. Finally, Rickey considered yet another piece of the puzzle:

How would the Dodgers win without Walker's bat? As usual, Rickey wanted everything. He wanted his integration plan to succeed and he wanted the pennant. He wanted to punish Walker and help him find salvation. So, when he asked the Pirates to include the young slugger Ralph Kiner in the deal and the Pirates refused, Rickey decided to stand pat. The owner and part-time operator of Hueytown's hardware store remained a Dodger, at least for the time being.

When the Dodgers left Havana and returned to Brooklyn, Robinson went, too, but he made the trip as a member of the Montreal Royals. The Dodgers and Royals would play a series of exhibition contests at Ebbets Field before each team began its regular-season games. Robinson, still unsure whether he would spend the season in the majors or minors, viewed the exhibition games as one last chance to prove he belonged with the Dodgers. Though his stomach remained queasy, there was never any doubt in his mind he would play.

On April 9, the Dodgers received a surprise from the commissioner's office. The commissioner, Happy Chandler, was the former governor of Kentucky and a former

U.S. senator. Chandler strongly backed Rickey's plan for integration, and he seemed to be in full support of Robinson's ascension to the major leagues. It was Leo Durocher with whom he had a problem. Religious leaders had been complaining for months about Durocher's recent marriage to the newly divorced actress Laraine Day. The Catholic Youth Organization was vowing a boycott of baseball if something wasn't done to punish the manager for his "moral looseness." Chandler said years later that Durocher was out of control and Rickey seemed incapable of reining him in. The only thing to do, he thought, was to put him out of action. In March, when the Yankee general manager Larry MacPhail sat beside a couple of well-known gamblers at an exhibition game, Durocher complained publicly, saying in effect that if he'd been seen sitting with a couple of gamblers, he would have caught hell for it. Durocher's comments gave Chandler the excuse he was looking for. Citing an accumulation of unpleasant incidents, the commissioner suspended Durocher for one year.

The news hit Branch Rickey like a fastball to the forehead. The start of the season was less than a week away. Now the Dodgers had a right fielder threatening not to play with the team's black first baseman, and the manager who had been expected to keep the peace was gone. Rickey decided there was nothing to do but carry on.

The next morning, he had his secretary call Robinson, telling him to come to Brooklyn for a meeting. It was on that morning, April 10, that Robinson got the news he'd been waiting for. But, still, Rickey asked him to play one more game with the Montreal Royals, one more game as a minor-leaguer, before telling anyone of his promotion.

In the sixth inning of that game, with Robinson at bat, the Dodgers handed out a press release to reporters. "The Brooklyn Dodgers today purchased the contract of Jackie Roosevelt Robinson from the Montreal Royals," it read. "He will report immediately."

At that very moment, Robinson bunted into a double play.

FOUR:
OPENING DAY

Robinson woke early for Opening Day. By now, his wife and five-month-old son, Jack Jr., had joined him at the McAlpin Hotel in Manhattan. The room was a mess, with diapers drying on the shower rod, baby bottles sitting on the bathroom sink, and a small, electric stove perched precariously atop one of their trunks on the floor. Silverware and dishes were often shoved under the bed, out of sight, in case a newspaper reporter dropped by. Though Branch Rickey had tried to think of everything, it would appear he hadn't given much consideration to the Robinsons' living arrangements, which were growing more difficult by the day.

Robinson dressed and got ready to leave.

"Just in case you have trouble picking me out," he told Rachel on his way out the door, "I'll be wearing number forty-two."

She looked up at her husband, her Jack,

100

who wore the pride and determination of his mother on his face in his strong chin and his bright smile. He was Hollywood handsome, with a high forehead, stern eyes set far apart, a wide nose, and full lips. He might flash a boyish smile from time to time, but for the most part his dark face cast an image of manly strength. If he was nervous before his big first day, he didn't betray it. He joked like a man born to privilege, a man whose lifetime of experience had taught him that one way or another everything was going to work out to his advantage.

He took the subway to work, tabloid newspaper in hand, dressed in a suit and tie and a warm, camelhair overcoat. He was twenty-eight, big and strong and ready. He understood the importance of the day. He was about to become, as the *New York Post* put it, "the first colored boy ever to don major league flannels." The black-owned *Boston Chronicle* gave the story a more rhapsodic spin with its top-of-page-one headline: "Triumph of Whole Race Seen in Jackie's Debut in Major-League Ball."

Truly great athletes tend to be those blessed not only with physical skills but also with a gift for psychological segregation — keeping complicated thoughts apart from

101

the simple ones needed to perform the task at hand. Whether he is smart as a whip or dumb as an ox, getting married later that evening or in the process of losing his wife to another man, whether he is playing before a crowd of fifty thousand or fifty, the great athlete knows how to draw lines, keeping emotion at a distance. Some ballplayers focus so tightly on the ball hurtling toward them that they wouldn't notice if the grass were on fire beneath their feet. Others concentrate on nothing more than the wad of gum crackling in their mouths. Others still become convinced they can read a pitcher's mind and foresee the next pitch he will throw. Robinson was different. He tuned out nothing — not the catcalls from the grandstand, not the cold shoulders turned by teammates, not the angry glares from the opposing dugout, not the expectations of the millions of black fans across the country who were counting on him to prove *they* belonged. He sucked it all in the way competitive swimmers suck in air. He turned it into energy.

When he reached the clubhouse at Ebbets Field, a few teammates nodded at him. Ralph Branca and Gene Hermanski came over and shook his hand, saying they were happy to have him on the team. Robinson grinned but didn't say anything. The rest of the Dodgers ignored him. As Robinson sat on a folding chair and began to get undressed, reporters lobbed a few easy questions. He smiled and answered briefly. The Dodgers had not yet assigned him a locker, so he found his uniform hanging on a hook attached to a bare wall. He took off his suit, hung it on the hook, and began putting on his uniform, a white undershirt and long blue socks beneath a crisp white jersey and pants.

The team held a brief meeting before the game, but nothing was said of Robinson. Clyde Sukeforth — "Sukey," the players called him — was managing the team while Rickey searched for Durocher's permanent replacement. It was Sukey who had scouted Robinson in 1945, seeing something in the infielder's character he liked, and it was Sukey now who penciled Robinson's name into the starting lineup.

It had not been clear until that moment that Robinson would be the starting first baseman. Even Robinson was unsure. Some who favored the slow and cautious approach to integration had hoped baseball's first black player would be used as a pinch hitter, at least at the start. But Rickey wanted Robinson to jump in with a splash, and

Sukeforth, a firm believer in the young man's talents, was happy to go along with the plan. Though he liked to think of himself as an old blueberry farmer from Maine who might leave the game and return to the fields when his services were no longer desired, Sukeforth's life was wrapped in horsehide. The game meant everything to him. Though he was pleased to tell Robinson he would be starting for the Dodgers, he was sensible enough, too, not to make a big fuss about it. He decided not to call a special meeting, not to tell the players how he expected them to behave, and not to fight for Robinson with a fiery speech like the one Durocher had made in spring training. He would let them all work it out on their own.

Robinson was relieved. On his way out of the clubhouse, with the start of the game still hours away, he stopped and checked the mirror, admiring the clean white wool and blue script letters across the front of his Dodger uniform. "It fit me . . . ," he recalled, "but I still felt like a stranger, or an uninvited guest."

April 15 was a perfect day for baseball, with blue skies, a soft breeze, and just enough chill in the air to remind fans that a long season of baseball lay ahead. Soon, the fans would begin to arrive in Flatbush, catching their first glimpse of Ebbets Field, a bird's nest of brick and steel tucked inside one square city block. The ballpark had a sneaky kind of beauty. You turned a corner and there it was. The awning in front reminded you of your favorite soda fountain or candy shop, only this place was so much sweeter. Fans entered through a marble rotunda and under a grand chandelier with arms shaped like baseball bats and lamps shaped like balls. The roof was a mere eighty feet high. The grandstand wrapped so snugly around the playing field that you could see your favorite players' expressions, hear their shouts, share their jokes. Watching the Dodgers play at Ebbets Field — capacity, thirty-two thousand — was an intimate experience shared by a small and peculiar tribe, an experience that would bring people together and mark them for life. Never was it more true than in 1947.

On Opening Day, Lou Boudreau of the Cleveland Indians once said, the world is all future and no past. In Brooklyn, Opening Day was a holiday, a celebration for the kids who skipped school and the parents who slipped out of work. Most of all, it was a day of wild optimism. For at least one afternoon, the Bums were would-be champs. "Wait till next year" was the team's unofficial motto. It was an also-ran's motto, to be sure, but it nevertheless expressed hope, and hope blossomed in spring no matter how poorly the Dodgers had played the prior year. That was Brooklyn in a nutshell: a borough for strivers and connivers, a place where moxie counted for more than birthright, a place that reveled in its peculiarities and even in its defeats, a place where people moved up and moved out.

In 1947, hopes ran higher than usual. The Dodgers had come achingly close to winning the National League pennant in 1946. Many in the Brooklyn clubhouse believed this would be their year, but Robinson posed concern. Most of the Dodgers had never played with a black man. Many had never spoken to one in any meaningful way. Baseball teams, especially in the day of train travel, tended to be tightly knit groups with carefully constructed social orders. Some players knew their teammates better than they knew their wives. Now, as they waited to meet Robinson, many of the men were afraid he would destroy everything they knew and loved about the culture of the game.

Fans were fearful, too. So much had

106

changed since the war. Allies had become enemies. Enemies had become allies. Women had left their homes and gone to work. Farm workers from the South had moved by the hundreds of thousands to the North, remaking the shape and color of the nation. Unions were organizing. The Communist Party was making noise. Black activists were demanding equality. It was all terribly confusing. Baseball was supposed to provide comfort in such trying times. When the war ended, Ted Williams, Joe DiMaggio, and the rest of the big stars swung back into action after missing time to serve in the military, and fans couldn't get enough. Major-league baseball broke all of its attendance records in 1946, and it was poised to break them again in 1947 — assuming Jackie Robinson didn't change the equation. No one knew what effect his presence might have. Some owners of major-league baseball teams predicted that Robinson would drive white spectators away from the game. Black fans would certainly come out in greater numbers, the owners said, but not enough to offset the loss. Baseball was supposed to provide an escape from the mayhem. Now the purest and simplest of American traditions was about to become as complicated as the rest of the world.

■ ■ ■ ■

"This is my first ballgame in ten years," said Norman Hazzard, a firefighter from New Haven, Connecticut. "I came out to look at the Negro boy play."

All of Brooklyn's ethnic groups converged. They funneled into narrow lines to get through the turnstiles, and then spread out across the stadium. The Italians, the Irish, and the Jews were always strong in number, while black fans were usually sprinkled lightly about the ballpark. Maybe they made up 5 percent of the crowd, but probably not 10. Whatever the number, their presence was not ordinarily strong enough to make an impression on white fans in attendance. On this day, though, as the Dodgers prepared to face the Boston Braves, the proportions had changed. By one estimate, nearly three-fifths of the fans were black. It was a stunning phenomenon, evident to the Ebbets Field regulars from the moment they entered the park. But the most stunning thing of all was that only about 27,000 people came through the gates — 2,000 fewer than on Opening Day in 1946, and 5,000 fewer than the ballpark's capacity. Simple math suggests that the crowd included a mere 12,000 white fans. For Opening Day, for the Dodgers, for a team that had finished the 1946 season tied for first, for a community with such a passionate base of fans, and on a day with pretty fair weather, such a turnout was unbelievably poor.

One reporter suggested a smallpox scare, but everyone knew the real reason. White Brooklynites were not accustomed to being surrounded by black Brooklynites, and they were not eager to discover how it felt. Neither did they know how black fans would behave. Brawls were common in the stands at Ebbets Field in the best of times. Fans fought because they'd had too much to drink, or because they couldn't agree on whether the situation called for a sacrifice bunt, or because someone blew cigar smoke in someone else's face, or because someone thought they heard someone say something about someone's mother. Many fans were concerned that Robinson's presence would set off more than the usual number of skirmishes.

Before the season began, aware that such concerns could kill his business, Branch Rickey had summoned some of Brooklyn's leading black citizens for a frank discussion. If Robinson failed, he told the gathering at the Carlton Avenue branch YMCA, it won't be because the media or his teammates mistreated him. "The biggest threat to his success," he said, "is the Negro people themselves." No doubt some jaws dropped. But Rickey continued: "Every one of you will go out and form parades and welcoming committees. You'll strut. You'll wear badges. You'll hold Jackie Robinson Days. . . . You'll get drunk. You'll fight. You'll be arrested. You'll wine and dine the player until he is fat and futile. You'll symbolize his importance into a national comedy . . . and an ultimate tragedy." Somehow, Rickey got away with his ill-mannered speech. In fact, in the weeks and months ahead, Rickey's message spread throughout the black community. Newspaper columnists used their space to echo Rickey's warning. "Robinson will not be on trial as much as the Negro fan," wrote Fay Young in the *Chicago Defender.* "The unruly Negro . . . can set us back 25 years." Preachers pounded their pulpits to remind congregants not to drink or use profanity in National League ballparks. "LET'S TAKE IT IN STRIDE," read the banner headline in the *Pittsburgh Courier.* Still, fear remained palpable among whites. "The conduct of 'SOME' of your race in the stands (drinking and

110

boisterousness) could be improved upon," one fan wrote to Robinson during the first week of the season, in a letter that reached him at his hotel.

Rachel and Jack Jr. waited until late in the morning before heading for Ebbets Field. Ever since their plane trip from California a few days earlier, the baby, referred to by his parents as "Sugar Lump," had been sick with diarrhea. When they finally got dressed and left the hotel, Rachel had a hard time finding a taxi driver willing to take them to Brooklyn. She began to worry about missing her husband's first trip to the plate. Most taxis were not yet equipped with roof lights to signal when they were vacant, so she threw her arm up and out as dozens of yellow cabs passed her by. For black passengers, hailing a taxi was often an unpleasant experience made more trying by the absence of roof lights. One never knew for certain if the driver kept his foot on the gas because he saw a black face or because his backseat was already occupied. After a long wait, Rachel managed to corral a cab. The meter started at twenty cents, and she and Sugar Lump were on their way.

Her first order of business when she reached Ebbets Field was feeding the baby, so she stopped a hot dog vendor and asked him to warm the baby's formula in a steaming vat of water where he kept his franks. Then she settled into her seat behind the Dodger dugout in a section filled mostly with black men and women. The men in the section wore jackets, ties, overcoats, and hats. The women, their hair done up as if for a night on the town, wore heavy coats, scarves, and gloves. These were not their baseball clothes, not even their Opening Day clothes; these were their Sunday church clothes. This day was special.

Though temperatures were approaching sixty degrees, it felt colder in the grandstand's shade. Rachel, not yet familiar with New York weather, hadn't brought a heavy jacket for herself or the baby, who wore a light-blue suit and matching cap. Rachel handed Jack Jr. over to the woman seated to her right, who tucked him under her fur coat. Fussing over the baby helped distract her from what was happening on the ball field, from all the countless ways in which her husband might be hurt or disappointed that afternoon. Finally, though, Rachel, who had been watching baseball for only about a year and had not yet mastered its nuances, sat back to watch her husband play.

Hilda Chester, the team's unofficial mas-

112

cot, wore a flowered print dress and clanged her cowbell. The musicians in the Dodger Sym-Phony, a disheveled bunch of Italian-Americans from Williamsburg, banged their drums and honked their horns. Umpires wandered about the field, while the ballplayers around them behaved like children, running and throwing balls and teasing each other, giddy for the start of another season. In the dugout before the game, the Dodgers for the most part left Robinson alone. But when he stepped out onto the field, there was no ignoring him. The sight jolted some of the spectators, as if a man in shoulder pads and a football helmet had run across the baseball diamond. Not much of his skin was visible — he wore a white, long-sleeved undershirt beneath his jersey, and a blue Dodger cap shaded his face — but his deep darkness could hardly be missed, even from the bleachers and high up in the grandstand.

Robinson posed for pictures on the dugout steps with the rest of the Dodger infield, John "Spider" Jorgensen (who in spring training had beat out Arky Vaughan), Pee Wee Reese, and Eddie Stanky. Stanky rested an arm on Robinson's shoulder, and the rookie smiled broadly and naturally, as if he were completely at ease and unapologetic. When the pictures were done, the men went about the work of getting ready for the game, loosening their arms and fielding some soft ground balls. Game time approached.

"Jackie is very definitely brunette." That was broadcaster Red Barber's description, as one fan remembered the announcer describing the team's newest player over the WHN airwaves that afternoon. Bobby Parker, fourteen years old, stayed home from school that day to listen to the game. A Dodger rooter from the time he was eight, he lived in Springfield, Massachusetts, where most of the New York City stations came in clear as crystal. He liked to make his own scorecards on lined paper and mark the games' progress while he listened. Bobby had been in some trouble with his mother that year for befriending a Negro boy in his neighborhood. "My mother worried that if we hung together people would react badly," he recalled years later. Her biggest concern seemed to be that someone might want to hurt the black boy, and that her Bobby would be the victim of collateral damage. Listening to the game that afternoon, Bobby felt vindicated in his choice of friends. Parker loved words as much as he loved baseball, and now his two loves came together, because baseball provided him with a vocabulary to talk about race for the first time. If Pee Wee Reese and the other Dodgers could associate with a Negro, he would ask his mother, then why couldn't he?

Under the byline Robert B. Parker, he would go on to write novels, many of them bestsellers, including one set in 1947 in which he imagined Jackie Robinson dodging an assassin's bullets and befriending his white bodyguard. In his most popular series of mysteries, the detective Spenser is often accompanied by his friend Hawk, a tough black man with a knack for escaping trouble. "Looking at a ball game is like looking through a stereopticon," Spenser once said. "Everything seems heightened. The grass is greener. The uniform whites are brighter than they should be. Maybe it's the containment. The narrowing of the focus."

Parker never forgot the way a ballgame narrowed the nation's focus in 1947, nor did he forget the elegance of Red Barber's call: "Jackie is very definitely brunette." The attention of an entire nation was concentrated on Robinson's Opening Day appearance, even if some people, including at least a handful of Robinson's teammates, were trying to pretend it wasn't happening. In the Dodger clubhouse, some of the players failed to acknowledge the presence of the new player. Dixie Walker went so far as to turn from the camera, and away from Robinson, when the Dodgers posed for their annual team picture.

Years later, after Robinson had become a legend, several of his teammates would say they empathized with him that day. They said they could see how difficult it must have been for him, that they were in fact proud to be a part of such a historic moment, that they respected the rookie for his dignity and strength. But no one said such things at the time.

As the baritone Everett McCooey sang a painfully slow rendition of the national anthem, the pitcher Ralph Branca lined up on the field next to Robinson. Branca, twenty-one years old, was tall and dark-haired, with a long face, a hawk nose, and dark patches under his eyes. The son of Italian and Hungarian immigrants, Branca grew up tossing baseballs on the streets of Mount Vernon, New York, with anyone who wanted to play. "Blacks lived right next door to me," he recalled, "then there was an empty lot, then there was a little bungalow with two Paisans, then there was Reverend Tucker's family, they were black, then there were the Levines, who were Jewish. . . . I

116

lived in the League of Nations." That explains why he went out of his way to position himself alongside the team's only black player for the anthem. After the game, Branca's brother John teased him about it, saying, "Are you crazy standing next to him? What if some sharpshooter missed him by three feet and got you instead?"

The Dodgers were optimistic, but few objective observers picked them to win the pennant in 1947. In 1946, they had won — or almost won — with trickery and aggression, leading the league in fist fights and dirt-stained pants. But they had made no obvious improvements over the winter. Their pitching remained shaky, and they had not a single legitimate power hitter in the lineup. Their two best hitters, Pete Reiser and Dixie Walker, were prone to injury. The third-base job was still up in the air, and Robinson was a huge question mark. To make matters worse, the team was opening the season minus a manager.

Without Durocher, the popular *New York Post* columnist Jimmy Cannon wrote, "the Dodgers are inept and helpless." The team's greatest strength was its reckless style of play, which Durocher, the madman, had always orchestrated so well. Durocher was loudmouthed and foul, but his instincts for the game were exquisite. He never exactly said the words most closely associated with him — "Nice guys finish last" — but he embodied the philosophy. Leo the Lip was no nice guy, and thus far he had never finished last. He seemed to know almost without fail when to call for the steal, when to try the squeeze play, when to hit-and-run, when to curse out his players, and when to let his silence scare them silly. With Durocher gone, New York's sportswriters didn't give the Dodgers much chance. More specifically, they wondered who would stand up for Robinson when his teammates tried again to get rid of him.

Robinson trotted out to first base in the top half of the inning, a smile creasing his face. The Braves sent their first batter, Dick Culler, to the plate. Culler hit a ground ball to third base, where Jorgensen scooped it up and threw to first. Robinson squeezed it for the out. It was a simple catch, but the crowd expressed its delight as if they'd never seen anything quite like it.

It was official now. The game had begun. A black man was playing big-league ball.

Stanky started the bottom half of the first inning with a ground-out. Then came Robinson, greeted by another cheer, this

118

one much bigger than the last. In the stands, some fans stood to get a better look. Shouts of "C'mon, Jackie!" and "We're with you, boy!" rang out across the field. The great Johnny Sain, winner of twenty games the prior year, stood on the mound, ready to go. The Braves' third baseman, Bob Elliott, crept in on the grass in case of a bunt. Catcher Phil Masi crouched behind the plate.

Robinson squeezed his Louisville Slugger, roughly thirty-three ounces and thirty-five inches long, holding the bat high. Sain pitched not at Robinson's head or at his rib cage, as some had feared. He threw wicked curves and whistling fastballs, better pitches than most Robinson had seen, and he threw them for strikes. Robinson swung at one and slapped a sharp ground ball to third base. Elliott grabbed it and tossed to first for the easy out. As Robinson jogged back to the dugout, the crowd roared yet again.

There were more cheers when he came to bat in the third inning. This time he hit a soft fly ball to left for another out. By the fifth inning, the score was tied, 1–1. The Dodgers had a man on base when Robinson, stepping to the plate for the third time, had a chance to play the hero. Once again, the Braves' infielders crept in on the grass, looking for a bunt. As the pitch arrived, Robinson took a hack. It was not a pretty swing — too much shoulder, not enough wrist, same as usual. He hit it hard and up the middle, but not quite hard enough. Just as the ball was about to skip safely into center field, shortstop Culler dove, gloved it, and, while lying on his stomach, flipped to second base to start a double play. If there were highlight reels in 1947, Culler's gem would have been all over them.

"Too bad about that double-play," said Harry J. Boger, an insurance broker from Brooklyn, talking to a reporter as he watched the game, "but that colored fellow is just under terrific pressure."

Stanky began the bottom of the seventh with a walk — his specialty. With Stanky leading off first, Robinson stepped to the plate once more. The Dodgers trailed, 3–2. The crowd buzzed. Long shadows fell across the field as Robinson raised his big bat high once again, and, once again, the Braves looked for him to bunt. This time he didn't disappoint. He pushed the ball delicately up the first-base line, perfectly placed. Earl Torgeson, the first baseman, grabbed it and spun around to throw to first. But by now Robinson was dashing down the line, and Torgeson had to hurry.

120

He threw to second baseman Connie Ryan, who was covering the bag, but the throw sailed wide to the right. The ball glanced off Robinson's right shoulder and rolled into foul territory. Stanky zipped to third and Robinson to second. When Pete Reiser followed with a double, Stanky and Robinson both scored to give the Dodgers a 4–3 lead.

Later, the left-fielder Gene Hermanski drove in another run to push the score to 5–3, where it remained. Nearly sixty years later, his memory smoothed by time, Hermanski would tell friends and strangers that it was he who had driven in Robinson with the winning run on Opening Day. "George Washington and Abraham Lincoln didn't know what people were going to say about them twenty-five, fifty years later," he noted. "We didn't know this was history. You wouldn't realize it until later on. Jackie was the first black guy to touch home plate in a big-league game, and I was the one who knocked him in. At least I think I was."

How closely was Robinson being watched? One reporter, Sam Lacy of the *Baltimore Afro-American,* took a seat opposite the Dodger dugout in order to provide his readers an inning-by-inning account of Robinson's seating choice and facial expressions.

Throughout most of the game, the story said, Robinson sat next to Sukeforth, like a new kid at school sticking close to the teacher, although at times he was joined by Pete Reiser, catcher Bruce Edwards, or Tom Tatum, the part-time outfielder who had been his teammate at Montreal. At other times he sat alone. In the bottom of the seventh, after he'd scored the winning run, according to Lacy, Robinson allowed himself a yawn.

The *Pittsburgh Courier* devoted almost its entire front page to Robinson. The *Chicago Defender* ran pictures above the masthead and included four stories and a photo essay on its inside pages. The *Richmond Afro-American* led with two big headlines, Robinson's debut and a report that the city's police department planned to double the number of Negro officers on the force, from four to eight. In the communist *Daily Worker,* Lester Rodney wrote: "It's hard this Opening Day to write straight baseball and not stop to mention the wonderful fact of Jackie Robinson." The *People's Voice* of Harlem ran a picture of Robinson in uniform on its front page but dedicated its biggest headline to the story of a black artist beaten by a white mob in Greenwich Village. The *Boston Chronicle* described Robinson as "very colored" and predicted he would open doors for black Americans well beyond the baseball field.

Elsewhere, however, the response was subdued. There was no notice made from the White House, and no pronouncement from Mayor William O'Dwyer. *The New York Times* confined the story to the sports page, and even then Robinson was not deemed headline-worthy. His actions on the field were described in the day's game story, but there was no mention of his race and no description of how he was received by fans. Arthur Daley, a sports columnist for the *Times,* waited until the tenth paragraph of his dispatch to mention Robinson's breakthrough, which he described as "quite uneventful." It was much the same in New York's *Daily Mirror,* where Robinson went unmentioned until the fourth paragraph of the game story.

It was a pattern that would repeat itself all season long. White journalists had little experience writing about integration, and sportswriters were even more unfamiliar with the subject. Rather than plunge into unfamiliar waters, they stuck close to the shore, treating Robinson as just another ballplayer, except when some unavoidable piece of news like a death threat or a threatened boycott came across their desks and forced the issue.

"Having Jackie on the team is a little strange," one member of the Dodgers told Daley of the *Times* that day, "just like anything else that's new. We just don't know how to act with him. But he'll be accepted in time. You can be sure of that. Other sports have had Negroes. Why not baseball? I'm for it if he can win games. That's the only test I ask."

Only a handful of people fully appreciated what had happened during the ballgame's two hours and twenty-six minutes. Seldom do heroes recognize their heroics in the instant. In 1947, Chuck Yeager broke the sound barrier; Jackson Pollock dripped paint on canvas for the first time; Jawaharlal Nehru declared the people of India free at last from British colonial rule; scientists at Bell Labs assembled the first transistor from strips of gold foil on a plastic triangle, held down gently by a piece of germanium; Thor Heyerdahl sailed a balsa raft called the *Kon-Tiki* from Peru to Polynesia; Miles Davis joined Charlie Parker's quintet, which reshaped the sound of jazz; and Jack Roosevelt Robinson, as ambitious as the rest, played nine innings of baseball. When he was done, a mob of 250 people, most of them white, waited for him outside the ballpark. It took him thirty minutes to work his way through the crowd of backslappers and autograph hounds. When he finally escaped into a friend's car, his body sagged into the cushioned backseat, and he released a heavy sigh.

Back at the McAlpin Hotel that evening, he and his wife took turns going out for dinner so that one of them might stay in the room at all times with the baby. Early in the evening, Ward Morehouse, a drama critic for the *New York Sun,* knocked on the door of the Robinsons' room and asked for an interview. It took a writer who didn't cover sports to land the best story of the day.

How was your first game? Morehouse asked, as Robinson and Jack Jr. sat on the bed swatting at toys.

"It was all right," Robinson answered. "I did all my thinking last night. Before I went to bed I thanked God for all that's happened, and for the good fortune that's come my way. I belong to the Methodist Church in Pasadena and I used to be a Sunday school teacher at U.C.L.A.; they gave me the bad little boys, and I liked it. I was determined not to give too much thought to it being my first game and that's

125

the way I did it. I didn't want too much pressure. . . .

"I was comfortable on that field in my first game. The Brooklyn players have been swell and they were encouraging all the way. The Brooklyn crowd was certainly on my side, but I don't know how it will be in other parks. The size of the crowd didn't faze me and it never will.

"Now I realize that to stay in the National League, I'll have to hit. I hit .349 for Montreal last year and I was pretty fast, but I already realize there's a difference. The big league pitchers are smarter. I realize that, although I haven't seen but a few of them. Take that fellow Sain. . . . He works on you. He has good control. I'm aware that I have to make it this year — this is my great chance. Will I hit? I hope I'll hit. I believe I'll hit. I'm sure I'll hit."

He picked up Jack Jr., lowered him into his crib, and went right on talking.

"I know that a lot of players, particularly the southern boys, won't be able to change their feelings overnight on the matter of playing ball with a Negro. I can understand that. I have encountered very little antagonism, however; I really expected a great deal more . . . I guess now it's all up to me.

". . . I know that I have a certain responsibility to my race, but I've got to try not to feel that way about it because it would be too much of a strain. I'll do my best."

As Rachel returned from dinner, the reporter said good-bye and moved for the door.

Robinson gave him one final instruction: "Just say that I know that this year is the test."

FIVE:
UP IN HARLEM

After two games at Ebbets Field, the Dodgers traveled across town to play the Giants at the Polo Grounds. At that moment, it was still not clear if Robinson would be an everyday player.

The team had a new manager, Burt Shotton, known to friends as Barney. Shotton hadn't been to the Polo Grounds since 1922, when he'd played there as a member of the St. Louis Cardinals, and he had a hard time finding the place again. At one point, he said, he wound up "on that Triple-Borough Bridge, traveling east in a westbound lane," and as a result arrived too late to introduce himself properly to his players before the game. Gray-haired and gray-eyed, Shotton was a soft-spoken, grandfatherly man. He'd been around professional baseball since 1908, and now, at sixty-two, he considered himself too old to be strutting around in a baseball uniform. He would wear street clothes in the dugout, he declared: proper slacks, starched shirt, bowtie, topped by a Dodger windbreaker on cooler days. Sometimes he would put on a ball cap, and at other times a fedora. Without a uniform, he would be prohibited by the rules of the game from stepping onto the field. That meant no shouting at umpires, no cajoling of pitchers, no chance for the fans ever to set eyes on him. Shotton didn't care. He would be managing a team of misfits, a pennant-contending lineup if all went perfectly well, but nonetheless a team full of obvious flaws. Staying out of sight might have struck him as a good idea.

Then there was his biggest challenge: Robinson. There was no blueprint for the job ahead. No one had ever managed under the conditions now facing Shotton. He didn't seem worried. He stared out placidly from behind his wire-rimmed glasses and made clear that he saw nothing to get excited about. Ever. In fact, though he had agreed to take the job, he had not bothered to ask Rickey for a contract, or even to inquire how much the job paid.

"Heck," he told Red Barber's radio audience before his first game, "I don't even have a hotel room to sleep in tonight!"

On the eve of the Dodgers' first game with

the Giants, there were at least three men hoping the new manager might park Robinson on the bench. One was Ed Stevens, who had been the leading contender for the first baseman's job before Robinson came along. Stevens was known by his teammates as "Whistling Ed" for the bizarre whistling noises — part bird call, part taxi-hailing screech — he made while fielding his position. He did it to keep his fellow infielders on their toes, he said. Stevens had grown up in poverty in Galveston, Texas, and played sandlot ball with kids of every color. He had no problem being on the same team as a black man. It was losing his job that bothered him.

"I was considered one of the best-fielding first basemen in the league," he said. "I had power. I could hit home runs. I was a clutch hitter. I felt my abilities were major-league stature." But he felt he wasn't getting the playing time he needed to show his talent. Branch Rickey's big experiment was getting in his way. He considered himself a victim of something like affirmative action, a term not yet in use, but he decided to keep his mouth shut.

The second was Howie Schultz, the team's other first baseman, although by now Schultz had a good idea that his Dodger days were numbered. He was thinking about giving up baseball and trying his luck at professional basketball.

The third man who may have wanted to see Robinson take some time off was Ford C. Frick, the former sportswriter now serving as president of the National League. The Giants played in the Polo Grounds, in Harlem, and it was Frick's fear that Harlem's enormous black population might celebrate Robinson's arrival with more enthusiasm than the nation's grand old game could handle. He had no qualms about integration, just as long as people didn't get too worked up over it. Frick suggested that it might be a fine idea if Robinson were to sprain an ankle and miss a few games.

Harlem was a place of extraordinary wonder and woe. As black families moved to the North throughout the 1940s, the community grew painfully crowded and desperately poor. In 1940, 458,000 black people lived in New York City. By the time of Robinson's debut, the number was approaching 700,000. Harlem wasn't just packed, it was packed with anxious energy. Lines at the unemployment office in Harlem were growing longer by the month in 1947, even as prices for everyday goods soared. Men who had proved their competence in the army were out of work and they were angry about it. Businesses all over the neighborhood were struggling with the drop in income, which led to more lost jobs. Black families in New York tended to earn less money than white families. They spent a greater portion of their income on rent. They paid more for groceries. They sent their children to inferior schools. They received inferior medical care and they tended to die younger.

Now, in the years after the war, discontent rumbled through Harlem like a subway train. In the vast trench between hope and reality, a political movement took root. "The Negro people," said Adam Clayton Powell, the black congressman who represented Harlem, "will be satisfied with nothing short of complete equality — political, economic, educational, religious, social."

America's history books tend to set the birth of the modern civil rights movement in 1954, with the Supreme Court's decision in *Brown* v. *Board of Education,* or in 1955, when Rosa Parks defied an order to move to the back of the bus in Montgomery, Alabama. But a case can be made, as Martha Biondi contends in her book, *To Stand and Fight,* that the struggle really began in Harlem in 1945, at about the time that

132

Branch Rickey signed Jackie Robinson to a minor-league contract. As Biondi and others have noted, Rickey's decision to sign Robinson had a lot to do with the political heat rising from Harlem. Businesses all over the city, from big military contractors to small, family-owned restaurants, faced pressure to integrate. Labor leaders, church ministers, Communist Party organizers, Jewish activists, and famous entertainers led the campaign, and they won some impressive victories, raising hopes throughout all black America.

Robinson had connected with at least two left-wing groups in 1946, according to his FBI file and newspaper clippings. An article in the *People's Voice* newspaper said Robinson had agreed to become chair of the New York State Organizing Committee for United Negro and Allied Veterans of America, and to speak at one of the group's conferences in Harlem. The organization sought to help black veterans adjust to life after war, although the increasingly suspicious FBI later described it as a communist front. "I consider it a great honor. . . ." Robinson wrote in a telegram. "The burning problems of discrimination in housing, employment, education and on-the-job training facing Negro veterans demand an

133

immediate solution. I am happy to join Joe Louis, honorary national commander of UNAVA, in the fight to solve these problems."

Robinson was also identified in a newspaper article as a member of the advisory board for a new cultural center in Harlem. The center was created by the International Workers Order, a left-wing labor group with alleged communist ties. And in December of 1946 he had agreed to speak at a couple of fund-raising events for the Detroit Committee to Fight Racial Injustice and Terrorism, another group that the government would later label subversive. Robinson canceled his appearance in Detroit at the last minute, perhaps on orders from Rickey, a staunch anticommunist, who said repeatedly that he wanted his player to focus entirely on baseball.

"Branch Rickey was not favorably inclined toward his involvement, and in fact he was hostile toward it," recalled Lester Rodney, the sportswriter for the communist *Daily Worker,* who covered Robinson and the Dodgers in 1947. "Jackie was personally an outspoken and intelligent guy. . . . His instinct was to get involved. . . . [But] he knew in this particular situation he couldn't alienate Rickey."

But before Rickey intervened, Robinson had tipped his hand. Free of restraint, he had aligned himself with the radical left. He was an athlete first, but he was a battler to the core, and he appeared eager to place himself at the center of the fight for civil rights. He was proud to be a symbol of the push for integration, but he was prepared to do more. Athletes and entertainers had always been at the front of the civil rights movement. Even before Robinson, the actors Paul Robeson, Lena Horne, and Canada Lee had been outspoken in their political views. After Robinson, black athletes from Muhammad Ali to Arthur Ashe would use their fame to push for social change. They were fighting for their people, but they were also fighting for themselves. Racial discrimination in housing would have a direct effect on Jackie Robinson's family in the months and years ahead. When Rachel Robinson had difficulty hailing a cab in Manhattan to take her to Ebbets Field on Opening Day, she learned something black New Yorkers had known for years — and know still today — about the city's taxi drivers.

In the years ahead, the crackdown on communism and a growing strain of politi-

135

cal conservatism would cool the civil rights movement in Harlem. But in 1947, as Robinson and the Dodgers prepared to play their first game at the Polo Grounds, Harlem remained thrillingly volatile. It was unclear if black Americans were on the brink of great gains or terrible troubles, but they were clearly on the brink. The community's tensions went on display whenever the Giants played at the Polo Grounds. As thousands of white New Yorkers traveled to Harlem by Checker cab and train to see the games, scores of police officers — most of them white — kept careful watch to make sure fans got in and out of the neighborhood safely. Fights in the stands were common in the 1940s, particularly in New York, where ethnic groups that avoided each other on the streets wound up close together, and drunk, in the bleachers and grandstands. Dodger-Giant games were among the most contentious of all, dividing ethnic groups and even families. But there had never been big black crowds at Giants games, at least not that anyone could remember. Suddenly, with the arrival of Robinson, much of black Harlem began pulling for the Dodgers, as Langston Hughes noted in a poem called "Passing."

On sunny summer Sunday afternoons in
  Harlem
when the air is one interminable ball game
and grandma cannot get her gospel hymns
from the Saints of God in Christ
on account of the Dodgers on the radio . . .

And while Frick considered himself an enlightened man, he worried about how Harlem's new Dodger fans would express themselves. He wasn't asking the Dodgers to set aside their experiment, merely to go slowly and avoid unnecessary risk. Before the game, Harlem's *Amsterdam News* cautioned its black readers to behave. "There is no need to take the bottle to the stands," its editorial pronounced. "Profanity is not necessary and the grandstands certainly are not picnic grounds. Don't think that we want you to go to the park and sit like a mummy or portray a saint. We want you to have fun — all the fun there is — but in a clean, healthy manner. . . . It will be well to remember that we are on the spot just as Jackie. We cannot afford to let him down!!!"

Even Branch Rickey warned that Robinson's fans were making his job more difficult. "Jackie's greatest danger is social," he pronounced, pounding on his desk as he

137

spoke to reporters. "Why, he gets 5,000 invitations to attend all sorts of events and on top of that he scarcely has time to eat or change into his uniform. The boy is on the road to complete prostration. . . . There are too many well-wishers and too many seeking to exploit him. It would be best for all these people to let him alone."

Dan Burley, a sports columnist for the *Amsterdam News,* was more worried about the action on the field than on the streets or in the grandstand. "Somewhere down the line," he wrote, "it's going to come, and by that I mean Jackie's biggest moment when some opposing player calls him something we hate to be called and he's either got to get down with it or lose prestige in the eyes of the fans and maybe his teammates. But that is where the issue will narrow down: Jackie isn't supposed to punch anybody in the jaw for insulting him or intentionally roughing him. He's got to be so set with the whole Dodger club that they will take charge of the situation themselves, waving Jackie to the sidelines while they swing their bats and boots. . . . That coming about will be the biggest hurdle for Jackie as a Dodger. Then he'll belong and start being the sensation that destiny marked him out to be when he was a tot in Georgia."

As excitement built among black fans for the Polo Grounds meeting, apprehension grew among some whites. Bob Cooke, a writer for the *Herald Tribune,* told a couple of his colleagues that before it was over the Robinson experiment would destroy the national pastime. Cooke supposedly believed an anthropologist's theory that longer heel bones gave black people greater speed, and those heel bones, he argued, constituted an unfair advantage. "The Negroes have the legs," he said, in a story told by the writer Roger Kahn. "It starts with Robinson but it doesn't end with Robinson. Negroes are going to run the white people out of baseball. They're going to take over our game."

The crowds were in fact enormous at the Polo Grounds: 38,736 for the first game, which was on a Friday afternoon, when people with jobs couldn't break away. If there were an unusual number of black fans in the crowd, none of the writers at the game mentioned it, although the *Times* did report that vendors on Eighth Avenue were doing a lively business selling "I'm For Jackie" lapel pins. Creole Pete Robertson, a Harlem resident, announced formation of the Jackie Robinson Booster Club, and said five hundred Harlemites had signed on for membership in the club's first week. James

Baldwin, a young black writer from New York who had just published his first big magazine piece, wrote: "Back in the thirties and forties, Joe Louis was the only hero that we ever had. When he won a fight, everybody in Harlem was up in heaven. On that April day the large contingent of blacks in the crowd of nearly 40,000 had another hero to be 'up in heaven' about, another hero to stand beside Joe Louis."

It was a cool Friday afternoon, April 18, with temperatures creeping up toward sixty degrees at game time, not a cloud in the sky. Shotton sent Vic Lombardi to the mound. Lombardi was a little man with an array of mostly soft pitches, but against the Giants, he was huge, having won nine straight. Dave Koslo, a slender lefty, pitched for the Giants. In the top of the first, after Eddie Stanky tapped one back to the pitcher for an easy out, Robinson stepped to the plate and heard a sudden, thunderous roll of applause, like a crashing wave. He watched one Koslo pitch go by, a high, inside curve. On the next pitch, a high fastball, he swung, hitting it on a soft arc into the glove of center-fielder Lloyd Gearhart for the second out.

In the third inning, he came to the plate

140

again, greeted by the clamoring crowd. By now the score was tied, 1–1. Koslo went into his windup, kicking his right leg high in the air and throwing high and inside for ball one. The next pitch was the same, high and inside, but not so high and not so far inside. Robinson swung and connected. The ball zipped on a long line drive and pinged against the upper-deck scoreboard in left field for a home run, his first. As Robinson trotted around the bases, toes turned inward, his fans stood and laughed and hollered and hugged one another, celebrating their good fortune as well as his.

Bob Cooke, seated in the press box behind home plate, meanwhile, took some sassing.

"That's because their heels are longer," cracked one of Cooke's fellow scribes.

Robinson ran quickly around the bases, without smiling or tipping his cap. As he stepped on home plate with his right foot, Tommy Tatum, the next batter, reached out and shook his hand. A photographer captured the moment, a black man and a white man hand in hand on a baseball diamond on a glorious afternoon, and the picture ran on the back page of the *Daily News* the following day.

With two homers from Bobby Thomson, one from Johnny Mize, one from Bill

Rigney, and another from Willard Marshall, the Giants went back on top, 6–2. But Robinson wasn't finished giving thrills. Leading off the eighth, he fell behind in the count, no balls and two strikes, then swung at a high fastball, this one on the outer half of the plate, and hit a bloop fly to right field, where it landed in front of Marshall. As the outfielder collected the ball and looked up, he saw Robinson running around first and headed toward second. The routine play for the outfielder is to throw to second to keep the runner from advancing, but Marshall couldn't tell yet if Robinson was going to second or back to first. When Robinson hit the brakes, Marshall thought he had a chance to catch him off first. It looked as if Robinson had overcommitted. But in his rush, Marshall threw wildly, and the ball sailed beyond the first baseman's reach. Robinson scampered to second. Then he scored from there on Carl Furillo's hit. It was the sort of play that would make Robinson famous, a reflection of his speed and daring, of his fearlessness. It wasn't enough to win the game for the Dodgers, but it was something to see.

For the second game, on Saturday afternoon, 52,355 fans paid to get into the Polo Grounds, and another 736 servicemen were admitted at no charge, making this the biggest Saturday audience ever to attend a single game at the Polo Grounds. And this time there was no mistaking the strong turnout among Harlemites. Robinson, in turn, enjoyed the best performance of his young career, with two singles and a double in three at-bats. After he smacked a single off the leg of pitcher Monte Kennedy, Robinson waited until the end of the inning and asked the pitcher if he was okay. The Dodgers lost 4–3, but for many of Harlem's black fans, it was an ideal outcome: Robinson had a great game *and* the home team got the win.

Afterward, Jackie and Rachel enjoyed a rare evening away from home and without Jack Jr., dining at Lawson Bowman's Café in Harlem, where cameras flashed, guests approached for autographs, and the proprietor pulled up a chair.

By the end of his first week with the Dodgers, Robinson owned a .429 batting average and a locker all his own. The Dodger clubhouse was a rectangular concrete block, about forty feet long and twenty-five feet wide, tucked beneath the Ebbets Field grandstand. Each player had a gray metal locker, with a mat on the floor and a small stool in front. The team's four biggest stars — Reese, Reiser, Walker, and Hugh Casey — had the biggest lockers at the center of the room, while the other lockers were lined up along the walls. Filtered light and the sound of traffic came in through windows high along Sullivan Place. Robinson was assigned the worst locker in the clubhouse, far back in the corner, next to the grouchy old equipment manager, Dan Comerford, as far out of sight as possible. His locker was near the clothes dryer, the toilets, and the showers. The manager's office and training table were at the opposite end of the room.

Sitting on his wooden stool, Robinson would have stared across at the red Coca-Cola cooler, where cold bottles of Coke (ten cents each) were stored. Players were supposed to mark a chalkboard above the cooler every time they took a bottle so that the bat boy, Stan Strull, would know who owed how much. They were honest about it. To the right of Robinson, on the floor near the entrance to the trainer's room, sat the money trunk. Each player would take his rings, watches, and wallets, slip them into bags, and put the bags in the money trunk, which would remain locked during the game.

By now Jackie felt confident enough about his spot on the team that he and Rachel had begun looking for an apartment in Brooklyn. When the Dodger front office pitched in to help in his search, reporters interpreted it as a sign that he would be sticking around, and several writers urged their readers to phone their newspaper offices with tips on available housing. With so many black families moving up from the South, and with so many soldiers returning from Europe, the competition for affordable apartments in black neighborhoods was intense. But a woman named Mabel C. Brown, who had an unused bedroom in her own Bedford-Stuyvesant apartment, read about the Robinsons' problem. She phoned the couple at the McAlpin Hotel and offered to rent them her empty space. Brown's apartment was on MacDonough Street, between Ralph and Patchen avenues, in a neighborhood full of row houses, small groceries, tobacco shops, and corner churches. The two-bedroom unit was small — about one thousand square feet — and had only one bathroom. But Brown pointed out to the Robinsons that she was single and had no children, so there would not be much competition for the bathroom and kitchen. Without having seen the place or having

145

met the woman with whom they'd be rooming, they decided to take it, a decision they would later regret.

On the day they moved in, Robinson gave an interview to Gilbert Jonas, a seventeen-year-old aspiring journalist from Brooklyn's Lafayette High School. Gil's sister was dating a man who knew Robinson from Montreal and had arranged the interview. When he was twelve, Gil had worked as a turnstile boy at Ebbets Field. The team would pay him fifty cents and let him watch the day's game from a general admission seat. At about the same time, he took up photography so that he could get closer to some of his favorite athletes. By the time he was fifteen, the *Brooklyn Eagle* had begun purchasing his pictures. He also wrote letters to his favorite baseball players, asking for autographs. He'd received a handwritten reply from Ty Cobb and managed to arrange a meeting with Babe Ruth. He invented something he called "The National Sports Fan Club," printed his own letterhead, and sent invitations to some of his favorite athletes to become honorary members. All they had to do was sign autographs on the index cards Gil conveniently enclosed. He sometimes sent dozens of cards at a time, without offering explanation, hoping to reap a bounty of signatures. There was no club, of course. It was strictly a ploy by Jonas to enhance his autograph collection, and it worked. He acquired thirteen Hank Greenbergs, thirty-four Marty Marions, sixteen George Cases, five Dolph Camillis, thirteen Bob Fellers, five Walter Johnsons, six Eddie Collinses, seven Leo Durochers, seven Casey Stengels, and sixteen Babe Ruths.

There were no black athletes in his collection, nor had he ever engaged in a conversation of any depth with a black person to that point in his life. "When my father had some money, he would get a cleaning lady for a couple of days," he said. Lafayette High School had one black student in 1947, as best he could tell, and Gil didn't know his name. He noticed that black people sometimes stepped into the gutter when they passed him on the street, but he didn't think much of it.

He took two subways to Brooklyn's Bedford-Stuyvesant neighborhood, walked to the Robinsons' apartment at 526 MacDonough, and rang the buzzer. Robinson came out and sat with him on the stoop. Jonas was struck at once by the man's size — wide shoulders, thick chest descending into a narrow waist. The ballplayer wore a long-sleeved V-neck sweater and pleated trousers. With his hair trimmed short on the sides and slightly longer on top, he appeared even taller than he was. His face was soft yet strongly masculine. He smiled easily and answered Gil's questions patiently, never making the young man feel like anything less than a serious journalist.

"Would you prefer playing another infield position rather than first base?" Gil asked on behalf of readers of the *Lafayette News.*

"Most definitely," Robinson said, smiling. "I'd rather play second base, but as long as I am benefiting the club at first, I'll remain there."

While they were talking, Rachel Robinson and Jack Jr. arrived by taxi from the McAlpin. Gil helped Robinson unload suitcases and crates from the taxi's trunk and carry them into the first-floor apartment. Gil was a short, slender kid, the son of a garment manufacturer, Jewish, with a head full of dark curls that he combed up and back. He was a graceful athlete but too small to compete for a spot on the baseball team at Lafayette, which is why he hoped someday to become a sports journalist. His plan was to graduate early from high school and go to college as far from Brooklyn as

148

he could.

He and Robinson spent about an hour talking that day. Not once did the subject of race or integration enter the conversation. Gil asked the same questions he would have asked had he been interviewing Duke Snider or Gil Hodges, a couple of other young players who were, coincidentally, sharing apartments with strangers that summer in Brooklyn. Gil asked about the competition for the National League pennant. He asked about Robinson's days at UCLA. He asked about Jackie's greatest thrill as an athlete. When he was done, he snapped a picture of the athlete standing on the sidewalk in front of his new apartment, left hand on his hip, a gentle smile creasing his face, eyes not quite on the camera.

Gil knew a little bit about the world. He knew that Jewish kids got beat up for walking in certain Irish neighborhoods. He knew that World War II had been fought in part over Aryan supremacy. But he had never thought about how black Americans were treated in America — not until soon after his interview with Robinson, anyway, when the Philadelphia Phillies came to Brooklyn to play the Dodgers on April 22.

The *New York Post* that morning carried a story saying Robinson's debut with the

Dodgers was off to such a fine start that he might soon supplant the popular Stanky at second base. If the Dodgers could find a power hitter to play first base — and Branch Rickey was said to be looking — then the light-hitting Stanky might have to go. "All hands agree now that he [Robinson] can't be kept off the ball club. He's too sound and solid a player." It was a generous conclusion, given that Robinson had only a few games under his belt. No one knew yet how he would respond to his first slump, to the first beanball, to the racist abuse that would be heaped by fans and players when the team traveled, to the physical demands of a long season.

It was a Tuesday afternoon, and a chilly one. The ballpark was quiet as Robinson stepped to the plate for his first look at old Dutch Leonard, the Phillies' starting pitcher. There were a lot of empty seats and a lot of fans wearing gloves and mittens. But while the grandstand remained virtually silent as Robinson dug his cleats into the back of the batter's box, a torrent of foul language, harsher than anything Robinson had heard in his professional baseball career, poured from the Phillies' dugout. Robinson recalled a few snippets of the invective in the autobiography he wrote at

150

the end of his rookie season:

"Hey, you black Nigger! Why don't you go back where you came from?"

"Yeah, pretty soon you'll want to eat and sleep with white ballplayers!"

And those were just the two he deemed suitable for print. His accounts in later years, and accounts by others who were there, say the Phillies mentioned Robinson's thick lips, thick skull, and sores and diseases his teammates and their wives would likely contract by associating with him. They were powerful words delivered at high volume by a surprisingly large number of players. Bench jockeying had always been a part of the game, and the taunting often centered on ethnicity. Babe Ruth had been called "Nigger Lips" by players who speculated that at least one of his ancestors must have been black. Hank Greenberg, the game's greatest Jewish star, had been referred to as a kike and a Christ killer. But even veterans of the game had never heard anything like the insults hurled at Robinson. Ben Chapman, the Alabama-born manager of the Phillies, was leading the cry and had reportedly ordered his players to join him. They would incur fines if they didn't obey, some players later recalled. "Figuratively, he was still fighting the Civil War," recalled Howie

151

Schultz, who was in the Dodger dugout that day and later played for Chapman in Philadelphia. "He was just embittered when Robinson joined the league."

White people said such things and worse all the time. Even white people with no particular animosity toward black people spouted off among friends from time to time. Occasionally, on a factory floor, in a bar, or aboard a bus, a white person might launch a verbal assault in the face of a black person. Relations were tense, conflicts inevitable. But seldom did such raw attacks occur on a public stage, with real emotions flashing, and with thousands of people watching and listening. Fortunately, it was a weekday afternoon, and few children were in the crowd. But for everyone who heard Chapman and the Phillies that day, the outburst served as a sort of Rorschach test. Instantly, instinctively, they may have been repulsed, shocked, embarrassed, horrified, humiliated, discomfited, ambivalent, mildly pleased, or perhaps even genuinely delighted. Gil Jonas, who was at the game, was startled and confused. Robinson wanted to put his fist through someone's face.

"For one wild and rage-crazed minute I thought, 'To hell with Mr. Rickey's noble experiment,' " he recalled years later. "I

152

thought what a glorious, cleansing thing it would be to let go. To hell with the image of the patient black freak I was supposed to create. I would throw down my bat, stride over to the Phillies dugout, grab one of those white sons of bitches and smash his teeth in with my despised black fist. Then I could walk away from it all."

He didn't. The first two pitches to Robinson were curveballs, high and inside, perhaps intended to send a message. The second one was close enough to the strike zone for Robinson to hack at it, which he did, raising a routine fly ball to left field. The Dodgers and Phillies played tense, scoreless baseball through seven-and-a-half innings. By the end of the seventh, some of the cold, damp crowd had gone home. In the top half of the eighth, Robinson made a great, spearing catch to snuff a Philadelphia rally. Then, in the bottom half, he took a curveball on the outer half of the plate for a strike and then swung at a fastball, poking it softly but in just the right spot, a few feet past second base. The grandstand murmured with excitement; no one wanted to see extra innings on such a frigid afternoon. With Pete Reiser at the plate, Robinson took a long lead from first, his right foot scratching at the infield's soggy clay, and then took off. Reiser swung and missed, strike three. Andy Seminick, the Phillies' catcher, tried to throw Robinson out but never had a chance; his throw sailed into center field. Robinson hopped up from his slide and started running again, speeding safely to third. After a walk to Walker, Hermanski smacked a single to center, scoring Robinson.

In the top of the ninth, with the Dodgers clinging to a 1–0 lead, the Phillies had the tying run on first when Robinson committed his first error of the season, letting a sharp grounder shoot under his glove. Now the Phillies had runners on first and third with two outs. Chapman sent the slugger Nick Etten in to pinch hit. Etten smashed a hard grounder past the pitcher. It looked like a certain hit, which would have tied the game. But Pee Wee Reese, the slick shortstop, gloved the ball just before it touched down in the center-field grass and flipped to Stanky at second for the game-ending out. "Greatest play I ever saw," said the pitcher Hal Gregg. Robinson, his error erased, was even happier than Gregg. He sprinted across the field to slap Reese on the back.

The victory helped Robinson feel better about what had been one of the most trying afternoons of his life. But the next day, Chapman and his men continued their taunting. This time, at least, some of Robinson's teammates stood up for him. They knew that Robinson had promised Branch Rickey he would not respond to any such attacks. "Listen, you yellow-bellied cowards," Stanky was said to have shouted across the field, "why don't you yell at someone who can answer back." Even Dixie Walker supposedly told his fellow Alabaman Chapman that he had gone too far.

In the third game of the series, Chapman called in sick, letting one of his coaches take over for him in the dugout. But the storm over his behavior didn't end. In the days and weeks ahead, fans and sportswriters weighed in on whether Chapman had a right to harass Robinson. *The Sporting News* noted that all ballplayers faced insults, and cited the case of the great pitcher Lynwood "Schoolboy" Rowe, saying "few players had ever had to take in more copious doses" of punishment than Rowe. But Rowe was teased about a dumb remark he'd once made on the radio, not the color of his skin, and the attackers never once suggested that they wished to see him permanently expelled from the game of baseball. If the literate men at *The Sporting News* couldn't see

155

the difference between Rowe and Robinson, it was little surprise that ballplayers were no better. And they weren't. "We will treat Robinson the same as we do Hank Greenberg of the Pirates, Clint Hartung of the Giants, Joe Garagiola of the Cardinals, Connie Ryan of the Braves, or any other man who is likely to step to the plate and beat us," Chapman said, naming some of the game's prominent ethnic ballplayers, and suggesting that the taunting was more a strategy than an expression of his personal feelings. "There is not a man who has come to the big leagues since baseball has been played who has not been ridden." Chapman may have been right. Maybe he did mean to give Robinson the same treatment any rookie might expect. But his claim wasn't helped by his reputation. As an outfielder for the Yankees in the 1930s, Chapman had made a specialty of baiting Jewish ballplayers, and he'd been in a huge brawl with one of them, Buddy Myer of the Senators. There were several Jewish stars in the 1930s, including Myer, Harry Danning, and of course, Hank Greenberg, and more Jews of marginal talent, but their presence was still small enough that they stood out. Now, with the arrival of Robinson, Chapman found an easier target.

Robinson didn't know whether Chapman would be the worst or merely the first of many. But, as it happened, Philadelphia's manager might have done him a favor. Some fans seated near the Phillies dugout wrote to Commissioner Chandler to complain about what they'd heard, and Chandler in turn warned the owner of the Phillies to control his manager or face punishment. Walter Winchell, the most popular journalist in the country — and the most spiteful — used his Sunday night radio broadcast to attack Chapman's behavior. "Ballplayers who don't want to be in the same ball park with Robinson don't belong in the same country with him!" Winchell trumpeted. Robinson had his own column in 1947, as did many popular sports figures at the time. Robinson's was ghostwritten by Wendell Smith of the *Pittsburgh Courier,* and thanks to Smith's accommodating nature and long-range view of the integration effort, the column tended to deflect most insults. Thus Robinson announced in his column that Chapman's assault "didn't really bother me."

Gil Jonas was neither convinced nor calmed. As the days and weeks went by, the teenager returned to those taunts again and again, replaying them in his mind, puzzling

157

over what could have inspired them and wondering what the black people sitting in the grandstand around him must have thought as they listened.

"I didn't know people could be that cruel," he said.

Only at that moment did the teenager begin to realize that Robinson was not like the other ballplayers he'd followed through the years. Only then did he begin to realize that life in America was different for black people, harder, more complicated, more painful. Only then did it occur to him that he had failed to ask Robinson some important questions in his interview. From that point on in the season, he began attending games not only to see whether the Dodgers would win but to see how Robinson was holding up, to see how black fans maintained their decorum, and to see if the race-baiting would let up. It was as if a new set of senses had become available to him. Week by week, he would notice a change. Some of the white fans who might have let slip a few snide remarks on race seemed to stop. Some of those who had sat in silence, unsure what to make of baseball's lone black man, broke down and began to cheer him. "I watched people who were hard-hearted or antagonistic . . . ," he recalled.

". . . and they changed. It was palpable. It changed so completely, and it changed me over the course of the season. Just watching the pain this guy felt, hearing the shouting across the field, it became very personal."

When Gil graduated from high school in 1948, he fulfilled his wish to go far from Brooklyn, enrolling as a freshman at Stanford University, where he was surprised to discover that the campus had not been integrated. Had it not been for Jackie Robinson, he said, he never would have noticed. But he did, and he wrote a letter to Roy Wilkins, the second in command at the NAACP, an organization he had never heard of previously, asking if anything could be done. Wilkins advised him to form a campus chapter of the NAACP, which he did, and within a year, he and some of his classmates succeeded in getting the school integrated. A year later, when the second black student came to campus, Gil summoned the nerve to ask her out on a date.

He started to become interested in politics and world affairs and gave up on becoming a sportswriter. When he graduated from Stanford, he went to work for the NAACP and spent most of his career with the organization, eventually becoming its leading fundraiser and helping to bring in about

159

$110 million in donations. Jackie Robinson became a member of the board of directors.

In 1960, Jonas and Robinson met for the second time, at a fundraiser. They shook hands. Jonas, a little nervous, asked his hero if he remembered their interview in 1947, when they had sat together on the stoop on MacDonough Street and talked about nothing but baseball. He tried to explain to Robinson how that meeting had changed the course of his life.

Robinson smiled politely. He said he didn't remember it.

SIX:
PRAYING FOR BASE HITS

The camelhair hat looked too big, like a garbage can lid perched atop his head. The coat, also camelhair, billowed in the wind. His face was tanned, but he did not look like a man who'd been spending time outdoors. If anything, he looked like a man who'd just been in the hospital and soon would wind up back there.

"Hiya, Babe," said an umpire to the most popular player in baseball history, now fifty-two years old, as he walked under the stands at Yankee Stadium, headed toward the home team's dugout. Two other umpires stuck their heads out a door to catch a glimpse of the great George Herman Ruth. "Get back in there, you three blind mice," the Babe said, smiling at the umps. The rasping voice hinted at the source of his illness: throat cancer. As he walked on, peanut vendors stepped aside and shook their heads in silence.

More than fifty-eight thousand people packed the stadium to say good-bye to the player who had meant more to the game than any other. Baseball's history could be divided into two eras, before Ruth and after. Before Ruth, the game had been played by quick little men who scratched out hits and stole bases in low-scoring games. After Ruth, it became a fireworks show, a dazzling display of power, an American spectacular, with homers soaring like rockets and slow, thick-necked soldiers making glorious marches around the bags. Ruth hit so many home runs and hit them so far that he became more myth than man, and the game, in turn, became something more fabulous than ordinary life.

Of course, Ruth never had to hit against a black pitcher. It was somewhat easier to clobber the competition when Jim Crow played on your side.

When Ruth retired in 1935, he had 714 home runs, nearly twice as many as his closest competitor. In the twelve years since then, the country had been through Pearl Harbor, World War II, the dawn of the atomic era, and the onset of the Cold War. But it was remarkable how little had changed in baseball. Had Ruth been plopped into the Yankee dugout in 1947, he

162

would have fit in fine. He would have been the most popular man in the clubhouse, same as ever, the best and highest-paid player in the league, the greatest home run hitter, and the favorite attraction of every typewriter-pecking gent in the press box. The sources of revenue that would later come to dominate the game's economy — radio, television, and advertising — were still insignificant in 1947. The big leagues consisted of sixteen teams and extended only as far west as St. Louis. Air travel was becoming more common, but teams still traveled almost exclusively by train. The men who played were more or less the same in character and world view as those who had played in the twenties and thirties. They were the sons of fishermen, farmhands, and barkeeps. Baseball delivered them from lives of manual labor, but it did not make them so rich — not most of them, anyway — that they could afford to quit working winters. Babe Ruth, Walter Johnson, and Ty Cobb had been replaced by Joe DiMaggio, Ted Williams, and Bob Feller. These ballplayers may have been a bit slicker and more subtle, in much the same way that *Casablanca* was slicker and more subtle than *Gone With the Wind,* but there was nothing remotely revolutionary about them.

Then along came Robinson.

At Ebbets Field, where Ruth's farewell speech was heard on the public address system, the Dodgers and Giants were getting ready to meet for the fourth time in the young season. The stands were stuffed to capacity, mostly with Dodger fans, of course, but also with a strong contingent of Giants rooters, and once again with a larger-than-usual number of black Jackie Robinson followers. The crowd was giddy and tense, but the tension had little to do with race relations. Today it was about baseball. There was no matchup in Gotham more enthralling than Dodgers v. Giants.

Bobby Thomson, a rookie center-fielder for the Giants, felt some jealousy at all the attention given to Robinson. Thomson was a promising newcomer, too, and a New York City kid, to boot. But at game time he wasn't worried about which rookie got more attention. Nor was he interested in Robinson's color and its effect on baseball as a whole. He was focused on helping the Giants beat their rivals, and he was eager to see how Robinson's unique set of skills would affect the course of the game. "We knew he was pretty good," Thomson recalled. "He was fast and shifty, as good a base-runner as you'll ever find. But I still

164

never gave him any credit. I never gave any of the Dodgers any credit."

A swirling wind turned the game into a bumbling series of collisions and dropped balls, classic Brooklyn baseball, in a sense. The hometown fans were having a good time. In the fourth inning, spectators got a special treat when Joe Louis, the heavyweight champ, walked down the aisle of the grandstand near the Dodger dugout. Celebrity sightings were not unusual at Yankee Stadium, but at Ebbets Field they were almost as rare as a triple play. Louis waved to Robinson at first base as he took his seat.

If there was any man in America capable of understanding the pressures facing Robinson, it was Louis, a sharecropper's son turned full-blown hero. Louis was not the first black boxing champion, but he and Jesse Owens were among the first black men to be widely admired by white Americans. By 1947, Louis had already been champ for a decade, giving him a run of celebrity far greater than that enjoyed by Owens, who began slipping from view shortly after his Olympic triumph in 1936. Louis was respected for his talent. No one had ever dominated the sport so completely and for so long. But the Brown Bomber was also widely admired for the way he comported

165

himself. He never used his position as a pulpit. He showed little interest in politics. He never gloated after beating opponents. And, unlike the great Jack Johnson, Louis never made race an issue, in or out of the ring. He made it a point never to appear in public with white women, conveying an image of a soft-spoken, God-fearing man. For all of his ferocious power, Louis somehow made whites feel safe. He was not "too black," as some whites put it — by which they meant that he wasn't too threatening to their own notions of superiority.

By 1947, the champ was thirty-two years old, only four years older than Robinson, but, like Ruth, seemingly of another time. Before the war, he had been indomitable, a machine designed and created to administer punishment. After the war, he was merely human, a dangerous condition given his line of work. Louis had defended his title in 1946 by beating Billy Conn, but he'd looked sluggish in doing so, and while he won a purse of $625,000, he owed so much money to the IRS, his managers, and his ex-wife that he ended the night still in debt by about $200,000. He would go on fighting for a few years, but never convincingly. He would try his hand at business, but almost always with disastrous results. For the rest of his

166

life, the IRS, drug addiction, and mental illness would dog him. But in 1947, for yet a few more moments, he remained the champ, and the crowd at Ebbets Field, black and white, greeted him lovingly.

Louis and Robinson had met before, in 1942 at Fort Riley, Kansas, when Robinson was in basic training. They had played golf, ridden horses, and exercised together. Louis was poorly educated, but Robinson, no doubt flattered by the attention from such a famous figure, was impressed by the sharpness of his mind. Now, as Louis found his seat, Robinson leaned over the railing to say hello, presenting him with an autographed baseball. Photographers sprang from the dugout and surrounded the men. It turned out to be Robinson's best play of the day. Back on the field, he walked once and scored a run, but otherwise didn't do much else. The Dodgers pulled out a 9–8 win, improving their record to seven wins and two losses. Despite his unremarkable performance and a three-game stretch in which he'd gone hitless, Robinson had reason to be pleased. The Giants had treated him much more kindly than the Phillies. His team was in first place. And the sight of two strong, proud black men shaking hands had elicited nothing but cheers. Put that one in the win column.

Robinson's apartment on MacDonough Street was better than the room at the McAlpin Hotel, but not by much. The brownstone was two stories tall, with an iron gate that opened to the stoop. It was surrounded by buildings that looked almost exactly the same and faced still more. A few small trees sprouted here and there on the block, but no grass. The California Robinsons were not used to such harsh environs. Where were the lawns, the meadows, the golf courses, the hills?

Jackie and Rachel both came from large families. They were accustomed to sharing tight quarters, but nothing as tight as this. Sixty years later, Rachel would forget how much rent they had paid, but the apartment itself remained vivid in her memory, painfully so: the tiny bedroom, eight-feet-by-twelve, at best; tiny kitchen; tiny closets; tiny bathroom, shared with Mabel Brown; the tiny slivers of sunlight poking in through the back door by the kitchen. The Robinsons were confined most of the time to their windowless bedroom. They had no desk, no table, and no chairs; just a bed, a dresser, and a wooden crib, which took up much of the room's floor space. They made little use of the living room because Mabel Brown spent most of her waking hours there, usually in the company of her boyfriend. To escape, the Robinsons went on long walks around Bedford-Stuyvesant, down Mac-Donough to Ralph, over to Fulton, or along Atlantic, which was the neighborhood's main thoroughfare, past corner groceries, small churches, Laundromats, bars, diners, and tailor shops. They seldom went out at night, although they did manage to see two Broadway shows, *Finian's Rainbow* and *Brigadoon. Finian's Rainbow* was one of many mainstream entertainment vehicles taking on the subject of race in 1947. The play was mostly song and dance — the story of a leprechaun in search of gold. But it also included a character named Billboard Rawkins, a bigoted southern politician who was turned by magic into a black man so that he might learn the error of his narrow-minded ways. Sinclair Lewis tried a similar bit of racial transformation in his 1947 novel *Kingsblood Royal,* the story of a successful midwestern banker who discovers that he is part black and sees his life crumble as a result. Another writer, Laura Z. Hobson, published *Gentleman's Agreement,* the fictional story of a white journalist pretending to be Jewish in order to document the effects of anti-Semitism. The book was turned quickly into a movie and won the 1947 Academy Award for best picture.

Though they didn't get out much, the Robinsons knew these were special times. They were newly married and had just become parents. Now here they were, young and scared and enmeshed in something bigger than they'd dreamed. The feeling at times was one of pure exhilaration, "I think sometimes people miss that part, they're so focused on the troubles and the stress," Rachel recalled. "There's this wild exhilaration that you never expected this to happen." Many people also miss that while Robinson seemed the most solitary figure the game had ever seen, he had in Rachel a supremely powerful partner. The Dodger wives, who could be catty at times, could not help but acknowledge that Rachel possessed astonishing good looks and unflappable poise. She was smart, well-dressed, and well-spoken. She showed no fear, yet neither did she assert herself in too forward a manner. For a young woman who was new to the city, new to the big leagues, and new to the demands of fame, she seemed remarkably calm. Those who knew her well were not surprised. All her life Rachel believed she could accomplish anything she set her mind to. She was a tender and loving woman who inspired great warmth. Jack wrote her long, mushy love letters when he went on the road. She set high standards for those around her, including her husband.

Jack, a muscular figure of independence, relied on her hugely. They had no phone and no television, no distractions at all, except for the baby's bleats and gurgles. So they talked and talked. Robinson would break down the events of the most recent game for his wife. Rachel would ask the sorts of questions any novice might: What does the catcher say to the pitcher when he visits the mound between pitches? What do the third-base coach's signals to the batter mean? What does the manager say to the players in the dugout? Robinson explained patiently. They talked about what it would take for him to last in the big leagues. Just now he was slumping. He had no hits in three tries in the first game against the Giants, and went 0-for-4 in the second game. When the Cubs came to town for three games, he managed only one hit, a double, in eleven tries. His batting average fell, as he later described it, "like an elevator in the Empire State Building." He told reporters that a bruised shoulder was crimping his swing. Rachel could see that more than his

171

shoulder was bruised. He never spoke of his anxiety, but in his sleep he gnashed his teeth and tossed and turned beneath the sheets. The whole experiment, his whole life, it seemed, rode on how well he played. It was the only thing he ever admitted being worried about.

Years later, Branch Rickey would insist that Robinson's job was never in jeopardy, but that did not appear to be the case at the time. The Dodgers had recently sent "Whistling" Ed Stevens back to the minors, but they were still carrying Howie Schultz on the roster as Robinson's backup. Every day, when Burt Shotton filled out his lineup card, Robinson wondered if he would see Schultz's name instead of his own. He wondered what Rachel would think if she came to the ballpark and saw another man playing first base. Then there were the reports that Rickey, flush with cash after unloading a bunch of spare players, was trying to deal for the Giants' slugging first baseman Johnny Mize. There were even rumors that Rickey was trying to pry Stan Musial from the Cardinals. It was unlikely the Cardinals would give him up, but what message did it send to the Dodgers' starting first baseman that the boss was trying to land a star to replace him?

Robinson worried that his big-league career might end at any moment. He felt certain he would start hitting eventually, but he didn't know how much time he would be allowed. His biggest fear, he explained to Rachel, was that his own teammates would lose faith in him before he had a chance to prove he could help the team. He could feel their eyes on him. A great divide stood between Robinson and the rest of the men. Robinson tried to bridge it, but he did so cautiously. He was a quiet man, not quite shy, but far from gregarious. He tried chatting a bit in the dugout. He congratulated his teammates on good fielding plays. But he also kept to himself, holding a part of himself back. Such restraint was something black men and women often learned in the 1940s if they spent much time around white men and women. No doubt it was something Robinson had seen in his mother's wary behavior all those years she worked in the homes of wealthy white families.

The rest of the Dodgers were equally circumspect. Not one of them invited Jackie and Rachel to have dinner or see a movie. Not one made an effort to help the couple learn the ins and outs of Brooklyn. Neither did the ballplayers' wives attempt to welcome Rachel to their informal club. The other women would shop, knit, and dine together. Some of the women from small towns were frightened to stay by themselves when their husbands were on the road, so they would organize impromptu slumber parties. Rachel remained an outsider. After one game early in the season, Norma King, the wife of pitcher Clyde King, noticed Rachel standing outside the ballpark waiting for her husband to get dressed. Norma wondered why she didn't join the other wives in the tunnel beneath the grandstand where they usually waited. "You belong in here with us," she recalled telling Rachel. It hadn't occurred to Rachel until then.

Rachel had dreamed of the day she would get married and have children and make her own home. She would hang curtains and pick the wallpaper and arrange the furniture just so. The Robinsons' apartment was a far cry from the place she'd dreamed of, but at least in one important way it felt like a home. Jack's intensity melted when he walked in the door, happy to be with his family, happy to have shelter from a world that expected him to be perfect all the time, a credit to his team and his race. He would coo at the baby and bounce him on his lap. He would read a newspaper or magazine.

He would hold his wife in his arms.

And every night before turning in, he would kneel by the side of their bed and pray.

"ROBINSON'S JOB IN JEOPARDY," read the headline in the *New York Sun* of May 1. That same day, Dick Young informed his readers in the *Daily News* that the rookie "should be given a rest in view of his ailing right arm and slump-pressing at the plate, but the Dodger powers appear reluctant to bench him for attendance and possible public relations reasons." Young, the best-informed of the Dodger beat writers and no great fan of Robinson, had got it right. The first baseman wasn't playing well enough to hold on to his position. He came into the game on May 1 with only nine hits in his first forty at-bats, for a .225 average. Branch Rickey was urging him to bunt more, to use his speed to get on base, where he could wreak havoc stealing bases. It was Rickey, back in spring training, who had encouraged Robinson to make himself conspicuous, to be aggressive, to put the opposition on edge. But he couldn't steal first base. One writer said Robinson could hit .260 if he did nothing but bunt every time. But Robinson was already bunting more than he cared to. He

175

wanted to prove he had more than speed. "Right now Jackie Robinson doesn't shape up as a first baseman," Pat Lynch wrote in the *Journal American.* "His weak hitting is something the shrewd assayers of baseball have been on to all along."

In the 1940s, black New Yorkers had low expectations in their encounters with white society. In *Black Boy,* Richard Wright described in 1945 the "essential bleakness of black life in America," and wrote that blacks "have never been allowed to catch the full spirit of Western civilization." Robinson, in his fight for dignity, supplied a morale boost of almost unimaginable consequence, and yet he never completely vanquished the fear of humiliation among his constituents. "Our approach was almost humorous, because that kind of humor was part of the culture," recalled Colin Powell, who was ten years old and a Giants fan, living in the Bronx at the time. "We said, 'Oh, Lord, don't let him strike out.' The greatest fear was that he wouldn't do well, and that would be a mark against all of us." Years later, when Powell became secretary of state, the highest-ranking black man in the history of United States government, things would be different. "There were still no black Greyhound bus drivers, no black airline pilots," he said of 1947. "I still remember joking when Greyhound . . . hired its first black bus driver, 'Oh, Lord, just don't let him run into anything. . . . You're living as a group through those selected individuals."

Robinson's shoulder ached every time he threw the ball, but he nevertheless stopped taping it before each game, perhaps hoping to convince the coaches and writers it had mended. If the Dodgers hadn't been winning, he might already have been benched, and once benched, he might easily have been sent back to the minors. Robinson was of the opinion that even a brief return to Montreal would mark a complete and indisputable failure, confirming in the minds of skeptics "that blacks weren't ready for the majors." The pressure to succeed, he said later, was much greater than anything he'd ever faced. "There were times," he wrote, ". . . when deep depression and speculation as to whether it was all worthwhile would seize me." He assumed he would start hitting, but he had no idea whether his teammates would reject him, and that made it more difficult to concentrate on his game. "There were things some people take for granted that we couldn't take for granted," Rachel Robinson recalled. "Mainly whether the team would accept it.

Would he become a teammate? You can't play alone, no matter how good you are."

At least one of his teammates spoke openly. Eddie Stanky was only thirty, but he looked older, his face all bumps and angles. He made up for his limited physical gifts by acting tough, even in his own clubhouse. Intimidation was a part of his game, a part of his life. So he may have been trying to scare Robinson when he told him, "Before I play with you I want you to know how I feel about it. I want you to know I don't like it. I want you to know I don't like you."

"All right," Robinson told Stanky. "That's the way I'd rather have it. Right out in the open."

Stanky might not have liked it, but then again, he didn't pretend to like much of anything. He was a baseball man to the marrow, and any peculiar emotions that might have crept in as a result of his new association with a black teammate would not distract him from the game. From the season's start he proved a comfort on the field to Robinson, helping to set his position before each pitch, telling him when to shade a batter toward the line and when to move toward the hole between first and second. Later, Robinson would say he was sorry for making the initial assumption that the second baseman was a bigot. "Stanky, although he was from the South, or raised down there, was a guy that took up battles, and a guy I respected. . . . He was gruff, but helpful."

While Robinson tried to make his way among his teammates, sorting the friends from the bigots and the malignant bigots from the benign, he was fortunate to have Shotton for a manager. Shotton seemed aloof and enigmatic, but in fact, he was as easy to read as the little notepad he kept in hand during each ballgame. In the pad, Shotton kept his own crude scorecard, scratching an F for a fly ball and an O for an out. He took note when a player hit the ball hard, even if it didn't result in a hit. "That's a hit in my book," he'd say, consoling a batter whose effort deserved a better outcome. Shotton's notebook reminded him that Robinson wasn't striking out much, and that gave the manager confidence that the hits would start to fall. "There's no reason to get all excited," he said of the slump, "no reason to panic."

The hitless streak came to an end that May 1 afternoon, in the first inning of a soggy game against the Cubs. Robinson lined a Bob Chipman fastball into left field for a double. After that, the Dodgers did not play again for five days, as heavy rains pounded New York. The reprieve gave Robinson time to contemplate his tenuous position — and to rest his shoulder.

SEVEN:
CARDINAL SINS

Branch Rickey never forgot anything, and he certainly had not forgotten the abortive spring training rebellion in Cuba, which had threatened to undermine his great experiment in integration. He still couldn't bring himself to trade Dixie Walker, who was leading all of baseball with a .439 batting average, but he remained determined to show the southern mutineers that his commitment to Robinson was genuine and permanent. So, while the Dodgers waited for the rain to stop, Rickey picked up the phone and put in a call to Frank McKinney, president of the Pittsburgh Pirates.

Rickey had burned every team in the league at one time or another with one of his seemingly guileless trades. He had outsmarted his trading partners so often that almost all his customers and would-be customers had grown wary. But he could still count on McKinney to return his calls.

This time, McKinney believed he had the upper hand for a change. Rickey's roster was bloated. Because of major-league regulations, the Brooklyn boss had two weeks to cut nine players or else release them and get nothing in return. McKinney offered Rickey cash for some of the players, knowing that Rickey had a fondness for fat profit margins. But he insisted that Brooklyn throw in one of its top pitchers — Kirby Higbe, Hal Gregg, or Joe Hatten.

Rickey, telling the *Daily News* that the Pirates had him "over a barrel," agreed to give up Higbe, along with pitchers Hank Behrman and Cal McLish, infielder Gene Mauch, and catcher Dixie Howell. In return the Dodgers got the considerable sum of $250,000, plus a throw-in: an outfielder named Al Gionfriddo whom neither team wanted. At five-feet-six and 150 pounds, Gionfriddo was the smallest man in the majors. The New York sportswriters predicted that he would soon be the smallest man in the minors.

The deal infuriated Dodger fans. Higbe — or Higelbee, as they called him — was a Brooklyn favorite and the ace of a shaky pitching rotation. He'd won seventeen and lost only eight in 1946, and he'd already won his first two starts in 1947. He was

182

thirty-two years old, with a lively arm that showed no signs of weakening. Rickey had a habit of trading good ballplayers at their peak, saving himself the hassle of owning them when they began to complain of aches and pains and the expenses of taking care of big families and high mortgages. But this time the fans and writers complained that he'd gone too far. They said he'd let greed get in the way of smart baseball. More than one writer predicted that Rickey would look back at the end of the season and recognize that he'd traded away the Dodgers' shot at the pennant.

Rickey did love money, and as one of the owners of the team, he would benefit directly from the sale of all those players to Pittsburgh. He held a 25 percent stake, as did each of his co-owners: Walter O'Malley, James and Deare Mulvey, and John Lawrence Smith. But what most of the writers failed to mention was that he had another powerful motivating force guiding him at all times: a sense of moral righteousness. Though none of the newspapermen made the connection, Rickey had begun trying to cast off several of his Cuban rebels. His message to the Dodgers who remained was that he intended to build his team around Robinson. It wasn't enough to promote the rookie to the majors. He had to make sure Robinson succeeded, and that required a comprehensive strategy.

More black players were on the way. Campanella and Newcombe were too good to keep in the minors for long. Rickey knew that racial chemistry in the clubhouse would get more complicated. It made sense to remove the most dangerous elements now, in preparation for the seasons to come. As usual, he was thinking two and three steps ahead. He had committed to fighting for both justice and a pennant, at times sounding more like a politician than a baseball man. At a charity dinner that spring, Rickey warned that "poverty and distress, want and sickness" would breed discontent among the less fortunate, and possibly lead them to embrace communism. The business community must give generously to charities and pay fair wages to workers, he said. The world was changing. Everyone would have to keep his eyes on the ball.

If Rickey had global concerns in mind, Higbe, meanwhile, was thinking only about himself. He liked being with the Dodgers and liked living in New York, and, while he had mixed feelings about playing with Robinson, he had resigned himself to the inevitable. He was saddened by the trade.

"I remember when I was a young boy, my grandfather used to tell me about the Civil War," he told the writer Peter Golenbock years later. "One grandfather fought for the South, the other fought for the North. Neither grandfather had anything to eat. When I was growing up, it never was no problem. Sure, we were segregated. I reckon that was the old Southern custom. I don't know. I don't suppose anyone would have objected if a colored wanted to come to our church when I was growing up as a boy."

The southerners playing with Robinson in 1947 were coping, in essence, by splitting themselves in two, just as Higbe had learned to share his love with a northern grandfather and a southern one. Even in the first weeks of the season, the Dodgers were learning to master living in two distinct worlds. During the baseball season, they would refrain from using the words "nigger," "coon," and "shine." They would censor their jokes. But when the season ended, they would go home and fall back into their segregated lives with ease. Higbe had made up his mind that he could do the same. Now, however, he wouldn't have to. He was headed to Pittsburgh, and vowing to wreck the Dodgers' pennant hopes if he got a chance.

■ ■ ■ ■

The mighty Cardinals, defending champs, started slowly. They dropped two of three to the Reds to open the season, dropped two of three again to the Cubs, and then, to everyone's astonishment, went on to lose nine straight. The season had barely begun, and the team expected to be king of the hill had dug itself an enormous hole, falling seven games back in the standings. If Jackie Robinson was the biggest story of the season, the Cards were the biggest surprise.

"That there's dissension on the club is doubtful," wrote Jim McCulley in the *Daily News.* "It could be that some dry boredom has set in. . . . But hardly inner discord. There are more close friendships on the Redbird club than anywhere else in baseball, it seems." But Sam Breadon, president of the team, was concerned enough that he decided to travel to the East Coast to watch his team play.

"Sure, we're down in the dumps," said Breadon, a native New Yorker who still had the accent to prove it, "but any day now we're going to break out. And when we do, you'll see the same hard-hitting and tight pitching outfit that won the world champi-

186

onship in 1946." With reliable stars such as Red Schoendienst, Stan Musial, and Terry Moore all hitting around .200, Breadon assumed the team's fortunes were bound to improve. Ironically, the man who had built the Cardinals into consistent winners was Branch Rickey. Before coming to Brooklyn, Rickey had run the Cardinals for twenty-three years, from 1919 to 1942. It was in St. Louis that he established his reputation as one of the game's finest minds, as well as one of its best evaluators of talent. "He could recognize a great player from the window of a moving train," the sportswriter Jim Murray once said.

After winning the World Series in 1946, several key members of the Cardinals demanded raises. Breadon resisted. He granted a few raises, including one to Stan Musial, but no one was happy. Those who got pay increases were insulted by the slender margins by which their salaries had risen, and those who didn't get raises at all were miffed at having been left out. Breadon was the most frustrated of all. A milk-chugging, vitamin-popping, ulcer-ridden man, he found himself in 1947 paying more than ever for a team that wasn't winning games.

Perhaps then it was frustration that led

some of the Cardinals to lash out at Jackie Robinson. Perhaps it was Dixie Walker's influence on his younger brother, Harry, an outfielder for the Cards and a more abrasive character than his brother. Maybe it was the rain drenching Brooklyn, which left the players with too much time to sit around and gripe. Whatever the motivation, some players began discussing their discomfort with the idea of sharing a baseball field with a black man. They wondered if they might be better off refusing to play. If enough players on enough teams boycotted, they seemed to believe, they might force cancellation of their games with the Dodgers, and maybe even shut down the league and force an end to the integration experiment.

"I heard talk," Musial told the writer Roger Kahn many years later. "It was rough and racial and I can tell you a few things about that. First of all, everybody has racial feelings. We don't admit it. We aren't proud of it. But it's there. And this is big league baseball, not English tea, and ballplayers make noise. So I heard the words and I knew there was some feelings behind the words, but I didn't take it seriously. That was baseball."

In Brooklyn, where the fans had trouble saying his name, Musial was called Musical.

Elsewhere, he was Stan the Man. He'd played with a black boy in high school, a kid named Griffey (whose son and grandson would go on to some renown as big-leaguers), and never had any problem with integration. He was a quiet man, by no means a leader, who would sit in front of his locker with a knife and some sandpaper, carving and smoothing the handles on his bats, oblivious to the noise of the clubhouse. To Musial, it seemed that Jackie Robinson wanted the same thing his own parents had wanted when they came to America: economic opportunity. But either he lacked the courage to tell his teammates or he didn't know how. "For me at the time — I was twenty-six — saying all that would have been a speech and I didn't know how to make speeches. Saying it to older players, that was beyond me. Besides, I thought the racial talk was just hot air."

It probably was. Most descriptions of the conflict suggest that the Cardinals who discussed a boycott were indeed trying to talk tough, to impress one another, to kill time on a couple of rainy days. They never came close to striking. Bob Broeg, who covered the Cardinals for the *St. Louis Post-Dispatch,* said Harry Walker was the only one he'd ever heard complaining, but Walker had a tendency to "beat his gums," Broeg said. He talked about all the trouble his brother was having in Brooklyn, trying to stir up trouble. Whether it was bluster or not, it soon became real enough for the Cardinals.

When Breadon got wind of the uprising, he met with some of the players rumored to be causing the dissension. Still, he wasn't sure his message got through, so he took a taxi to the office of Ford Frick, the National League president, to tell him what was going on. Like Breadon, Frick was a mild-mannered man, the son of an Indiana farmer. Frick learned to type at fifteen so he could be a sportswriter, but he turned out to be better at public relations than reporting and writing. He ghostwrote columns for Babe Ruth when the Babe was in his prime, then switched sides and became the publicity director for the National League in 1934, and in 1935 became the league's president. He was adored by baseball's owners, in no small part because he had a knack for avoiding conflict. It was a trait that had served him well in service of the Babe, and one that would serve him well again now. The plot against Robinson may have been nothing more than a low-grade rumbling and unworthy of attention under normal circumstances, but these weren't normal circumstances, and Frick was not one to take chances. He knew that the best way to avoid bad press was to get in front of it, to tell the story on his own terms before any of the newspapers got hold of it. The truth? As any good PR man knows, the truth isn't half as important as what the newspapers print.

The truth, as Frick recounted it in his autobiography and again in an unpublished interview many years later, was so simple it's a wonder the story became such a fuss. Frick spoke to Breadon in his New York office that day, the league president recalled. Breadon explained that some players were shooting their mouths about Robinson and hadn't responded to his order to cut it out. Frick didn't name the players, but he said he told Breadon to send the players a message: "Tell them this is America, and baseball is America's game." In recollecting the conversation, he added: "I don't know how Sam delivered the message, or to whom he talked. I do know that he called the league office a day or two later to report that the whole matter was settled, and everything was under control."

In Frick's view, the ballplayers were merely blowing off steam. The same sort of resentment existed in the Dodger clubhouse, and probably in quite a few more, he said. The only difference was that Sam Breadon didn't feel equipped to handle it himself and asked for help. "You know baseball players," he said. "They're like anybody else. They pop off. Sitting around the table with a drink or two they commit many acts of great courage but they don't follow through. My feeling was that it was over and done with. We had no more trouble."

Then came the newspaper version of events. Stanley Woodward broke the story in the *Herald Tribune*, and according to Woodward's story, it was not a small strike by a few Cardinal players that had been averted but a league-wide work stoppage. Woodward claimed the strike was "instigated" by a member of the Dodgers and "formulated" by "certain St. Louis players." And if that wasn't fuzzy enough, he went on: "Subsequently, the St. Louis players conceived the idea of a general strike within the National League on a certain date." Woodward didn't name any of the players involved in the alleged uprising. Nor did he reveal how many there were, or on what date they had intended to strike. But he did offer a transcript of Frick's address to the players, which went like this:

"If you do this you will be suspended from the league. You will find that the friends you think you have in the press box will not support you, that you will be outcasts. I do not care if half the league strikes. Those who do it will encounter quick retribution. They will be suspended, and I don't care if it wrecks the National League for five years. This is the United States of America, and one citizen has as much right to play as another. The National League will go down the line with Robinson no matter what the consequence. You will find that if you go through with your intention that you have been guilty of complete madness."

Less than a week earlier, at the army prison in Fort Leavenworth, Kansas, a race riot had left one prisoner dead and five guards and six more prisoners hurt. At the same time, school officials in Albany were battling in court over whether to let the left-wing activist Paul Robeson sing in a school auditorium. Now, Frick was proclaimed a hero for defusing what could have been an ugly uprising in baseball. Woodward's story was praised far and wide as one of the most important pieces of journalism ever to grace a sports page. But in the days after the *Herald Tribune* story appeared, and for years to come, players up and down the Cardinal roster denied any conspiracy. They denied everything in the story, in fact. Breadon labeled the Woodward article "ridiculous." Manager Eddie Dyer called it "absurd." Burt Shotton didn't believe it either.

The next day, Woodward submitted a follow-up story in which he said his first report had been "essentially right and factual." Then he added a few small caveats, admitting, for starters, the fact that he had never tried to interview Frick before writing his initial account. "Knowing him to be an honest man," Woodward said of Frick, "we decided he would not deny the story. Therefore, we went ahead and printed it."

Woodward went on to say he had never intended to suggest that the Frick quotation was entirely accurate, despite the quotation marks surrounding it and the fact that it formed the backbone of his story. "We were wrong, apparently, in stating he personally delivered it to his players. It seems he delivered it to Breadon for relay to said operatives." Whatever the precise words, the writer went on, "it obviously is the most noble statement ever made by a baseball man."

Whereby Woodward printed it again.

■ ■ ■ ■

At game time on May 6, the Cardinals took the field. All of them.

Nothing about the contest suggested there had been any behind-the-scenes turmoil. No one threw at Robinson's head. No one tried to spike him. No one taunted him with any particularly pungent epithets. A big crowd came out — big for a Tuesday afternoon, anyway — to see the rematch of the series that had ended the Brooklyn season seven months before. "You'd have thought it were September the way pennant hysteria gripped the 18,971 flamboyant faithful," wrote Dick Young.

The Dodgers scored first, but the Cardinals bounced back to take a 6–3 lead after four innings. Seated behind the Dodger dugout, watching his first game of the year, was Leo Durocher, his Hollywood bride, Laraine Day, at his side. Durocher had been out in California since his suspension, playing golf and chopping down trees on the land where he and Day planned to build a home. He had given up hope of returning to the Dodgers in 1947, but he was campaigning to make sure the job would still be his in 1948.

In the sixth inning, with the Dodgers still trailing by three, Robinson singled off Red Munger with two outs. As Robinson danced his familiar dance off first base, darting back and forth, Munger lost his control, walking first Reiser and then Walker to load the bases. That brought up Carl Furillo. After watching one pitch go by, Furillo swung and connected, lining a triple to the right-center alley, driving in three runs, and tying the score at 6–6. In the next inning, Pee Wee Reese, stuck in a slump even worse than Robinson's, poked his first home run of the season into the left-field seats to give the Dodgers the win.

In the end, the response to Woodward's story proved far more informative than the story itself. Most of the nation's big-name columnists and countless letters to the editor came through in support of Robinson, essentially labeling the Cardinals a bunch of ignorant bigots. Woodward's story, followed by his clumsy partial retraction, offered no help in making clear how many Cardinals were involved, much less which ones. As a result, the whole team was tarred. Dan Parker of the *Mirror* wrote: "Sports writers have been studiously trying to avoid the racial angle in Baseball this Spring but, despite their best efforts, it keeps bobbing up. Obviously, it must be faced squarely, sooner or later. . . . If it is our national pastime, embodying American ideals, let us proceed to conduct it along those lines with no more racial barriers in its playing fields than there are at its turnstiles."

Even the *Sporting News,* based in St. Louis and generally skeptical of Robinson, suggested ballplayers had better get used to him because "the presence of Negroes in the major leagues is an accomplished fact."

Between the purported strike and the attack by Ben Chapman, Robinson's most bitter foes were turning out to be his best friends. Their feeble attacks served mostly to help paint a picture of the black ballplayer as a victim and to coalesce support for him. Suddenly, the newspapers weren't talking about Robinson's batting slump but about his enormous strength of character. Jimmy Cannon called Robinson "a big leaguer of ordinary ability" but said that was beside the point. "There is a great lynch mob among us and they go unhooded and work without rope," the *New York Post* columnist wrote. "We have been involved in a war to guarantee all people the right to a life without fear. . . . In such a world it seems a small thing that a man be able to play a game unmolested. In our time such a

197

plea should be unnecessary. But when it happens we must again remember that all this country's enemies are not beyond the frontiers of our home land." Cannon's column struck such a chord that left-wing political groups purchased advertising space in order to reprint it in newspapers throughout New York.

By checking his temper and remaining stoic, Robinson established an image of strength and courage. Still, he would admit at the end of the season that the controversy affected his performance on the field, and he worried that he would survive the taunting only to find himself back in the minors because he couldn't hit.

The Cardinals bounced back after the first game to take two out of three from the Dodgers. Though he made solid contact several times and seemed to be swinging the bat somewhat better, Robinson managed only four hits in fourteen tries. Less than a month into the season, he was hitting a dispiriting .241. Dan Burley of the *Amsterdam News* reported on an overheard snippet of street-corner conversation: "Man, they just don't pitch Jackie the kind of balls they throw them white fellows."

But Burley went on to say that Robinson was getting a break at the moment — thanks to the color his skin. He wouldn't be pulled from the starting lineup as long as the Dodgers kept winning, predicted the columnist, because Branch Rickey didn't want "a whole lot of hemming and hawing about Jackie being benched because he's colored."

Robinson wasn't so sure. He checked the lineup card every day, still expecting to see someone else's name penciled in at first base. He remained a Dodger in uniform but hardly felt like a part of the team. It was at about this time that Cannon, called him "the loneliest man I have ever seen in sports."

EIGHT: THE GREAT ROAD TRIP

The Dodgers' train hissed out of New York early on the morning of May 9, headed for Philadelphia. Along the way, the players read and discussed Woodward's article about the purported strike by the Cardinals, which appeared in that day's paper. Rather than quieting as the season went along, the strife over baseball's integration seemed to be growing. The men who had predicted in spring training that Robinson's presence would be a distraction may have felt some validation. Now there would be more news stories, fresh mobs of fans, and a higher degree of scrutiny with every town the Dodgers visited on the National League circuit.

Baseball players were not adventurers. They did not choose their line of work to see exotic places, meet new people, or learn new languages. They were lovers of routine, revelers in the familiar, heroes in a world of countless precise rules and consistent facts. Change was not what they'd expected. Ralph Branca, as sensitive as any of his teammates to Robinson's plight, said he couldn't remember anyone talking to Robinson during the trip to Philadelphia. It hadn't occurred to Branca to ask his teammate how he was doing.

The Dodgers still hadn't played a game outside New York City. A week before the team left on its first road trip, Rickey answered a call from Herb Pennock, the former Yankee pitcher now running the Philadelphia Phillies. Pennock, referred to by the scribblers as the Squire of Kennett Square, Pennsylvania, was fifty-three years old, tall, silver-haired, and dignified, though not exactly enlightened. The Dodgers' traveling secretary, Harold Parrott, walked into the room during the conversation, and Rickey motioned for him to pick up another extension. ". . . just can't bring the Nigger here with the rest of your team," Parrott heard Pennock say. "We're just not ready for that sort of thing yet. We won't be able to take the field against your Brooklyn team if that boy Robinson is in uniform."

It's not clear who wasn't ready. Did Pennock mean the fans, the players, manager Ben Chapman, or all of the above? Rickey didn't care. "Very well, Herbert," the Dodger president said. "And if we must claim the game nine to nothing, we will do just that, I assure you." Nine to nothing was the official score of a forfeited game.

Commissioner Chandler had already been on the phone to Chapman and others in the Phillies organization warning them that he did not want to see a repetition of the brutish behavior displayed in Brooklyn. Chapman promised to obey and issued a statement in defense of Robinson's right to play ball. "Jackie has been accepted in baseball, and we of the Philadelphia organization have no objection to his playing, and we wish him all the luck we can," he said. "Baseball is a national game, and there are no nationalities, creeds nor races involved. Jackie Robinson is an American."

All that proved, however, was that Chapman wasn't stupid enough to defy the commissioner's order. Across baseball, there were still plenty of players hoping to see Robinson driven out of baseball. Some of them were racists. Some of them feared losing their jobs to black athletes. Among owners, some were angry because they feared they'd been fleeced again by Branch Rickey, who had already signed some of the best black talent in the country. Despite Chandler's warnings, Chapman's praise, and Rickey's confidence, there remained a strong feeling among the writers covering the Dodgers that Robinson remained in a precarious spot, especially as long as he wasn't hitting.

Stanley Woodward's story on the Cardinals had all the baseball world talking, and in some clubhouses news of the quashed uprising seemed to rally southern players who remained uncomfortable with integration. Some books and articles written years after the event have suggested that Dixie Walker engaged in a letter-writing campaign to stir dissension throughout the National League and promote a league-wide strike. The letters were never mentioned in press reports from the 1947 season, however, and Robinson never referred to them in any of his subsequent books or speeches. Nor has a copy of any such document ever surfaced. Nevertheless, decades later, several players around the league would insist they heard talk or saw evidence of a plot.

Freddy Schmidt, a pitcher with the Phillies, insisted he saw a letter being passed around the clubhouse. Fifty-nine years after the fact, though, he refused to name its author, not wanting to smudge anyone's reputation. Schmidt grew up playing with black kids in his hometown of Hartford, Connecticut, and had seen Josh Gibson and Satchel Paige play in Negro-league games. He knew the "colored boys," as he called them, could play, and believed they ought to have every chance to compete. "They were Americans," he said. "It was a shame they were held back." But when the letter came around, he decided not to speak up in Robinson's defense. He was thirty-one, just traded from the Cardinals, and clinging to his roster spot by a shoelace. He regretted his inaction for the rest of his life.

Hank Wyse, a pitcher for the Cubs, told the writer David Falkner that a letter from someone on another club — again, no name — prompted his teammates to meet before their first game at Ebbets Field. "We voted not to play," Wyse said. "I'm not sure, but I think the vote was unanimous." Other Cubs insisted they heard nothing of a letter, meeting, or vote. When the Cubs and Dodgers played, there were no signs of trouble.

The baseball season was only a month old, but it was already shaping up to be a messy one. In the National League, Robinson created the most confusion, but there were plenty of other strange occurrences. The Cardinals kept losing, dropping thirteen of their first eighteen, leaving them deep in last place. The order of the universe was similarly disturbed in the American League. The Red Sox, led by "Boo" Ferris on the mound and Ted Williams on the field, were favorites yet again, with the Yankees posing their only real challenge. But Williams, a left-handed pull hitter, was having trouble adjusting to the defensive shifts applied by opposing teams. "Well, that's the end of Williams — he can't hit to left field," proclaimed the former big-league slugger Al Simmons. That wasn't Boston's only problem. The team lacked depth on the bench and in the bullpen. They were not strong on defense, and in particular suffered the absence of a strong shortstop. Most of all, though, they lacked leadership. Bobby Doerr was too mild-mannered. Johnny Pesky was tough, but not tough enough to change the character of the team. Williams set the tone in the clubhouse, and Williams worried only about Williams.

The Yankees were entirely different. They had a strong bench. They played solid defense, especially at shortstop, where the nifty Phil Rizzuto roamed. They had a promising young catcher named Yogi Berra, who looked awkward, especially on defense, but hit the ball a mile and entertained the older players with his silliness. And, of paramount importance, they had Joe DiMaggio. DiMaggio hit about as well as Williams, but he also did two big things Williams didn't: He played brilliant defense, and he inspired his teammates to play up to his high standards. Like the Red Sox and the Cards, the Yanks started sluggishly. Rizzuto wasn't hitting much, and the slugger Charlie Keller was hitting even less. Berra showed flashes of brilliance but had yet to prove that he could be trusted to handle the team's pitchers. DiMaggio, recovering from a heel injury that had threatened to end his career, came back sooner than expected and seemed slower by several steps than he had in his prime. The Yankees had a lot of young talent, especially on the pitching staff, but it was not yet clear if the talent would mature quickly enough. Detroit and Cleveland looked strong in the early going, but it remained to be seen if they were legitimate contenders.

In each league, there was a sense that the pennant was up for grabs. With so much apparent parity, the first team that got hot and built a strong lead would have a chance to grab the title. It was an exciting time. Every game counted. The fans loved it.

■ ■ ■ ■

In Philadelphia, the Dodgers stepped off the train and onto a bus for the short drive to the Benjamin Franklin Hotel, where they would enjoy a few hours of rest before getting back on the bus to go to Shibe Park. Though the team had been staying in the same hotel for years, though their block of rooms had been reserved for weeks, and though it was certainly known that the team now included a black player, this time they were turned away before they could unload their bags. "And don't bring your team back here while you have any Nigras with you!" they were told, according to Parrott, the traveling secretary. Thirty years later, when writing his memoirs, Parrott recalled that he sent the players to the ballpark while he began looking for another hotel. But memory has a way of emboldening men, and Parrott was no exception. The truth is that he let the rest of the team check into the Ben Franklin and helped Robinson find a room at an all-black hotel called the Attucks.

Somehow, in the middle of this mess of a morning, another story surfaced: New York City police were investigating death threats received by Robinson. Commissioner Arthur Wallander had assigned a secret squad of investigators to find the authors, according to the *Daily News,* which didn't reveal the precise language of the so-called "get-out-of-baseball-or-else" letters.

Rickey confirmed the reports. "At least two letters of a nature that I felt called for investigation were received by Robinson," he said. "These letters proved to be practically anonymous. Investigation showed the names signed to them were of persons not living at the addresses given. I think the whole matter can be called ended now." Robinson said that a police investigator had come to his house that morning, before the team had left for Philadelphia. He said he told the officer that he had turned over all the threatening letters to the Dodgers. Beyond that, he had little to tell the reporters preparing their stories that afternoon. A few days later, in his column for the *Pittsburgh Courier,* written with the help of Wendell Smith, Robinson downplayed the threats, saying, "The police wanted to know about some threatening letters I have received. I admit that I've received some, but by the way they were written I would say they were from scatter-brained people who just want something to yelp about." Neither

Robinson nor Smith ever described their journalistic collaboration, so there's no telling whether the words came entirely from one man or the other, although most athletes who hired ghostwriters at the time had little to do with the finished product.

The police believed the letters serious enough to warrant investigation. But the interesting question is why they surfaced at just that moment. Reporters had been hearing rumors of threatening letters since Opening Day. They'd noticed on several occasions that Robinson had left Ebbets Field with police escorts, which he said had been provided to ease the crush of autograph seekers. Yet they'd never mentioned it in their columns. What happened on May 9 to change that?

Rickey had noted the powerful response to Ben Chapman's racist outburst. Fans, editorial writers, and even the crusty Eddie Stanky had rallied to Robinson's defense. Letters of support poured in from around the country. And the response to the Cardinals' reported planned protest had been even more powerful. No one tried to argue that the Cards were within their rights. With that in mind, Rickey decided to publicize the threatening letters. If he could show the world that Robinson was suffering, he believed, support for his great cause would grow. He was setting up Robinson as a Christlike figure, a humble man capable of turning his cheek no matter how fierce the assault, a man willing to suffer and perhaps even die for the cause. There's no evidence to suggest that he conferred with Robinson in making his decision. If he did, Rachel knew nothing about it. The success of the plan depended on Robinson's ability to shoulder the growing burden. Rickey accepted on faith that the ballplayer would cope.

"Mr. Rickey thought it would get Jackie and the Dodgers some sympathy," Buzzie Bavasi, one of Rickey's top executives that season, recalled in a recent interview. Rickey gave the story first to the *Daily News.* Then he started calling more reporters. The letters, never traced and neither seen nor quoted by the media, made news all over the country. Robinson's celebrity grew. He was portrayed as a victim of cowardly racists, and, more important, as a proud man who refused to back down. He did not hide in the dugout. He took the field and played ball.

By now, even players with no special hostility toward Robinson were getting nervous about whether they would be perceived as racist if they tangled with him. "Some of the fellows may be riding Jackie," one unnamed player told *The Sporting News,* "but an even greater number are going out of their way to avoid him. They just don't want to be involved in a close play where Jackie might be accidentally spiked or knocked around. . . . I don't want to be the first fellow to be involved in a collision with him — no matter how accidental or unavoidable. Jackie wouldn't squawk, but I think some of his fans would, and they'd probably boo me all around the circuit."

Chapman knew what it was like to get on the bad side of Robinson's fans. Now he had promised to be on his best behavior, but as Freddy Schmidt recalled, the manager had not changed his mind about Robinson. As the Dodgers and Phillies prepared to play a night game, Chapman told his players he was worried about a race riot at the ballpark. It was a Friday night, and the stands were filling up fast, with a lot more black faces than usual in the mix. He warned the men not to walk out of the park by themselves after the game but to make sure they had an escort. An hour before the game, Chapman sent word to the Dodger clubhouse that he wanted to pose for a picture with Robinson, and not in the

211

depths of the locker room but on the dugout steps, where everyone could see. Perhaps it was conciliation, perhaps it was stagecraft. Schmidt said he thought Chapman did it to keep the crowd from exploding. In any case, Robinson agreed to take part in the stunt. Chapman grabbed a bat by the handle and Robinson held its barrel as the men posed.

While the photographers snapped away, Schmidt said he heard his manager murmur loud enough for Robinson and just a few others to hear: "Jackie, you know, you're a good ballplayer, but you're still a nigger to me."

Yet Robinson said that week in his *Courier* column that he didn't mind the handshake. In fact, he seemed to enjoy it more than Chapman did. "I was glad to cooperate," he wrote. "Chapman impressed me as a nice fellow and I don't really think he meant the things he was shouting at me the first time we played Philadelphia." If Chapman did in fact call Robinson a nigger during their photo opportunity, Robinson must have decided to let it pass, or perhaps it secretly pleased him to have gotten so deeply under an opponent's skin. As is so often the case where Robinson's rookie year is concerned, fact and legend intertwine. Were watermelon pieces thrown at Robinson in Phila-

212

delphia? Was a black cat set loose on the field? These legends have been reported as fact, and some claim to have witnessed such things, but there is no reporting to back up the reports, at least not in 1947.

One thing is certain: They played ball that day, though the Dodgers might have wished they hadn't. Robinson managed two hits, scored two runs, and started a nifty double play on a popped bunt, but the Dodgers lost their third straight and fell into third place, a game behind the Braves and Cubs. The Phillies did not completely abandon their attacks on Robinson, but the assault was milder than it had been in Brooklyn.

After the game, Rickey made one more move to solidify support for Robinson: He sold Howie Schultz, the backup first baseman, to Herb Pennock of the Phillies for fifty thousand dollars. (Schultz became the regular first baseman in Philadelphia and established himself over the course of the season as among the worst in the league, hitting .223, with only six home runs and thirty-five runs batted in.) So at the same time that Rickey was subjecting Robinson to one of his most difficult trials, letting the whole world know of the racist squall his player faced, he was also giving him a sturdy tree to cling to until the storm passed. As of

May 9, Robinson was the only first baseman on the Dodger roster, and on May 10 Rickey announced that he was no longer pursuing a trade for Johnny Mize.

In the *New York Post,* Leonard Cohen said he was glad to see Robinson getting the chance to establish himself. "But if the Dodgers should start losing and Robbie still looks ineffective at the plate, no one would accuse the Dodger management of unfair treatment if Robbie were benched. That's been the plea of all fair-minded sports fans: Let the chap rise or fall on his merits as a ballplayer."

The Dodgers dropped two out of the next three in Philadelphia. Robinson got three hits, all singles, in eleven times at bat. He had hits now in eight straight games, but he was hardly tearing the cover off the ball. His average was a so-so .257. He had but one home run, two doubles, and no triples. Despite his terrific speed and daring style, he had stolen only one base. Yet public opinion was beginning to turn his way, so much so that the Dodger business office began handling the enormous task of responding to his fan mail. As Rickey suspected, men and women around the country were reading about the attacks on Robinson and sympathizing. Their letters arrived at

Ebbets Field by the hundreds.

From a machinist in New Jersey:

I know what you are going thru [*sic*] because I went through the same thing in a much smaller way. I was the 1st Negro machinist in a big shop during the war (about 400 men). They did all the little dirty underhanded things to me that they must be doing to you. I came out alright after a while because I developed a thick skin. . . . I couldn't fight back because my side never would have been considered in a show down. My work had to be better than the other guy's but I had to see that there wasn't to [*sic*] much attention drawn to any of my better work I did because I knew I'd never make any friends if they envied me or thought I was a show off. I'm writing this for two reasons. One, is to let you know that there are plenty of people, black and white rooting for you that aren't the type that will hurt you by yelling their heads off every time you catch a simple pop fly. The other reason is I know how much guts it takes to go out on that field and play the kind of ball you're playing under such pressure. There are plenty of people who would

215

have been in a fright long before now. If your batting average never gets any higher than .100 and if you make an error every inning, if I can raise my boy to be half the man that you are, I'll be a happy father.

From Richmond, Virginia:

I happen to be a white Southerner. But I just wanted you to know that not all us southerners are S.O.B.'s. Here's one that is rooting for you to make good. . . . Judging from what I've read in the papers you have had a particularly hard road to travel. . . . I know that very few of us whites can understand the terrific pressure put on you — but I know, at least, that you are doing every bit as good a job for your race as a Booker T. Washington, a George Washington Carver, or a Marian Anderson. I should also say that you're doing a darned fine job for all Americans. Stick to it, kid, don't worry. You've got a lot more friends in this country of ours than enemies. The main thing to remember is that it's the unthinking few who generally make the biggest noise. Unfortunately, too many of us are apt to say nothing when a man's doing a swell job. I hope you get a lot more letters like this. You're carrying a terrific load on your shoulders. And I, for one, think you're man enough to shoulder it! Keep plugging, Jackie!

From a bellboy in Kansas:

Saw you play in Wichita, Kan an also in St. Louis about 30 days ago. An dicided I wanted to name my expected child for the first negro in league baseball. An above that a good sport an gentleman. Something our race needs as bad as they do a square deal. Little Jackie Lee was born the 8-15-47 — 2 pm.

A group of students in Connecticut addressed its letter to Commissioner Chandler's office:

We are members of the sixth grade and we have been thinking over the Jackie Robinson case. Many of us are fans of teams in both leagues. Not all of us are Dodger fans but we still think that Jackie Robinson should play on any Major team in the Leagues. All who are Americans have equal rights as American citizens and should be able to do as others can do, even if his race is different. We all are born the same, eat the same, and sleep the same, why can't we play the same? Why not give everyone an equal chance? Since baseball is the national pastime we think that we should not allow any mention of race to hurt its future. We are the future baseball players and fans of the U.S. and for the good of baseball we think Jackie Robinson should continue playing in the Majors.

No doubt there were angry letters, too. Rachel Robinson recalls many. But neither she nor the Dodgers saved them. Only a handful survive. One, addressed to Rickey from a Louisiana attorney, read:

Your decision to break big league tradition by playing a negro on the Brooklyn team is indeed deplorable. In fact, it is inconceivable that any white man would force a Negro on other white men as you have done. . . . I tell you Rickey anything the Negro touches he ruins and your club will be no exception. His presence will create dissension on the Brooklyn team that will impair its efficiency and break its morale. You have many southerners on your team who are forced to keep silent but mark you they do not like this Negro in their midst. Remember southerners have been born and bred believing in the segregation of the races and your disastrous decision will not get it out of their bones. . . . You can compel them to play but you cannot compel them to accept.

For Robinson, each game was not just a battle but a crusade. The weight of it at times seemed too much. His teammates would watch him come into the locker room, take his seat in the back corner of the room, and prepare himself emotionally as he pulled up his long blue socks and laced his shoes. Robinson had no problem being at the center of a storm. He'd shown that in the army. But in the army he'd been able to lash out at his attackers. He did so at some personal risk, but it was an equation he'd worked out to his satisfaction. Anger fueled his success. Now, however, he was unable to express the anger, and he suffered for it.

"I can't take it anymore. I'm quitting," he told his sister, Willa Mae, in a telephone conversation that came in the early part of the season. His mood darkened. He made little or no effort to find friends among his teammates. The relationships were too complicated. Later, hitting golf balls would provide him momentary relief, but not in 1947. In 1947 he had nothing to do with his anger but swallow it. He withdrew, even at times from his wife. Rachel decided it was best not to try too overtly to get him to open up. He wasn't capable of it yet. "He was the kind of person who if he had things bothering him, he'd be unusually quiet," she recalled. "He was not stormy and he wasn't tearful. He wasn't shaky. Just very quiet. You had a feeling that he was figuring it out, so just let him figure it out." There was no use asking how he felt or what he would do if the team blamed him for their losses or if he was sent back to the minors. He had to fight through these things in silence, and Rachel had to wait for him. "I learned that about him in those early days," she said. "Let him work that out quietly on his own."

Rachel told the biographer Arnold Rampersad of tension in their little apartment on MacDonough Street, especially early on. Jackie changed wet diapers, but never soiled ones. He expected peace and quiet when he read his morning newspapers, and he wanted "a loving send-off" each day when he left for the game. Rachel could see he was anxious. She heard him mumbling in his sleep, watched him twitching beneath the covers. Though they had practically no space of their own, she did all she could to make their home a haven for her husband, to help him escape. And she waited.

In the beginning of May he ordered a new batch of bats, half an inch shorter and an ounce and a half heavier than the ones he'd started with — an R-17 instead of a G-7, in the Hillerich & Bradsby nomenclature — and he seemed to like the new lumber. He was beginning to hit the ball hard. Some ballplayers never make the adjustment to big-league pitching, where fastballs fly so fast you can hear them buzz and curveballs break at unhittable angles. They never feel any sense of control at the plate. But Robinson, whose athletic abilities had thus far never let him down, knew he was starting to get the hang of it.

But some of the other changes taking place around him were more subtle, and not necessarily apparent to him yet. Some of his teammates were beginning to think about what he was up against. "He was under such pressure, such tension and stress," Ralph Branca recalled years later. Some respected him for taking his lumps. They appreciated the way he kept to himself

221

instead of trying to force himself upon the group, the way he stared out the window on the train instead of elbowing his way into card games or conversations, the way he waited for an invitation before sitting down to eat with a teammate, the way he never pretended to be one of the boys and yet never berated them for not treating him more kindly. He didn't care if the men liked him or not, Robinson said years later, recalling his first days with the team, just so long as they respected him.

Some of the Dodgers had expected Robinson to play ball in the Negro-league style, running the bases recklessly, hamming it up, horsing around, taking unnecessary risks for the sake of entertainment. "I wasn't much in favor of black players if they acted like black players," said Jack Banta, a Dodger pitcher. "Sometimes they were inclined to showboat a little." But Banta, like most of the other Dodgers, had never played with a black man. Coming into the 1947 season, all they had were their stereotypes. Robinson was not an easy man to figure out. His face revealed little of his emotion, high or low. He didn't say much, either. But now some of his teammates were beginning to replace their stereotypes with flesh-and-blood images.

Reporters, too, were subtly changing their approach, dropping some of the references to race that had routinely accompanied his name during spring training and the season's first weeks. After the stories about the hate mail, the sportswriters were more likely to mention Robinson's color only when they deemed it relevant. Maybe they simply assumed by now everyone knew he was black, or maybe they found the racial piece of the story too complicated to deal with. Integration was a new and daunting topic for white writers at the time. In his 1947 novel *Kingsblood Royal,* Sinclair Lewis described a white character's perception of black America this way: "To be a Negro was to live in a decaying shanty or in a frame tenement like a foul egg-crate . . . to sleep on unchanged bedclothes that were like funguses, and to have for a spiritual leader only a howling and lecherous swindler. . . . It was to be mysteriously unable ever to take a bath, so that you were more offensive than the animals who clean themselves."

Robinson preferred newspapers and magazines to books. If he read *Kingsblood Royal,* his wife couldn't recall it. Nevertheless, the issues raised in the book were familiar to him. Robinson was a race man, fixated on the effects of skin pigmentation.

He wanted to be given a fair chance, same as any other player, but he didn't want to see all mention of his color dropped from the dialogue. He wanted to be perceived as a black man *and* a fully nuanced human being. One or the other wasn't enough. "I happen to be a bit proud of the fact that I'm a Negro," he said once, reflecting on the early media coverage. "When they start talking about me . . . as a Negro they are certainly not intending to flatter me, but they are patting me on the back, as far as I'm concerned."

After the series in Philadelphia, Robinson and the Dodgers went back to Brooklyn on May 12 for one home game before shipping out west. That day, in an 8–3 win over the Boston Braves, Robinson flashed some of the skills that made him special. In the first inning, after reaching first on a fielder's choice, he advanced to third on a hit by Reiser. When Walker followed with a ground ball to first base, Robinson dashed toward home and then abruptly stopped, arms flailing, cleats kicking up clouds of dirt, as he put on the brakes, hoping to distract the Braves' infielders. It worked. The first baseman gave up the easy out at first base and turned his attention to Robinson. But Robinson had the play measured perfectly.

224

By the time the throw came in to third, he was back on the bag. Everyone was safe. Gene Hermanski followed with a single and the Dodgers had a 2–0 lead.

With Branca pitching beautifully, the Dodgers coasted. Along the way, Robinson singled, walked, reached base after being hit by a pitch, stole two bases, and scored another run. From the box score, at least, it looked like the sort of game he might have enjoyed.

NINE:
TEARING UP THE PEA PATCH

Baseball's great legends often turn out to be fictions, but here's one that checks out: It really was possible in the 1940s to walk down certain blocks in Brooklyn at certain times of day and hear Red Barber's delightfully soft voice echoing from one apartment window after another, as if God were speaking with a southern accent through tinny speakers and shilling for Old Gold cigarettes over WHN-1050 on the radio dial. Maybe it wasn't every window. Maybe there were gaps that forced pedestrians to miss a pitch or two of the action as they strolled through Bushwick, Brighton Beach, and Bensonhurst. But Barber's voice did indeed blanket the borough, competing with the cries of infants, the churning of heavy machinery, and the clattering of elevated trains.

The voice didn't fit Brooklyn. It was too calm, too respectful, and, most of all, too southern. But Barber's drawl made baseball more magical, as if the game belonged to another place and time. The heartland had crickets. Brooklyn had Red Barber.

In 1947, hardly anyone owned a television set. Some apartment buildings banned their installation that year for fear that rooftops would become congested with the enormous antennae required to get good reception. A few bars were beginning to install TVs, and the early reports were encouraging. One bartender reported that the television set attracted a dozen extra customers during day games. With the average customer buying ten beers at ten cents a beer, he noted, the bar cleared an additional forty dollars a week. But most people who watched television in 1947 still did so through the window of their local hardware store, where the latest models were displayed. With an RCA television set priced at about $375, or roughly 10 percent of the average family's annual income, a glimpse through the store window would have to suffice. American manufacturers produced 20 million radios in 1947 but only 178,000 television sets. "People will soon get tired of staring at a plywood box," predicted Darryl F. Zanuck, head of the 20th Century Fox film studio.

Before Red Barber came to town, baseball games in New York were seldom heard on the radio. Other cities enjoyed regular baseball broadcasts, but not New York, where the three ball clubs each were owned by old-fashioned men who believed fans were less likely to buy tickets when they could listen to the action at home. Games could be heard on Opening Day and during the World Series, yet seldom in between. But in 1939, the Dodgers decided to break ranks and embrace the new medium. They had the least popular team in New York and needed some kind of boost. They turned to Barber, and, suddenly, the team developed a passionate following, one that included plenty of men and women who seldom had the time or money to go to the ballpark. Baseball became a core part of the borough's identity, like the Brooklyn Bridge and the Cyclone at Coney Island.

Walter Lanier Barber was born in 1908 in Columbus, Mississippi. While attending the University of Florida, he tried broadcasting on the campus radio station, reading a paper entitled "Certain Aspects of Bovine Obstetrics," and thrilled to the notion that he could communicate across long distances instantly and without wires. In 1934, after four years of radio work in Gainesville, Florida, he was hired by WLW in Cincinnati to broadcast baseball for the Cincinnati

Reds. He had never seen a major-league game.

Years later, it struck no one as strange that the voice of Brooklyn baseball was so heavily southern in accent. Perhaps it was because so many of the game's players were southerners, or simply because New York listeners had never heard any other voice describing their ballgames. Barber was first, and he was awfully good. He was a small man, thin, with wispy curls of orange hair. He tended not to mingle after hours with the players, favoring the company of his wife, Lylah. Neither did he travel with the team, because the Dodgers were not yet offering live broadcasts of their away games. Instead, Barber would sit in a studio in New York and read the play-by-play as results came in from a teletype operator at the ballpark where the team was playing. He made no attempt to hide the fact that he was miles away from the action. His listeners didn't care. Barber could describe the comings and goings of a parking lot and make it sound interesting.

"We've got a great game today," he'd say, "right he-ah in Brooklyn." But it was his choice of words more than his pronunciation that really tickled fans. When the Dodgers were sitting pretty, Barber had them "in the catbird seat." When they were scoring runs in a hurry, Barber said they were "tearing up the pea patch." When things turned sour, he would say the Dodgers had "one foot and five toes in the pickle bag." When he saw something astonishing, he might say, "Well, I'll be a suck-egg mule," the notion being that there were few things more amazing than a mule that could suck down eggs. A close game was "tighter than a new pair of shoes on a rainy day." A bobbled ball was "slicker than oiled okra." A hard-throwing pitcher "could toss a lamb chop past a hungry wolf."

It was Barber's enormous popularity that inspired Branch Rickey to confide in him early in 1945, months before he'd made up his mind to sign Robinson to a minor-league contract. Rickey wanted to know if Barber would give his support to the team's first black player. The broadcaster sang the praises of all Dodgers, no matter how weak, how old, or how inept. His job was to make the home team sound appealing, and he had never been anything less than loyal and enthusiastic. But the boss wanted to make certain that there would be no hint of disapproval, no subtle digs, no awkward moments of silence during Barber's play-by-play when Robinson came to bat. The men went for a late lunch one afternoon at Joe's Restaurant, around the corner from Rickey's office on Montague Street, and sat down at a table in the back. Rickey stabbed at a roll with his butter knife, scattering crumbs, as he told a story that he would go on to recount dozens, if not hundreds, of times in the years to come. It was the story of a college ballplayer named Charlie Thomas whom Rickey had coached at Ohio Wesleyan. Rickey described Thomas as "a fine young man, fine family, good student and my best player." One day, he said, when he and his players were checking in to a hotel in South Bend, Indiana, the desk clerk informed Rickey that Thomas would not be welcome. Only when Rickey agreed to share a room with Thomas did the clerk relent. Later, when Rickey went to his room, he said he found Thomas, "this fine young man, sitting on the edge of a chair, crying. He was crying. He was pulling at his hands as though he could tear the very skin off. 'It's my skin, Mr. Rickey. . . . If I could just pull it off.' "

Rickey started to stab at another roll and told Barber he'd been haunted for years by that scene and had made up his mind to do something about it. He didn't want to see other Americans shamed the way Charlie

Thomas had been. Now he knew what he had to do. He looked Barber in the eyes and said, "I'm going to bring a Negro to the Brooklyn Dodgers."

He dabbed some butter on his roll and took a bite.

Barber said nothing. He offered no support and made no complaint. He simply stared. He was an open-minded man, active in his church, pleased to use his fame to help raise money for homeless families. But the taboos ingrained since childhood gripped tightly. "He had shaken me to my heels," Barber recalled.

Rickey had told no one but his wife and children of his intention to breach baseball's color barrier (and his wife and children all thought it a mistake, or so Rickey liked to tell it). But he wanted Barber to be on board early, or at least have time to think about it, because he recognized the broadcaster's extraordinary ability to sway public opinion. Barber always said he had been raised to treat black people with respect and warmth, but he was also raised to believe that there was a line between the races, and the line was not to be crossed.

"I'm going to quit," Barber told his wife when he got home to Scarsdale that night. "I don't think I want . . . I don't know

232

whether I can. . . ." Usually, his sentences flowed fast and smooth, but now he was tongue-tied. Then he repeated: "I'm going to quit."

His wife urged him to wait. After all, the team hadn't hired a black player yet. There was no need to do anything rash, at least not for the moment.

"Let's have a martini," she suggested.

Time went by, and the matter was never spoken of again. "It tortured me," he wrote years later. "I finally found myself doing something I had never really done before. I set out to do a deep self-examination. I attempted to find out who I was. This did not come easily, and it was not done lightly." He decided he wasn't afraid of losing his job. He loved the Dodgers, loved Ebbets Field, but there would always be another team, another ballpark, another radio station. From there, he took the next logical step, asking himself why the thought of a black ballplayer troubled him so? "What was it that had me so stirred up?

"Well, I said, I'm Southern. I'm trained. . . . I was a product of a civilization: that line that was always there was indelible. . . . And then — I don't know why the thought came to my mind — I asked myself the basic question that a human being, if he is fair, ought to ask. How much control did I have over the parents I was born to? The answer was immediate: I didn't have any. . . . Then I figured out that I didn't have anything to be so proud of after all, this accident of the color of my skin."

At about that time, the rector of a church in Scarsdale asked Barber to give a talk on the radio about the growing tensions in Scarsdale between Christians and Jews. "Men and Brothers" was the suggested title for the broadcast. Barber's father was a Baptist, his mother a Presbyterian, his wife an Episcopalian. He attended the Episcopal church with his wife. In working out something to say about relations between the religions, Barber's thoughts turned again to his lunch with Rickey. He was still trying to decide what to do, still trying to figure out who he was. "What was my job? What was my function? What was I supposed to do as I broadcast baseball games?"

Barber recalled how the great umpire Bill Klem had always said that he blocked out the crowd noise, the score, and the names of the players on the field so that he might concentrate entirely and objectively on the ball. He called it umpiring the ball. Was it fair or foul? A ball or a strike? Did it stick in the glove or pop out? Under Klem's system, it wouldn't matter if the man hitting the ball happened to be black or white, a star or a nobody. It didn't matter if he was working an exhibition game or a World Series clash. Maybe the same approach ought to apply to a broadcaster, Barber reasoned. It wasn't his job to decide who should play the game. His job was to describe what he saw, simple as that.

"If I did do anything constructive in the Robinson situation," he recalled, "it was simply in accepting him the way I did — as a man, as a ballplayer. I didn't resent him, and I didn't crusade for him. I broadcast the ball."

With Barber calling the action in 1947, Robinson came to life for fans in the best possible way. When he finally started to hit, he became a hero, his color not a factor. In person, Robinson could be irritating. He was standoffish at times. But over the radio, he was all action. Listeners heard of his deeds and were left to imagine the rest. Based on what they were reading in the newspapers, they imagined a man showing up every day to play despite enormous pressure and deeply personal attacks. Had there been television cameras waiting for him in the clubhouse, or outside his home, fans might have seen some anxiety furrowing his brow. Perhaps they would have detected some sadness in his voice. But Robinson came across largely as Red Barber described him. As far as anyone listening to the radio could tell, the Dodgers — black and white, northern and southern, Jewish, Italian, and Irish — were as undifferentiated as a bag of peanuts.

In New London, Connecticut, thirteen-year-old Margot Hayward and her cousin wouldn't go outside, no matter the weather, when Barber was broadcasting a Dodger game. Margot's mother finally draped an extension cord out the window and lowered the radio down from Margot's room so the kids could play in the yard and hear the game. Hayward sensed the excitement whenever Robinson reached base. The crowd got louder as Barber described Robinson taking his lead off first base, always a threat to steal. Hayward had read about the indignities the Dodger first baseman had been forced to endure. To that point in her life, she had given little if any thought to race. "I always thought their lives were fine," she said of black people. "They were just separate. It never occurred to me there was any injustice in the world." The black kids her own age, along with some of the poor white children in the community, usually attended technical high schools, training for blue-collar jobs, while she and her friends went to mainstream high schools. Margot didn't see anything wrong with that. In 1947, Robinson instantly became her favorite player, in part because he was so exciting and in part because he was different. As a girl of thirteen, she thought she knew something about feeling different. She began keeping a scrapbook dedicated exclusively to his rookie year. She began noticing black people in her community. One day she asked her parents if she could invite a new friend to a party she was having at her house. The girl was white, but she was the daughter of a garbage collector. Margot's father, a lawyer, said he didn't want his daughter mixing with someone not in her social class. But Margot thought of her scrapbook. Robinson wasn't her kind. He wasn't Red Barber's kind, or Pistol Pete Reiser's kind, or Eddie Stanky's kind. They mixed. She stood up to her father, saying she would rather not have the party if her friend couldn't come, and her father backed down.

"At age thirteen, that was total victory," she recalled. The arrival of Jackie Robinson, she said, "was something that changed a lot

237

of things in my life. You grow up in a society that's pretty rigid . . . and eventually you start to rebel."

Malcolm Little was another of Red Barber's regular listeners in the spring and summer of 1947. He, too, knew something about rebellion. He was twenty-one years old and following the Dodgers from his cell at the Charlestown State Prison in Massachusetts. Beginning with Opening Day, which created a huge sensation throughout the prison, and for every game thereafter, Little would sit next to his radio, pencil in hand, keeping track of Robinson's every at-bat. At the end of each game, he would calculate the Dodger first baseman's batting average.

A light-skinned black man from Lansing, Michigan, Little was serving a ten-year sentence for burglary. "Red," his friends called him, for the rusty color of his hair. Later, he would change his name to Malcolm X. Before he became a convicted criminal, Little had been engaged in a long series of auditions for the part. For years, he'd been dodging the law as a shoplifter, drug dealer, street hustler, numbers runner, and pimp. He was an angry young man, though thoughtful enough that he directed the anger mostly at himself.

As he listened to baseball on the radio, he might have recalled his own brief athletic career, as the only black basketball player on the Mason Junior High School team. Little was one of a handful of black students at the school, and the only one in the seventh grade. His father had been murdered, his mother had been confined to a state mental hospital. Their children were scattered among state institutions. Malcolm's gift for trouble landed him in a detention home in Mason, Michigan, which is how he came to enroll at Mason Junior High. He liked Mrs. Swerlin, the woman who ran the detention center where he lived, and he respected his English teacher, Mr. Ostrowski, who encouraged students to "become something in life." But he sensed, only dimly at the time, that these white people who offered their encouragement did not always have the best intentions. He felt as if he were accepted in Mason merely as a mascot, a curiosity, never as a fully formed human being. No one was able to see past his color, he believed.

As a member of the junior high basketball team, Little traveled to nearby towns such as Howell and Charlotte, where fans taunted him with cries of "nigger," "coon," and "Rastus." "It didn't bother my teammates

239

or my coach at all," he recalled years later, "and to tell the truth, it bothered me only vaguely."

After the games, there would be school dances. Whenever Little walked in with his white teammates, everyone in the room would freeze. Someone would lift the needle from the record player and the room would go silent, or so it seemed to him. People smiled, but Little usually understood that he was not supposed to dance with the white girls. Only when the others could see that that black boy was smart enough to show restraint and humility would the record player restart, with Glenn Miller's "Moonlight Serenade," or the Ink Spots' "If I Didn't Care," scratching through the public address system.

In his second semester at Mason, Little was elected president of his class. He was surprised and proud. He had good grades. He had friends. His teachers offered encouragement. But he understood — again, only vaguely at the time — that there was another force at work. He was elected because he was different, he sensed, not because he deserved to win. "I was unique in my class," he wrote years later, "like a pink poodle." In Little's mind, his election was part cruel, part kind; part joke, part tribute.

At the time, there were few role models for a young black man trying to fit into a white man's world. For every source of pride, like Joe Louis, there were a dozen or more sources of shame, like Butterfly McQueen, who played Prissy in *Gone With the Wind* and shouted "Lawzy, we got to have a doctor!" The movie, which Little saw that year in Mason, made him want to crawl under the carpet. Still, he was doing well in school, fitting in nicely, thankful for the attention. But one day he found himself alone in a classroom with Mr. Ostrowski, the English teacher he so admired. Mr. Ostrowski asked Little if he'd given any thought to a career.

"Well, yes, sir, I've been thinking I'd like to be a lawyer," he said. He hadn't been giving it any thought, in fact, but he had a job at the time washing dishes after school, and he knew for certain that lawyers didn't have to wash dishes.

Mr. Ostrowski half smiled. "Malcolm, one of life's first needs is for us to be realistic," he said. "Don't misunderstand me now. We all here like you, you know that. But you've got to be realistic. A lawyer, that's not a realistic goal for a nigger. You're good with your hands, making things. Everybody admires your carpentry shop work. Why

241

don't you plan on carpentry. People like you as a person — you'd get all kinds of work."

The remark poisoned Little. None of the white students in class had been told to scale down their ambitions, and his grades were better than most. He began to change, to pull away, to lose interest in trying to please his white teachers and classmates. Now, when he heard "nigger," he turned and glared instead of letting it roll off his back. Soon he would drop out of school and board a bus for Boston to live with his half-sister.

After years of petty crimes and misadventures in Boston and New York, he found himself locked up in the Massachusetts state pen, listening to Jackie Robinson and the Dodgers in the summer of 1947. Red Barber danced nimbly around the subject of race, scarcely mentioning the first baseman's color, but Little could think about nothing else. His own attempt at integration had failed. Mason Junior High's seventh-grade class had not been ready for him. Now he wanted to see if the Dodgers and the rest of America were prepared to do better. He passed his time to the steady rhythm of balls, strikes, and outs, monitoring Robinson's batting average, praying for it to stay above .300, the benchmark for excellence in the majors.

That same year, Little began to turn his life around ever so slightly. He took a correspondence course in English, working on grammar, vocabulary, and penmanship. He read as if books were food and he was starving. Five years later, when he was released on parole, he embraced the Muslim religion and dropped his last name, which he considered a vestige of slavery, and replaced it with the letter X. He did not become a believer in integration — at least not in the brand exemplified by Robinson and endorsed by mainstream civil rights leaders. He took a more militant approach, arguing for black separatism and urging black people to use violence if necessary to achieve power. In the 1960s, he would attack Robinson, saying the ballplayer had been "used by the whites," starting with Branch Rickey, throughout his career. He would ridicule Robinson for his conservative political stances. "You, yourself would never shake my hand," he wrote in a letter to Robinson, "until you saw some of your white friends shaking it."

But all that came later, much later. In 1947, Malcolm was spellbound by Robinson, captivated by his speed and daring, just as so many others were. He listened to Red

243

Barber's broadcasts and pictured this burglar, this black man stealing the white men's bases, running circles around them, making them look helpless. He was truly tearing up the pea patch. "Jackie Robinson had, then, his most fanatic fan in me," he wrote.

TEN:
PEE WEE'S EMBRACE

For one month Jackie Robinson had been a clenched fist — frozen, cramped, joyless. He had kept his mouth closed, backed down from provocation, made no waves, just as Branch Rickey had asked. It wasn't until the Dodgers made their first extended road trip that something clicked and he found a way to fight, and to play the kind of baseball he most enjoyed.

In Cincinnati, Pittsburgh, Chicago, and St. Louis, they waited for him. America was a nation in flux. Beginning around 1940, hundreds of thousands of black men and women had begun moving from the rural South to the urban North. The migration continued through the war, as black men arrived, hoping to secure some of the high-paying factory jobs abandoned by men off fighting. Even after the war, the waves continued to roll from south to north, strong enough to scare some people. "If tens of thousands of black Southerners descend upon communities totally unprepared for them psychologically and industrially, what will the effect be upon race relations in the United States?" David Cohn, a white southerner, wrote in 1947. "There is an enormous tragedy in the making." The African-American writer Richard Wright had reached much the same conclusion a few years earlier: "Perhaps never in history has a more utterly unprepared folk wanted to go to the city; we were barely born as a folk when we headed for the tall and sprawling centers of steel and stone. We, who were landless upon the land; we, who had barely managed to live in family groups; we, who needed the ritual and guidance of institutions to hold our atomized lives together in times of purpose; we, who had known only relationships to people and not relationships to things; we, who had our personalities blasted with 200 years of slavery and had been turned loose to shift for ourselves — we were such a folk as this when we moved into a world that was destined to test all we were, that threw us into the scales of competition to weigh our mettle."

That was Jackie Robinson, a man thrown into the scales of competition. But he was not the only one. Millions of Americans, black and white, were feeling the pressure. The black migration, the biggest internal resettlement in the nation's history, created enormous competition for jobs and housing and all sorts of consumer goods. Cars, for instance, were in short supply because for years auto plants had been cranking out jeeps and tanks instead of sedans. Men who had seen their bravery tested on the battlefields had come home to find that their wives, after working in factories *and* running households for a couple of years, had become more self-reliant. Some men could not be sure where they fit anymore. A nation united by battlefield triumphs and confident in the destiny of the American way suddenly found itself dazed and confused by the changes.

Black families moving north often set out with no fixed destination in mind. They would try St. Louis, or Cincinnati, or Dayton, and if they found no work, they moved on, perhaps to Cleveland, perhaps to Pittsburgh, or perhaps to Chicago.

Cincinnati was a fairly typical stop along the route, more North than South, more recipient than sender. The Queen City prospered in the 1940s, with a population approaching half a million, and booming factories that manufactured jet engines and machine tools. From 1940 to 1950, the black population in the city grew from fifty-six thousand to seventy-eight thousand. By 1947, roughly three out of every four black Cincinnatians were clustered in the West End, a sprawling slum filled with falling-down houses, aging factories, and empty lots. About 80 percent of black families lived in homes that the city deemed beneath acceptable standards. "Police rookies patrol the streets in pairs," reported the *WPA Guide to Cincinnati* in 1943, "and victims of knife slashing in this section are numerous among regular patients of the city's General Hospital. Despite the law-abiding nature of the better element, the reputation of the area is bad." The West End might have been shunned completely by white Cincinnatians if not for one concrete-and-steel structure, located at the corner of Findlay Street and Western Avenue: Crosley Field, home to the Cincinnati Reds, set in the northern end of the impoverishment, between a smoky railroad yard and a long bank of tenements, with the Superior Towel and Linen Service Building out behind left field.

Cincinnati, having never prepared for the huge influx of black families, was feeling the strain of its growth, its urban center breaking down. The war had helped postpone certain problems, as everyone rallied around the flag. So long as the manufacturing sector continued to boom, jobs remained in good supply for men black and white. When the war ended, though, everything and everyone felt the pressure. Jobs got scarce. Schools and playgrounds grew crowded. Crime rates ticked slowly higher. Poor people, unable to find affordable housing, began doubling up with brothers and sisters, aunts and uncles. Families that could afford it pushed beyond the city's boundaries, planting new suburbs on soil that had once been farmed.

This was no small demographic shift. This was an earthquake. A baby boom was coming, and while most social scientists would not notice for years, planners in Cincinnati were more alert than most. In 1947 they were at work on a comprehensive plan to repair the city's dissolving infrastructure. They would build highways through the West End slums. They would tear down countless thousands of dilapidated homes with little regard for their inhabitants. And though the city's black population was growing as its white population fell away, the black community in Cincinnati, with no elected representation, would have no say in the plans. The neighborhood never enjoyed a sustained period of glory, but if ever there were a moment when the West End swelled with pride, it was Tuesday, May 13, when Jackie Robinson came to town, making his midwestern debut.

This time he didn't stare out the window on the train. En route to Cincinnati Robinson played cards with a couple of the guys who'd been his teammates in Montreal: Marv Rackley and Johnny Jorgensen. Eddie Chandler, a rookie pitcher and an Alabaman, was their fourth. They played for no more than twenty-five cents at a time. From the train station, the Dodgers — including Robinson — went to the Netherland-Plaza Hotel, opposite the city's famous Fountain Square, where, seemingly, they had no problems at check-in. Reporters following the team congratulated the hotel manager on his progressive attitude, failing to mention that Robinson couldn't use the pool or dining room during his visit.

Down the block from the hotel, William Mallory bussed tables that afternoon at the Hub Café. He was a fifteen-year-old high-school dropout, wiping tables for the restaurant's white customers, making twenty-five dollars a week, and dreaming of a career as an elected government official. Sixty years later, Mallory couldn't recall whether he witnessed Robinson's first or second game in Cincinnati, but he remembered with clarity the mood of the city as the Dodgers came to town. It was just another ballgame for the white men who stopped in at the Hub Café for dinner on their way to Crosley Field. But not in the West End. "Oh, it was really something to see," he said. Black people filled the neighborhood as if from nowhere, like some magician's trick, pouring out of every bus, every taxi. But what looked like magic to Mallory was simply a matter of practicality to the travelers. They had taken off from faraway homes that morning, planning to make the trip back and forth to Cincinnati in one long day to avoid hotel charges. Unsure whether they'd find restaurants willing to serve them as they traveled, many carried shoeboxes lined with wax paper and filled with fried chicken, a whole day's supply.

Showers fell throughout the day, but the skies started to clear two hours before the game, just in time for a lovely sunset and night baseball. The parting clouds added to the West End's euphoria. "It was like a picnic, like a holiday," recalled Donald Spencer, who sat with his wife, Marian, in the bleachers for that night's game. Spencer was a teacher at the all-black Harriet

Beecher Stowe Junior High in Cincinnati, moonlighting a bit in real estate, helping black vets use the GI Bill to buy their first homes. Spencer and his wife both knew how Robinson felt, knew what it meant to be black in a white person's world. As undergraduates at the University of Cincinnati, they had fought to end segregation at school dances. Now, at Crosley Field, they stood and cheered every time Robinson stepped to the plate. If they embarrassed him with their overdone hoots and hollers, they didn't care. "Listen, it was quite an affair," Donald Spencer recalled. "It was kind of a revolution, you know?"

The Dodgers by now were accustomed to seeing a lot of black faces in the stands. One newspaper report said about half of the twenty-seven thousand people at the ballpark that night were black. But to some of the Cincinnati Reds, it looked like more. "The place was packed — all blacks," said Eddie Erautt, a rookie pitcher. "All Robinson had to do was foul a ball off and they cheered. You'd have thought he hit a home run." In the Reds dugout, players joked about it, wondering aloud if Robinson would get a round of applause for tying his shoe or successfully relieving himself in the bathroom.

252

The Dodgers played their sloppiest game of the year, walking eight, committing three errors, and going down by a 7–5 score. Twice the Reds robbed Robinson of hits on well-struck balls. Still, he came through with a walk, a single, a run scored, and a run batted in. But in the mythology of Robinson's rookie year, there was one more bit of action. According to reports handed down across the years, Robinson on his debut in Cincinnati was taking horrible abuse from the white fans at Crosley Field, worse than anything he or his teammates had heard all season, when he went to his position at first base in the bottom of the first inning. Pee Wee Reese heard the cries, the story goes, and left his position at shortstop. He walked across the diamond to first base, where he put an arm around Robinson's shoulder and spoke something in his ear, hushing the crowd with his gesture of brotherhood. Reese was a Kentuckian — "the Colonel," Red Barber called him. Many of his friends and family had made the short drive to see him play in Cincinnati. He was more popular at Crosley Field than most of the Reds. His walk across the diamond, his embrace of Robinson, would be described years later as one of baseball's most glorious and honorable moments.

"I was warming up on the mound, and I could hear the Cincinnati players screaming at Jackie, 'You nigger sonofabitch, you shoeshine boy,' and then they started to go in on Pee Wee," recalled the Dodger pitcher Rex Barney in Pete Golenbock's book of Dodger oral history, *Bums.* "Pee Wee went over to him and put an arm around him as if to say, 'This is my boy. . . .' Well, it drove the Cincinnati players right through the ceiling, and you could have heard a gasp from the crowd as he did it."

Lester Rodney, reporting for the communist *Daily Worker,* said he remembered the incident because it occurred on the only road trip his editors permitted him to cover all season. "I saw the incident in Cincinnati," he recalled. "A bunch of men before the game were shouting. Pee Wee dropped his glove at shortstop and walked over. I was there that day. That kind of drama, how do you measure it?" Rodney said he would kick himself years later for not writing about what he had seen.

But no one else wrote about it either; not in New York, not in Cincinnati, not in white papers, not in black — not in 1947. In fact, the *New York Post* called Robinson "the toast of the town" after that game, and the *Cincinnati Enquirer* reported that he "was

254

applauded every time he stepped to the plate." Robinson, in his weekly column, called his visit to Crosley Field "a nice experience." Even Rex Barney's account, which he provided only many years after the fact, contains a significant flaw. Barney says he was on the mound warming up in the bottom half of the first inning when he saw Reese walk over and put his arm around Robinson, but Barney didn't pitch that night until the seventh inning.

In the days and weeks after the game, no newspaper stories placed Robinson and Reese together on the diamond. No photos of the incident have ever been identified. Commissioner Chandler, a strong supporter of Robinson, watched the game from a seat near the dugout and never mentioned the gesture or any unseemly behavior by Cincinnati players or fans. At season's end, when Robinson sat down with Wendell Smith to write his version of the year's events, he didn't mention the purported incident, either. In fact, Smith and Robinson didn't even cite Reese as someone who went out of his way to make the rookie feel welcome. In later years, as Robinson and Reese developed a genuine friendship, Robinson would talk about the role the Dodger shortstop played in making him feel a part of the team. Reese did indeed become a leader among the Dodgers in matters racial, embracing Robinson physically and emotionally. But not in 1947. In 1947, he was one of the boys. He was an ally, but not a strong one, and certainly not an outspoken one. Rickey and Robinson, in accounts written shortly after the 1947 season, both rated Eddie Stanky as Robinson's earliest important backer.

In a book written many years later, Robinson did describe an incident in which Reese walked over and put a hand on his shoulder to hush a bothersome crowd, but he set the drama in Boston in 1948. There's no contemporaneous reporting and no photograph to support that account, either. It's possible that the Robinson-Reese moment took place just as Barney, Rodney, and others remembered it, in 1947. But it seems unlikely. What's more likely is that Reese and Robinson slowly became friends, and after Robinson became a second baseman in 1948, he and Reese enjoyed frequent chats on the infield between innings and during timeouts in the action. Perhaps Reese, as warm and kind a man as there was in baseball, sometimes put an arm around Robinson's shoulder. Perhaps he even did so intentionally to show support when catcalls were raining down, or simply to remind fans that black and white men now played side by side. There were still plenty of fans abusing Robinson in 1948, and throughout most of his career, so the sight of these two men getting on well would have been a memorable one — memorable enough that some would place it in the mental file for 1947, when it would have resonated most strongly.

The story of Reese's embrace has become a sermon, a children's book, even a bronze statue, dedicated in 2005 at Keyspan Park, home of the minor-league Brooklyn Cyclones, seven miles from the former site of Ebbets Field. "My father had done his own soul searching," Mark Reese, Pee Wee's son, said at the dedication of the statue depicting his father's most famous moment, "and he knew that some fans, teammates, and, yes, some family members didn't want him to play with a black man. But my father listened to his heart, not to the chorus." Years later, Pee Wee Reese would make a point in interviews to say his role in the Robinson drama had been exaggerated, that he had never tried to be an activist, had never intended to make any grand gestures. All he had ever tried to do, he said, was treat Robinson the way he treated everyone else.

"You know, I didn't particularly go out of my way just to be nice to you," he once told Robinson.

"Pee Wee," Robinson replied, "maybe that's what I appreciated most."

The Dodgers lost both games in Cincinnati, and Burt Shotton might have been forgiven for wondering what had happened to the team that had finished the regular season tied for first place in 1946. The Dodgers used eight pitchers in their two games against the Reds, and none of them looked good. Durocher had always been especially adept at juggling the pitching staff. Now some on the team began to wonder if Shotton knew what he was doing. Starting pitchers had completed only five of the team's first twenty-two games, and the Dodgers used an average of almost three pitchers a game, an unusually high number by the standards of the time. In the two games at Cincinnati, the pitchers issued thirteen walks. When Clyde King came in to pitch in the first game, three of his five warm-up pitches sailed high into the backstop behind home plate. It didn't get much better.

Pitching wasn't the only problem. With Jorgensen hurt, the team once again found

258

itself with no good third baseman. Shotton tried Cookie Lavagetto, Stan Rojek, and Arky Vaughan, but none hit. Pee Wee Reese was still slumping terribly at the plate, and Eddie Stanky was only slightly better. Pete Reiser, after missing time with an ankle injury, remained gimpy and in need of rest. If there was any consolation, it was that the entire National League thus far was a big clump of mediocrity, tightly bunched in the standings. Only the Cardinals were far behind. "Our team, baseballically speaking," Branch Rickey told a Rotary Club lunch, "is the youngest I have ever had. It's considerably different from the team we had last year."

Robinson was lucky in at least one respect. The Dodgers had so many problems that no one gave much thought to whether he was helping the team, even as he continued to struggle, and continued to torture himself. Don Newcombe compared him once to a boiler, always hissing and clanging, radiating heat. But in 1947, particularly early on, when he wasn't hitting, he had no release valve. He just got hotter and hotter until he thought he would burst.

"It is true that I had stored up a lot of hostility," he wrote years later. "I had been going home nights to Rachel and young

259

Jackie, tense and irritable, keyed up because I hadn't been able to speak out when I wanted to." And when he wanted to tended to be all the time. "That sounds as though I wanted to get even, and I'm sure that's partly true," he said. "I wouldn't have been human otherwise. But more than revenge, I wanted to be Jackie Robinson."

ELEVEN:
THE GLORIOUS
CRUSADE

From Cincinnati it was on to Pittsburgh, where Wendell Smith would enjoy a homecoming. Smith was proud of his contributions to Robinson's early-season success, and yet the sportswriter seldom bragged about his part in these historic events, not even to the beautiful young secretary at the *Pittsburgh Courier,* Wyonella Hicks, whom he would marry two years later.

Smith's stories on Robinson were a sensation. The paper's circulation soared higher by the week, to more than 250,000, and Smith was the *Courier's* biggest star. He was Robinson's Boswell, his roommate, and his friend. Yet the young reporter with the receding hairline, chubby cheeks, and dainty mustache went about his business with calm determination, unimpressed by all the attention and uninterested in claiming celebrity status for himself. Back in Pittsburgh, he let his bosses spend time with Robinson, permitting them to revel in the celebration of the newspaper's accomplishment, while he stayed in the office and finished up some stories.

Smith and Robinson had a great deal in common. Each had felt imprisoned at times by the nation's color caste system. Each had tried through the years not to let his white counterparts see how badly he had been hurt by segregation. Such feelings threatened to ruin black Americans in the 1940s. When he was a young man, wrote the scholar and activist W.E.B. DuBois, the first black person to receive a Ph.D. from Harvard, he viewed segregation as a challenge, as "a glorious crusade." But the crusade wore him down before long. The fight was rigged, he discovered, and he grew resentful. He came to feel like a prisoner in his own country, the shackles growing tighter the more he strained to break them. Robinson and Smith were younger than DuBois, and each in his own way still felt the desire to struggle, Robinson hammering away with his Louisville Slugger, Smith scratching with pencil and pen.

Like Robinson, Smith was a black man who had grown up surrounded almost entirely by whites. Smith came from Detroit, where his father had worked as a cook for

Henry Ford. As a boy, Wendell sometimes accompanied his father to work at Fair Lane, the automobile mogul's magnificent estate. Ford's grandchildren — Henry II, Benson, and William — would play ball on the mansion's plush lawns, and they invited young Wendell to join in. Yet even as a child he recognized the hierarchies in place. He knew that his father cooked for Ford but never ate with him. He knew that when the grandchildren grew tired of playing ball and moved on to the bowling alley or the pool, young black boys were not allowed.

Later, as the only black student at Southeastern High School in Detroit, he became a star in baseball and basketball. He wasn't terribly big or strong, but he was smooth and fast. "Everybody was great to me," Smith recalled of his high-school sports career. "You'd naturally run into some jerks once in a while, but that never disturbed me because there wasn't that much trouble, and I always had the feeling that if I had any problems the guys on the team were with me." Smith felt that he got along well with his white classmates because he was the only black student in the school. Had there been more of his kind, the white students might have felt more threatened. Right though he may have been, Smith failed to account for the effect of his personality. He was ambitious and determined, but also, by nature, a compromiser. His white classmates liked him because he was so affable.

When Smith was nineteen, he pitched in a big playoff game for his American Legion team, tossing a complete-game shutout. A big-league scout for the Chicago White Sox watched the game. But when it ended, Smith wasn't approached. Instead, the scout offered a contract to Mike Tresh, the team's white catcher. "I wish I could sign you, too, kid, but I can't," the scout said. Smith didn't argue. He didn't even answer. He simply went home and cried.

Smith played baseball and basketball at his all-black college, West Virginia State. But he didn't picture much of a future in sports, partly because of his color and partly because of his size. Instead, after graduating, he landed a seventeen-dollar-a-week job writing sports for the *Courier,* then the nation's leading black weekly. The *Courier's* influence was extraordinary. The nation's big black papers helped speed the black migration, encouraging black farmers to make the move and, upon their arrival, helping them find jobs and homes. The newspaper functioned at times as a social worker, at other times as a cheerleader, and at still other times as a fire-breathing lawyer — but always as an advocate. If you were a black person of good character, the *Courier* was on your side. In 1932, the paper urged its readers to drop their traditional support for Republicans and vote for FDR, forever shifting the nation's political balance. The paper's writers attacked the popular *Amos 'n' Andy* radio show for its racist portrayals of black characters. They chided the Red Cross for refusing to accept blood from black donors. And in the 1940s, the paper launched its extraordinary successful "Double V" campaign, demanding that black soldiers who risked their lives for victory in the war receive equal rights at home.

Campaigns such as these helped boost circulation, but they did much more. They created a sense among black Americans that they had a voice, that they had power, that they were living through an era of rapid change — in Europe as well as in America — and that they had a chance to come out of it in better shape than they entered. But if they hoped to make gains, the paper said, black Americans needed to prove they were worthy of respect. They needed to stand up and fight rather than wait for white men to implement reforms according to their own terms and timeframes.

Though he wrote sports, Smith saw no reason to approach his job any differently from reporters covering politics, crime, or the union movement. Late in 1938, just weeks after the Nazis attacked Jews throughout Germany in a night of broken glass and bloodshed that became known as *Kristallnacht,* Smith compared baseball's segregationists to the Nazis. "While Hitler cripples the Jews," he wrote, "the great leaders of our national pastime refuse to recognize our black players."

Thanks in large part to Smith, Robinson fast became the *Courier*'s favorite symbol of the struggle for equal rights. He was neither asking for nor receiving special treatment. His position on the team had been attained without a court order or armed guards. He offered a perfect symbol for the *Courier* and for supporters of the Double V campaign.

There were other black men and women making their marks in the white world in the summer of 1947. Adam Clayton Powell, a Baptist minister, was already serving in Congress, representing the people of Harlem. A. Philip Randolph had already turned the Brotherhood of Sleeping Car Porters into a powerful force for black workers. Ralph Bunche, a diplomat who helped plan the United Nations, made headlines that year as he began trying to negotiate peace between Jews and Palestinian Arabs in the Middle East, an effort that would earn him a Nobel Prize. Benjamin O. Davis, the army's first black general, had received a Distinguished Service Medal in 1945 for his work in advising the War Department on maintaining strong morale among black troops. Powell, Randolph, Bunche, Davis, and the countless other black men and women working in white institutions as doctors, teachers, and engineers faced pressures unimaginable to their white contemporaries, but they didn't have to perform in front of thirty thousand fans every day. Their performances weren't reviewed daily by a dozen reporters, with batting averages printed every day in the paper to measure in crisp clarity their worth.

The *Courier* had helped launch Joe Louis's career, but no story in the paper's history perked up circulation like the story of baseball's integration. It started as early as 1938, when Smith began polling white players, managers, and owners as they came through Pittsburgh to play the Pirates, asking if they thought black ballplayers ought to be allowed to compete with white players. Smith, because he was black, wasn't permitted in the press box for Pirates games. Rather than fight it, he conducted his interviews outside the ballpark and in the lobby of the Schenley Hotel. "Have you seen any Negro ballplayers you thought could play major league baseball?" he would offer as an opener. It was a nonthreatening question, and Smith was a nonthreatening figure, but it nevertheless took courage for him to ask. The results were encouraging: Roughly three out of every four interviewees expressed support for integration. Smith's editors liked the stories so much they gave him a raise.

Other writers around the country conducted similar campaigns. Smith was joined by Sam Lacy, who worked for the *Washington Tribune* and the *Chicago Defender* before joining the *Baltimore Afro-American,* as well as by Joe Bostic of the *People's Voice* in New York. The communist *Daily Worker* agitated on the issue, too. In 1943, Commissioner Landis and baseball's owners, responding to pressure brought by the black journalists, granted Smith, Lacy, and a few others an opportunity to state their case. It was a bit of showmanship on the part of Landis, who had hoped to get the journalists off his back. To heighten the drama of their presentation, the newspapermen brought the controversial singer and actor Paul Robeson along for the meeting. If a black man could play Othello as part of an all-white cast on Broadway, as Robeson had done, why couldn't a black man play baseball on an all-white team? the actor asked. The visitors' presentation lasted about thirty minutes. When it was over, the owners stared in silence. After the delegation departed, Landis said there would be no discussion. At first glance, the meeting seemed a disaster. But Smith thought he detected a glimmer in the eye of Branch Rickey, a small flicker to suggest Brooklyn's owner had taken more interest than the rest.

The following year, Landis was dead, replaced by Albert Benjamin "Happy" Chandler, lawyer, former U.S. senator, and former governor of Kentucky — a stubborn man and yet as difficult to dislike as his nickname would suggest. Chandler was a southern Democrat, but a fairly conservative man. No one knew for certain where he stood on integration. Smith, along with the communists and a few other interested writers, continued to pound away, picking up supporters in the mainstream press. Then, in April 1945, came a breakthrough: In Boston, a white city councilman named Isadore Muchnick, apparently trying to maintain his hold on office as more black families moved into his district, began pressing the Red Sox and Braves to integrate. Many years later, Smith would say he had phoned Muchnick and suggested to him that the integration of baseball would make a great campaign issue. Muchnick, a liberal, threatened to deny the teams the annual permits required to play baseball on Sunday if they didn't make some racial progress. Eddie Collins, general manager of the Red Sox, responded by telling Muchnick that no black player had ever asked for a tryout. When Smith heard the excuse, he contacted Muchnick and told him he had three black prospects eager for tryouts with the Boston teams. The prospects Smith chose for the job were Sam Jethroe, a speedy outfielder with the Cleveland Buckeyes; Marvin Williams, a second baseman with the Philadelphia Stars; and Jackie Robinson, then playing shortstop for the Kansas City Monarchs. Why Jethroe, Williams, and Robinson? Why not Paige or Gibson? For one thing, Smith wanted younger men. He wanted everyday players, not pitchers. He wanted intelligent men who had played with white athletes and who weren't afraid to take a little harassment. He wanted men capable of assimilation. In other words, he wanted men like himself. In explaining his choice of Robinson, completely unproven as a baseball player to that point, he said, he "wasn't necessarily the best player. He was the best at that time for this particular situation."

The Braves were out of town when Smith and his players arrived by train, but the Red Sox, after some hemming and hawing and delays for rain, finally agreed to grant the players a tryout. All three of the men played well in Boston, and Robinson played especially well, but it didn't matter. Team officials did just enough to get Muchnick off their backs, and then sent Smith and his crew packing. The Red Sox would wait another twelve years to bring a black man, second baseman Pumpsie Green, to the majors, making them the last team in baseball to integrate. For all the talk about Boston's Curse of the Bambino — the notion that the Red Sox went eighty-six years without a World Series championship as some sort of karmic punishment for trading Babe Ruth to the Yankees in 1920 — the curse of Jackie Robinson hurt them far more.

On his way back to Pittsburgh, Smith stopped in Brooklyn and visited Rickey at his office on Montague Street, telling him all about the tryout in Boston. At the time, the Dodger boss was talking about establishing a new Negro league to help fill Ebbets Field when his big-leaguers were out of town. Rickey asked Smith which black players he had brought with him to Boston. "And when I said 'Jackie Robinson,' " Smith recalled, "his bushy eyebrows raised, and he said, 'Jackie Robinson! I knew he was a good football player . . . but I didn't know he played baseball.' "

A week later, Rickey telephoned Smith and asked again about Robinson, although he never used his name, lending to the conversation a sense of mystery and urgency. Smith had the feeling that Rickey was intrigued by Robinson's fame as a college football player, that it might make him a strong attraction at the box office. Rickey told Smith that he was interested in hiring "that young man from the West" for his new Negro-league team, and that he was sending a scout, Clyde Sukeforth, to have a look at the prospect. Smith tipped off Robinson, telling him to be on his best behavior when Sukeforth arrived. And though he had a feeling that Rickey might be interested in Robinson for the major leagues, not for some new Negro league, Smith put his ego aside. He had more than enough evidence to splash a big story speculating on Rickey's plan, but he held off. The outcome meant more to him than the scoop.

Robinson, his shoulder aching, wasn't playing much when Sukeforth came around in late August 1945. But in one Monarchs game, with the scout watching, Robinson displayed some of the temper for which he had been well known in California. Some accounts of the incident have suggested that Robinson clenched a fist and prepared to throw a punch at the umpire. Sukeforth reported the incident to Rickey, and Rickey in turn called Smith. Was the young man from the West "a belligerent type of individual?" he asked. Smith lied: "I didn't want to tell Rickey, 'Yes, he's a bad guy to get along with.' . . . I told Robinson to watch his conduct. Sure, I knew he was belligerent."

A few months later, when Rickey agreed to sign Robinson, he added Smith to his payroll, too, at a salary of fifty dollars a week. It was agreed that Smith would continue writing for the *Courier,* where he also earned fifty dollars a week. But he would serve as Robinson's chaperone and Rickey's unofficial Negro-league scout. "Now, Mr. Rickey," the journalist wrote in a personal letter, "I want you to feel as though the publishers of the Pittsburgh *Courier* and I are a distinct part of this undertaking. We do not want you to take all of the responsibility with regards to help to strengthen these boys spiritually and morally for the part to play in this great adventure. For that reason I want you to feel you can call upon me for any cooperation which you think I may be able to render."

Smith rendered every kind of service. He bunked with Robinson; wrote the ballplayer's weekly newspaper column for him; helped find hotels and restaurants on the road when whites-only businesses turned them away; and turned his own column into a long-running advertisement for the benefits of racial integration. Dixie Walker and Ben Chapman may have done Robinson a favor by making him a victim, but it was Smith more than anyone who created the impression that Robinson was untroubled by the victimization, that he was letting the insults roll off his back when, in fact, he was absorbing them all like blows to the gut. Robinson was never going to be baseball's Gandhi, but Smith helped create the illusion of serenity, at least for one season.

"Through all of this," Smith said, "I always tried to keep it from becoming a flamboyant, highly militant thing. And I think that's why it succeeded. If there had been picketing and all that type of thing, this would never have developed the way it has. . . . There were agitators at that time, people who knew the part I was playing, Negro organizations who wanted to be a part of it, to push it faster, and I kept them out of it. . . . We always tried to play this thing in low-key. That was Rickey's idea, too."

The Pirates, like the Dodgers, had a new first baseman in 1947, one who knew a little something about discrimination. Hank Greenberg was a New York City kid, a product of James Monroe High School, and one of the game's greatest sluggers during the 1930s. Though there had been other Jews in baseball, Greenberg became the game's first Jewish superstar as a member of the Detroit Tigers. For Jews who were otherwise agnostic when it came to baseball, he was the only ballplayer who mattered. "Moses in Cleats," they called him, though only because it was catchy; Greenberg was not observant of his faith and never attempted to be a leader of his people. "Sure there was added pressure being Jewish," he wrote in his autobiography, noting that he heard cries of "Jew bastard," "kike," and "sheenie" from both players and fans. "I used to get frustrated as hell. Sometimes I wanted to go up in the stands and beat the shit out of them."

Playing for the Tigers, Greenberg led the American League in home runs four times, and twice won the Most Valuable Player Award. He was drafted into the army at the age of thirty, re-enlisted after the Japanese attacked Pearl Harbor, and missed more than four full seasons of baseball. When he returned in 1945, at age thirty-five, his swing was as sweet as ever, but his legs wobbled a bit. After the 1946 season, the Tigers sold him to the Pirates. Greenberg considered retirement but was lured back by a contract offering one hundred thousand dollars — the first six-figure salary in the game's history — and a promise that Pittsburgh would shorten the left-field fence at Forbes Field to about 335 feet. Reporters began calling the area behind the chicken-wire fence, where his home runs soon would land, "Greenberg Gardens."

Greenberg and Robinson met in the third inning of their first game at Forbes Field. Robinson of late had been hitting the ball nicely, well enough that he wasn't self-conscious about bunting anymore. So as pitcher Ed Bahr made his pitch, Robinson slid his right hand up the barrel of the bat, squared around, and tapped gently at the ball. It rolled back toward Bahr, who scrambled to field it and throw to first. When the throw sailed wide and toward the outfield, Robinson tried to make the turn toward second. But the first baseman, Greenberg, was in his way. The men collided. Robinson tumbled to the ground. He picked himself up and took off again for second, where he arrived in plenty of time.

"That particular play was the type that prejudiced writers and players and big league owners used to say would cause a riot," Smith wrote after the game. "Those who have fought against the entrance of Negro players into the majors have always contended that the kind of collision that Robinson and Greenberg had would only result in a free-for-all and the 'good' name of baseball would be smeared." Quite the contrary, Smith reported, later in the game, when Robinson reached first on another single, Greenberg expressed his concern and admiration for the rookie.

"Hope I didn't hurt you," he said. "I tried to get out of your way, but it was impossible."

"I didn't get hurt," Robinson replied. "I was just knocked off balance. . . ."

"How are things going?" Greenberg asked.

"Pretty good," he answered.

Greenberg offered Robinson a few encouraging words, and Robinson sang the big first baseman's praises after the game: "He sure is a swell guy. He helped me a lot by saying the things he did. I found out that not all the guys on the other teams are bad heels. I think Greenberg, for instance, is pulling for me to make good."

Smith visited the Dodger clubhouse after each game in Pittsburgh and reported that much of the tension seemed to be dissipating. Robinson, he wrote, "has actually become a part of the club." As an example, Smith cited the third game with the Pirates, when pitcher Fritz Ostermueller threw a fastball up and in. Robinson, unable to duck it in time, raised his arm to protect his face and fell to the ground.

"When the ball hit him a deathly silence hovered over the entire park," Smith wrote. "Jackie was on the ground grimacing in pain." The Dodger bench emptied as teammates checked to see if he was all right. As soon as Robinson got up and ran to first, some of his teammates began shouting threats at Ostermueller. Stanky was particularly loud and to the point, warning that the Dodgers would get even when Ostermueller's turn to hit arrived. Though the taunting was profane, Smith interpreted the Dodgers' attacks on the pitcher as "expressions of their regard for Robinson." Later in the game, Frankie Gustine singled and went to first, where he apologized to Robinson on Ostermueller's behalf. "I'm sure he didn't mean it," Gustine told Robinson, adding that he, too, was happy to see the rookie getting on well in the big leagues. That's how Smith, always looking on the bright side, reported it, at least.

The Pirates took two of three games. By now a pattern was emerging on the road trip. Huge crowds were coming out to see Robinson, he was giving them plenty of cause to cheer — hitting .428 since leaving Brooklyn, raising his average to .299 — and the Dodgers were losing. Robinson admitted to feeling more confident. "Perhaps I do look bad on a curve and a low outside pitch occasionally," he said. "But the pitchers haven't found any weakness yet, I guess."

Coach Sukeforth said the rookie had reason to feel good. "The guys on the team are all for him. Yes, sir," he smiled. "Mr. Jackie Robinson's going to do all right."

TWELVE:
"A SMILE OF ALMOST PAINFUL JOY"

It was a sunny Sunday afternoon, May 18, and Chicago Stadium was packed to its capacity, but the event had nothing to do with baseball. The fifteen thousand gathered came purely to express their patriotism as part of "I Am an American Day," the date thus proclaimed by President Truman. The crowd heard speeches by General George Churchill Kenney, commanding general of the Strategic Air Command; Governor Dwight Green; Mayor Martin H. Kennelly; and movie stars Edward G. Robinson and Dale Evans. Some five hundred immigrants became naturalized citizens on the spot. It was all part of the postwar rah-rah, the president's effort to enliven the spirit of democracy in a country still recovering from war.

Meanwhile, a bigger and more spontaneous display of Americanism was shaping up across town at Wrigley Field, home of the

Chicago Cubs. Fans filled every seat and every available space in which they were permitted to stand. When the last click of the turnstiles had been recorded, 46,572 paying customers were wedged into the cozy ballpark on the city's North Side, and 20,000 more clustered outside, trying to figure out a way in. It was another record. Not since 1930, on a day when 30,000 women were admitted free of charge and overflow crowds were permitted to stand on the field, had so many fans packed Wrigley. None of the reporters on hand estimated the number of black fans in the crowd, although photos from the game and eyewitness accounts suggest they turned out in massive numbers.

Chicago was the capital of the black migration, the epicenter of the nation's great demographic shift. The Negro problem, as the sociologists called it, had once been a southern problem. Now, almost overnight, it had become a northern problem, and an urban problem. In 1900, Chicago had been home to only about 30,000 black people. By 1945, that number had grown to about 350,000, or roughly 10 percent of the city. The most striking thing about the population in Chicago, beyond its great size, was its solidarity. "Its Negro district is immense and unbroken," St. Clair Drake and Horace Clayton wrote in the introduction to their 1945 book *Black Metropolis.* In New York, while Harlem was the African-American hub, there were several black neighborhoods of considerable size scattered throughout the city. But that was not the case in Chicago, where black residents clustered almost entirely on the South Side. In Chicago, it was possible for white people to live on the North Side and go days or weeks without seeing a black face. Nowhere else in America was the chasm so great.

That's what made for such a stunning sight on Sunday morning, May 18, as black fans from the South Side began arriving on the North Side by bus, train, and car, coalescing around the neighborhood that contained Wrigley Field. Allan H. Selig, known to friends as Bud, counted himself among the astonished. The future commissioner of Major League Baseball was just twelve years old, soon to give up his own dream of playing the game professionally. He traveled by train from Milwaukee to Chicago for the game, found himself sitting in the upper deck, and feeling as if he and his companions (one of them Herb Kohl, a future U.S. senator, the other a cousin who taught at the University of Chicago) were the only white people around. "It was so exciting," he recalled. "It made a lasting impression on me."

Once again, the black media had warned fans to behave. Fay Young, writing in the *Defender,* reminded spectators that they would be on trial as much as Robinson would — and that Robinson wouldn't face jail time if he messed up. "The telephone booths are not men's wash rooms," Young wrote. "The sun and liquor, even if you drink it before you head north, won't mix . . . Don't tell us all our fans are Sunday school members and behave like Emily Post would have us. Tain't so. . . . The Negro fans can do more to get Jackie Robinson out of the major leagues than all the disgruntled players alive. President Frick . . . and other fair minded men can regulate the players but they can't regulate the ignorant, loud-mouth, uncouth or whiskey crazed fans."

Mike Royko, who would become Chicago's best-known newspaper columnist, was fourteen years old at the time. He was half Polish, half Ukrainian, and 100 percent Cubs fan. On the morning of the game, he and a buddy walked five or six miles to the ballpark to see what all the fuss over Robinson was about. Years later, Royko remembered it this way:

As big as it was, the crowd was orderly. Almost unnaturally so. People didn't jostle each other.

The whites tried to look as if nothing unusual was happening, while the blacks tried to look casual and dignified. So everybody looked slightly ill at ease.

For most, it was probably the first time they had been that close to each other in such great numbers.

We managed to get in, scramble up a ramp, and find a place to stand behind the last row of grandstand seats. Then they shut the gates. No place remained to stand.

Robinson came up in the first inning. I remember the sound. It wasn't the shrill, teenage cry you now hear, or an excited gut roar. They applauded, long, rolling applause. A tall, middle-aged black man stood next to me, a smile of almost painful joy on his face, beating his palms together so hard they must have hurt.

When Robinson stepped into the batter's box, it was as if someone had flicked a switch. The place went silent.

He swung at the first pitch and they erupted as if he had knocked it over the wall. But it was only a high foul that dropped into the box seats. I remember thinking it was strange that a foul could make that many people happy. When he struck out, the low moan was genuine.

I've forgotten most of the details of the game, other than that the Dodgers won and Robinson didn't get a hit or do anything special, although he was cheered on every swing and every routine play.

He was right, Robinson didn't do anything special. In the first inning, he struck out on a big curve by Johnny Schmitz. The *Chicago Daily News* noted that Robinson "trudged back to the dugout, just like any white gent, to the jeers of a partisan Cub crowd." He went hitless in three more tries, snapping a fourteen-game hitting streak. Though he dropped a routine throw at first base, Robinson and the Dodgers still managed to win the game, 4–2. Afterward, thousands of black fans waited outside the clubhouse door and climbed all over the team bus, trying to get one last glimpse at their hero.

Shotton thought that Robinson, despite some recent success, was still too tentative at the plate. He talked to him in the clubhouse about loosening up, relaxing, about taking a more powerful swing, especially when he was ahead in the count. He wanted him to take the same aggressive approach at the plate as he did on the bases.

The Dodgers were tied for third place, with a 14–12 record. Shotton was desperate for some offense. With Walker slumping, Reese swinging feebly, and Stanky trying to get by on nothing but a sneer and hard slides, the team wasn't scoring runs. And if the hitting was weak, the pitching was worse. Only Ralph Branca was throwing well with any consistency. "The current Brook staff has about as much depth as a shot of whiskey in a clip joint — and half the potency," wrote Dick Young in the *Daily News*. Some of the writers blamed the manager, saying he was taking it all too calmly. Durocher had used fear tactics to get more from his modestly talented players, but Shotton was content to let the boys work things out on their own. He was such an unimposing presence that many fans outside Brooklyn didn't know his name. In Chicago, a radio station offered to give $375 to anyone who could answer the question, "Who is Burt Shotton?" The prize went unclaimed.

Somewhere between Chicago and St. Louis,

Robinson and Smith got word that they might not be welcome at the Chase Hotel, where the rest of the Dodgers planned to stay. They were hardly surprised. Smith knew when he signed up for the escort job that he would often be called on to make contingency plans. So when the team's train snorted to a stop at Union Station, Robinson and Smith peeled away from the rest of the Dodger entourage.

They spent the night at the home of one of Robinson's old army pals, Joe Neal, who ran a community center for some of the city's poor and working-class children. The next morning, heavy rains drenched St. Louis. There would be no baseball. Over at the Chase Hotel, players slept late. Once they were up and informed of the rainout, they broke into groups based on mutual interests. Groups of card players, moviegoers, drinkers, and skirt chasers each went separate ways. As for Robinson, recalled Gene Hermanski, no one gave him much thought. "We didn't see much of him on the road."

At some point that day, May 20, Robinson checked into the Deluxe Hotel, where the manager of the hotel turned over the keys to his own Cadillac and told Robinson to use it as much as he liked. Almost every

287

black celebrity stayed at the Deluxe when visiting St. Louis, and there was a pretty fair chance they also rode in a Deluxe Cab, bought records at the Deluxe Music Shop, and ate at the Deluxe Café, the Deluxe Chicken Shack, or the Deluxe Barbecue Shack. Many of the Deluxe operations were in the process of renovation or expansion in the years just after the war, its proprietors convinced that black consumers were on the verge of unprecedented economic good fortune.

The skies over eastern Missouri cleared on the morning of May 21, and Robinson went back to work. His first game of the season at Sportsman's Park came only twelve days after news of the Cardinals' strike threat had broken in the New York papers, but by now the writers barely mentioned it. More than sixteen thousand fans came out to see the game — about six thousand of them black — giving the Cardinals their biggest weekday crowd of the season. In the top of the first inning, Robinson showed patience, working a walk from Harry "The Cat" Brecheen, the Cards' best pitcher, and went to third on a single by Reiser. When Carl Furillo cracked a ground ball to first, Stan Musial grabbed it and stepped on the bag. Out of the corner of his

288

eye, he could see that Robinson was staying put, so he turned and threw to second, hoping to catch Reiser there for the double play. When Musial pivoted, Robinson, taking a chance, broke for home, scoring the first run of the game.

"Robinson was cheered each time he went to bat and the Dodgers as a team received more vocal encouragement than they usually get at Sportsman's Park," the *Post-Dispatch* reported. The only hint of trouble that afternoon was a skirmish, seemingly harmless, between Robinson and the Cardinals' catcher, Joe Garagiola. But even seemingly harmless skirmishes were tricky business in 1947, when black and white ballplayers remained almost entirely unacquainted. Garagiola was twenty-one years old, six feet tall and pudgy, the son of Italian immigrants. He was playing in just his second year with the Cards, and still trying to prove he belonged. His anemic hitting was one of the reasons the team had been struggling in the early part of the season. From the moment they met, Garagiola and Robinson clashed, according to Wendell Smith's account.

"Watch this guy!" the catcher shouted to third baseman Whitey Kurowski as Robinson stepped up to bat. "He gets all his hits bunting. That's the only way he can get them."

Garagiola kept it up. "This guy can't hit!" he said, as Robinson dug his cleats into the russet soil of the batter's box.

"What's your batting average?" Robinson asked the catcher over his shoulder.

"Oh, about two points lower than yours," he answered. "But if I could run as fast as you I'd have a real good average."

In fact, Garagiola was hitting .167, about a hundred points lower than Robinson.

"No matter how fast you run, Joe," Robinson shot back, "you couldn't hit as much as you weigh." Garagiola squatted behind home plate at about two hundred pounds.

Smith didn't bother to tell his readers how that at-bat turned out. Robinson went hitless in the game, but his aggressive baserunning in the first inning proved important as the Dodgers won it, 4–3, in ten innings. After the game, Robinson and his teammates piled on to a bus and headed yet again for the train station, Brooklyn bound at last. Robinson had no hits in his last three road games, and the Dodgers lost five of eight on the trip, leaving them in a tie for fourth place. Still, among the men in the clubhouse, attitudes had begun a subtle shift during their two weeks on the road.

Ralph Branca noticed the Dodgers still weren't talking much to Robinson, but they were talking *about* him more. They weren't saying they liked him. They weren't debating the merits of integration. They were talking about him as a baseball player, about his improvement as a first baseman, about the peculiar straight-armed way he swung the bat, about his speed and temerity on the bases. It seemed to Branca like a positive sign, a sign of acceptance.

Bobby Bragan, one of the opponents of integration who had refused to back down when confronted by Rickey before the start of the season, still hadn't made any effort to reach out to Robinson, nor did he have any intention of doing so. But he had been thinking a good deal about him, and Bragan admitted to himself now that some of the things he'd worried about in spring training had been no cause for concern after all. He'd shared a locker room and a shower room with a black man, and neither he nor his parents had dropped dead from shock. A black man had joined a team of white players, and no riots had ensued. Robinson had taken a job that otherwise would have gone to a white man, and the nation's social structure had not collapsed. Bragan wasn't ready to join the NAACP or to invite

Robinson to dinner, but two things were slowly dawning. The first was that the world was changing. The second was that he could probably live with the change.

At UCLA, where he ran track, starred at football, and dabbled in baseball, Robinson became known as one of the best all-around athletes in the nation. (National Baseball Hall of Fame, Cooperstown, NY)

Though they were dressed for success, the Robinsons' first trip to the South for spring training in 1946 proved disastrous. (Charles "Teenie" Harris, Carnegie Museum of Art, Pittsburgh; Heinz Family Fund)

In 1947, in order to spare Robinson from southern segregation, the Brooklyn Dodgers and their top minor-league team, the Montreal Royals, trained in Cuba, the Dominican Republic, and Panama. (*Pittsburgh Courier* Archives)

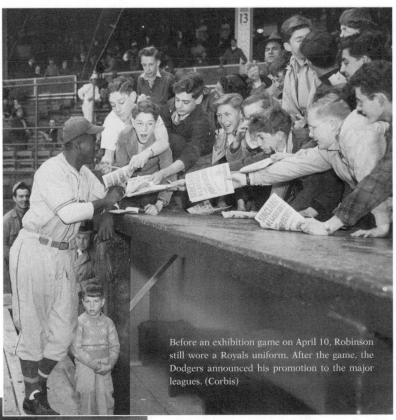

Before an exhibition game on April 10, Robinson still wore a Royals uniform. After the game, the Dodgers announced his promotion to the major leagues. (Corbis)

Branch Rickey, president of the Dodgers, faces questions from reporters after the suspension of the team's manager, Leo Durocher. (Brooklyn Collection, Brooklyn Public Library)

Robinson signing his contract for the league's minimum wage: $5,000. (Corbis)

In a scene staged by photographers, Robinson enters the Dodger clubhouse for the first time. (National Baseball Hall of Fame, Cooperstown, NY)

The uniform wouldn't stay clean long. On his first day with the Dodgers, Robinson prepares to face the Yankees in an exhibition game. (National Baseball Hall of Fame, Cooperstown, NY)

He's out at third. Billy Johnson of the Yankees applies the tag. (Corbis)

April 1947: Following a game at the beginning of the season, Robinson heads for home. (Corbis)

All year long Jackie, Rachel, and Jack Jr. lived in close quarters, beginning with a room in the McAlpin Hotel in Manhattan. (Brooklyn Collection, Brooklyn Public Library)

The Robinsons moved to a two-bedroom apartment on Mac-Donough Street in the Bedford-Stuyvesant section of Brooklyn, but they shared the tiny place with a stranger. (Courtesy of Gilbert Jonas)

Outside Ebbets Field, at least three varieties of Jackie Robinson pins were usually on sale. (*Pittsburgh Courier* Archives)

Robinson gets a handshake from Tommy Tatum after his first home run. Catcher Walker Cooper of the Giants looks on. (Corbis)

By 1947, Joe Louis was fading, and Robinson emerged as the nation's most popular black sports hero. (Corbis)

Robinson takes a swing at a Ewell Blackwell pitch. Critics called the Dodger rookie a "lunger" and said he would never hit well in the majors. (Corbis)

After Philadelphia Phillies manager Ben Chapman led a brutal verbal assault by his team, Robinson said the name-calling didn't bother him. Here, he poses with Chapman. (Corbis)

Heroes and Bums: Hugh Casey, Pee Wee Reese, Joe Hatten, Eddie Stanky, and (seated) Dixie Walker. (National Baseball Hall of Fame, Cooperstown, NY)

Wendell Smith of the *Pittsburgh Courier* roomed with Robinson on road trips and ghosted his newspaper columns. (National Baseball Hall of Fame, Cooperstown, NY)

Baseball in Brooklyn had a southern accent, thanks in large measure to the wonderful radio broadcasts of Red Barber. (National Baseball Hall of Fame, Cooperstown, NY)

Umpire Beans Reardon tries to calm Joe Garagiola of the Cardinals, but Robinson continues to goad the catcher. The spat between the ballplayers, immortalized in a popular children's book, would haunt Garagiola for years. (Corbis)

When Dan Bankhead joined the Dodgers late in the season, Robinson was no longer the team's only black player. (Brooklyn Collection, Brooklyn Public Library)

After clinching the pennant, the Dodgers were mobbed by fans at Pennsylvania Station. Here, Pee Wee Reese gets a lift. Elsewhere, Robinson was trapped in a phone booth. (Brooklyn Collection, Brooklyn Public Library)

Jackie Robinson Day at Ebbets Field: Bill "Bojangles" Robinson (no relation) presents the keys to a new Cadillac. Rachel Robinson is at left. (Corbis)

Burt Shotton, the soft-spoken manager of the Dodgers, greets Robinson after the opening game of the World Series against the Yankees. (Corbis)

Dodger fans wait through the night for World Series bleacher seats. (Brooklyn Collection, Brooklyn Public Library)

At the United Nations, reporters skip out on the General Assembly to watch the World Series on television. (Corbis)

In game one, the ever-aggressive Robinson gets trapped in a rundown. But as he draws the attention of four Yankees, he allows Pete Reiser to sneak into second base. (National Baseball Hall of Fame, Cooperstown, NY)

In game six of the World Series, Robinson tries to break up a double play—and flattens Yankee shortstop Phil Rizzuto. (National Baseball Hall of Fame, Cooperstown, NY)

Thirteen: Up and Down MacDonough Street

The spring of 1947 slid toward summer. As they took their meals at a small table in the kitchen and looked out the back door, the Robinsons watched the sky brighten. Life was getting better. Jackie was playing without pain, his shoulder healed. More important, he was playing well. Jack Jr. had recovered from the illness that had marked his arrival in New York. Rachel, while lonely, had thrown herself completely into the role of housewife. She made sure her husband's clothes were clean and ironed, that there was food in the cupboard, that their bedroom was cleared of clutter, their full-size bed neatly made, their crazy little closet-sized home in some semblance of order. She felt important. She felt like part of the team.

The 500 block of MacDonough had but a few wispy trees, all of them now fully in bloom. Other signs of summer were more abundant. Over on Ralph Avenue, Abe Kutner stacked melons, plums, and peaches on wooden tables in front of his fruit and vegetable store. Bicycles tilted against the window at Bill McDonald's sweet shop, where the kids came for egg creams, cream soda, and penny candies. The smell of baked bread wafted on warm air from the Capitol Baking Company.

When her husband was on the road, Rachel busied herself with long books and long walks through the neighborhood. She felt isolated at times, but never bored, as she recently recalled. She listened to the Dodgers on the radio and waited for the mailman to slip her husband's letters in the mailbox. But neither Red Barber's broadcasts nor her husband's handwritten notes on hotel stationery supplied the details she craved. She learned from Barber how well her husband was playing, but she had no sense of whether the fans and players were accepting him. She learned from Jack's letters, which began with "Darling," that he lusted and longed for her, but she didn't get any idea of how he was bearing the strain.

The Robinsons were still largely untested as a couple. As they padded about the apartment on MacDonough, Rachel discovered that Jack, though he loved to play with his son, was not much help with the cleaning, washing, and feeding. Rachel also noticed that her husband didn't like to spend money. He had earned $3,500 playing with the Montreal Royals in 1946, which was better than the national median family income by $500, and more than twice the national median for a black family. A barnstorming tour in the fall of 1946 had brought him another $3,500 or so (although some of the checks bounced and Robinson, taking advantage of his newfound prominence, turned to Thurgood Marshall of the NAACP for help in recovering what he was owed). Even if he didn't collect it all, it had been a good year. And now, with a salary of $5,000, he was making a solid income — not in the same ballpark as Hank Greenberg, to be sure, but well in line at least with a good many college professors, architects, and accountants. Still, he skimped. He bought no clothes. He bought no car. He treated his wife to no fancy nights on the town, no jazzy dresses, no ornate hats to match those worn by the more established Dodger wives. Even in later years, when his salary soared and he owned a big house in Connecticut and his family's future had been well secured, he would remain tight at times with cash. He would leave his home for the drive to Ebbets Field with twenty-five dollars in his pocket, and when he returned at night, he would brag about how much of the twenty-five dollars remained. Rachel didn't mind. He loved his family and took care of them, and that was all that mattered to her.

Other aspects of the marriage, however, were more complicated. In Montreal, Jack and Rachel had each been secretive at times, hiding their thoughts and feelings. When Rachel had been feverish during her pregnancy, she'd kept it from Jack, preferring not to worry him. When Jack had felt burdened by the pressures of the game late in that season, he'd lost sleep and quit eating. But he didn't open up to his wife. He had made up his mind to handle it on his own.

Now, with her husband back from his first road trip, Rachel was learning how to unlock his thoughts and feelings. Patience was the key, she found. If she came right out and asked him what was on his mind, he would burrow deeper into his shell. So she would offer a game of honeymoon bridge, played atop their mattress, whispering the bids and passes so as not to wake the baby. There was no real competition between them; Jack was the stronger player by far, and that was fine with Rachel. If he

296

managed to relax, that was victory enough for her. When they weren't playing cards, they would sit down to eat, and Rachel would exhibit a powerful appetite for the details of her husband's most recent ballgame.

Before Jack signed with the Montreal Royals, Rachel had never seen a baseball game. Now she became an avid student and an "active listener," paying close attention and, in the manner of a psychologist, gently moving the conversation in the direction she wanted it to move. How much did personality play into the game? If two infielders didn't get along, did it affect their ability to turn double plays? Were some hitters more selfish than others, always trying to make hits when perhaps a sacrifice bunt might be more helpful to the team? What effect did a coach's decisions have on the game's outcome? Why were some players used only occasionally while others played every day, and how did that affect morale? The questions were designed to help her learn the game but also to decode her husband's state of mind. They reflected her greater interest in human psychology than in athletics.

Baseball was so much slower and more thoughtful than basketball or football. So much more strategy was involved. Rachel never ran out of questions, and she soon discovered that her husband never tired of talking about the game. What's more, once he got going, he found it much easier to talk about how he felt. His sense of well-being, she discovered, was inextricably linked to events on the field. His batting average proved a pretty fair indicator of his happiness.

That spring, Rachel began taking classes several mornings each week at the New York School of Interior Decorating. An old friend who was studying piano at Juilliard would come by the apartment to watch Jack Jr. After class, she would come home and, if there was a day game at Ebbets Field, get the baby ready to go. Each game helped her think of new questions to ask her husband. Jack lectured patiently, interpreting her interest as a token of her love, as she hoped he would. Once, Rachel had aspired to be a doctor. Later, when she decided that a career in medicine would make raising a family too difficult, she steered toward nursing instead. She had always looked forward in five-year intervals, imagining where and how she would be living. In 1947, she still clung to the belief she would one day work outside the home, yet she was not sure anymore if that would be in five, ten, or fifteen years. Both her parents had been entrepreneurial by nature, and they'd always made her feel, even as a little girl, that the household could not operate without her help. Sometimes as a child she had felt like Cinderella. She washed her brothers' dirty clothes, she tended to her father when he became too sick to work, she scrubbed pots and pans for her mother's catering business. She knew that working around the house still counted as working — and at that moment in 1947 she couldn't think of any job more important than supporting her husband. It required a great deal of selflessness, especially given the enormous attention Jack was getting. Some wives — especially a strong, smart one such as Rachel — might have grown jealous. But Rachel wanted the glory to go to her husband. His pride was hers.

They had almost no social life, as best she could remember in interviews almost sixty years later. The baby was a light sleeper and Rachel a heavy worrier. When Jack Jr. slept, his parents tiptoed around in the dark. When Jack Jr. cried out in the night, it was Rachel who got up to feed him, ensuring that her husband would get his rest. Leisure time meant a long walk or a ride on a bus or trolley. There were squabbles, Rachel remembered, most of them attributable to their tight quarters, but she couldn't remember what they were, and, in retrospect, none seemed too severe. "The excitement, the joy, the growing confidence . . . it kept us going," she recalled.

The stress wounded Jack at times, but Rachel didn't see the fuming, tormented soul others have described. Most of the writers commenting on Robinson's emotional state didn't understand that baseball occupied just one part of his mind. He had wanted a family as much as he had ever wanted to play in the major leagues, maybe more. The fulfillment of that wish went a long way toward providing him peace of mind. "We were very, very much in love and we'd waited a very long time to get married — five years — so we had that, the strength of that going," Rachel recalled. The attacks by opposing players and managers made him furious, but he'd been hearing racial epithets all his life. He knew how to handle them. The racism of his own teammates pained him, but it never forced him to question his self-worth. He didn't lose sleep wondering if people liked him. His main concerns were those he could control, namely hitting and fielding.

It helped, too, that Branch Rickey remained so determinedly on Robinson's side. The Robinsons knew that Rickey was doing everything he could: hiring a manager friendly to the cause, making certain that Robinson played every day, spinning the media for sympathetic coverage. Rickey and Robinson met often that season, usually in the boss's office, and usually before games. They talked baseball. Perhaps they talked religion, too, a subject that stirred passionate feelings in both men (although the Robinsons never attended church that year, according to Rachel). Whatever the topics of conversation, Rachel noticed that the chats boosted her husband's confidence.

She realized something else about her husband that spring, something that eased her worries considerably. Despite his vow to avoid confrontation with his opponents, Jack had already found a way to fight back. Rachel might not have noticed it if Jack hadn't been teaching her the finer points of the game's strategy, but now she saw that her husband was playing a breathtakingly aggressive style of baseball unlike that of the other men on the team. If he'd wanted to fit in and maintain a low profile, at least until he'd become better established, he could have done so. He could have pounded out hits, advanced to the next base when the batter behind him moved him along, and at all times kept his mouth shut. Instead, he glared at his opponents. He crowded closer to the plate when pitchers tried to back him off. He stole bases and took wide turns even in games that weren't close, just to show that he could, playing at all times with the confidence of a man who knows something his opponents don't. The approach made him dangerous even when he wasn't hitting the ball particularly well. It made him the focus of attention. It sent jolts of electricity through the crowd. It stoked anger in some players and fear in others. It was, on her husband's part, a deliberate and cunning attack.

Rachel recognized that her husband was bringing a little bit of Negro-League baseball to the majors, and she loved him for it.

A few days after their return from the season's first long road trip, Robinson and the Dodgers traveled again to Harlem for a game against the Giants, the first night game of the year at the Polo Grounds, where some white fans preferred not to venture after dark. A bright quarter-moon shone in the cloudless sky. It was May 27. The Giants, to everyone's surprise, were in first place, thanks to a barrage of home runs by Johnny "Big Cat" Mize. The Dodgers now trailed by a game. Though the season had a long way to go, Dick Young of the *Daily News* wrote that this contest carried with it the flavor of a World Series. Reserved seats sold out weeks in advance.

At game time, the paying crowd was announced at 51,780, the biggest audience that had ever seen a night game at the Polo Grounds to that point. Across the Harlem River, less than a mile away, two top Negro-league teams, the Homestead Grays and the New York Black Yankees, were preparing to play at Yankee Stadium. It was, as *Daily Mirror* columnist Dan Parker put it, the first time since the advent of Jackie Robinson that "a battle was underway for Harlem's patronage." It turned out not to be much of a battle. Black fans — eight thousand of them, by Parker's estimate — began lining up outside the Polo Grounds six hours before the Dodgers-Giants game. At Yankee Stadium, meanwhile, the turnstiles clicked a mere twenty-six hundred times, hardly enough to turn a profit. Parker wrote that Robinson, while helping make money for the owners of the Giants and Dodgers, "will harm the Negro league whenever it comes within the orbit of his influence."

Harlem's loyalties were tested many times

over that night. Bill "Bojangles" Robinson, the tap dancer and actor who would become a symbol of the age when black stars settled for demeaning roles in white-operated productions, told a friend before the game that he rooted for Robinson to play well so long as he didn't play well enough to beat the Giants. His friend agreed that was the way to go, saying "that if Booker T. Washington himself was playing first for the Dodgers, I'd still have to root for the Giants."

Others who had not been so strongly attached to the Giants became instant Dodger fans. Sidney Poitier, twenty years old and recently arrived in Harlem from the Bahamas by way of Miami, knew nothing of baseball but kept hearing about Jackie Robinson and the Dodgers everywhere he went. The struggling young actor went to Ebbets Field to see what the fuss was about and instantly became a Robinson rooter. Kenneth B. Clark, a resident of Harlem and professor of psychology at the City College of New York, was usually too busy to trifle with baseball. Among other things, he was working on an experiment in which black and white children were asked to play with black and white dolls. It was of enormous concern to Clark that the black children, when asked which dolls were nicer and prettier, generally chose the white ones. It was a sign, he believed, that black children were being taught to believe in their own inferiority. But Clark took time from his studies in 1947 to cheer on the Dodgers, a team he had never cared about before Robinson's arrival. He took his four-year-old son, Hilton, to a few games, and though the boy was too young to understand what was happening, he never forgot the sight of his mild-mannered father, a slightly built man, on his feet, screaming at the top of his lungs, and cursing like a soldier, cheering on the only team he would ever love.

Robinson and his wife had only the vaguest idea of what was happening. New York was a big, complicated place, and they didn't see much of it from their little mouse hole on MacDonough. They sheltered themselves, as if the burden were great enough without firsthand knowledge of its precise weight.

Back in the winter, when Branch Rickey had gathered some of Brooklyn's leading black citizens for a pep talk, a few of those in attendance had determined to help the Robinsons get acclimated to their new home. One of the men at the meeting thought the Robinsons ought to get to know

Lacy and Florence Covington, who lived in a big brownstone on a tree-lined stretch of Stuyvesant Avenue, roughly four blocks from the Robinsons' place. Lacy Covington, forty-six years old, was a bricklayer and part-time minister, a big, handsome man with a full head of curly hair. Florence, thirty-nine, an elegant woman with a high-pitched, rippling laugh, stayed home and took care of the house. She shopped at thrift stores for linens and crystal and set an elegant table in her dining room. The Covingtons were one of those families that made a neighborhood feel like a community. Florence had four sisters, all of them single at the time, and the five women kept the house buzzing. They had a formal parlor for entertaining on the second floor, but everyone was more comfortable squeezed into the first-floor dining room, where Lacy held court at the head of the table and Florence, never sitting down, flitted around carrying glasses and plates and what seemed like a never-ending stream of hot, greasy, southern-style dishes. No matter how crowded the room, no one was ever turned away. The Robinsons became regulars at the Sunday dinners. The Covingtons treated Jack warmly but casually, as if he were nothing special. Every so often, though, another

306

dinner guest would react in amazement to Robinson's presence at the table, gushing about how much the ballplayer meant to his race, how proud everyone was, how astonishing it was to see him there in the flesh.

Robinson caught glimpses of his impact on the community. He noticed the kids who followed him home on the subway just to bask in his glow. He spotted the gaggle of elderly women, black and white, who waited for him outside Ebbets Field just to say, "Good game!" or "Good night!" But there were other scenes he could never have imagined. He could not have dreamed that George Marchev, owner of the Gordos Corporation in Bloomfield, New Jersey, would watch the Dodgers play in 1947 and decide to integrate his electronics factory. He didn't know that Lou Brown, the black man Marchev decided to hire, would show up for work every day in a shirt and tie, even though his job was to load and unload trucks and required no formal attire and even though none of the white men doing the same work were so sharply dressed. He didn't know that Brown felt the same responsibility as Robinson, that he sought to represent his race proudly every time he lifted a box of relay switches and set it down again. He didn't know that Marchev and

307

Brown would become lifelong friends. Nor did he know that at Brown's funeral years later, Marchev would eulogize Brown this way: "Jackie Robinson opened the door of baseball and all sports to all men. You opened the door for countless men and women in our lives. I think we got the better of the deal, Mr. Brown."

World War II reshaped the country's culture like nothing since the Civil War. Brooklyn, big and broad and beautifully complicated, full of Italians, Poles, Irishmen, and Jews, was the perfect place to explore the possibilities inherent in that transformation. In the South, local politicians were feeling the heat from the federal government to go after lynch mobs, to stop excluding black voters from primary elections, and to end segregated interstate busing. In the North, radicals were pushing businesses to hire more black workers. In both regions, the issues were contentious. Ground was lost and gained in such small increments that it was still tough to say which way things were going, forward or back. But Brooklyn was ever changing. People came and went. Transformation wasn't just possible, it was inevitable, which helps explain why Robinson's arrival was handled with such aplomb.

It also helps explain his special connection with Brooklyn's Jewish population. While Jewish Americans were better off than black Americans in 1947 by almost any statistical or anecdotal measure, Jews still faced enormous bias. When President Roosevelt banned discrimination in hiring by defense contractors and formed the Fair Employment Practices Committee to take complaints, Jewish workers filed 43 percent of the grievances in New York. Just as the war had prompted many black men and women to take up the fight for equality on the home front, it compelled Jewish activists to attack anti-Semitism. Members of both minority groups hoped the war for freedom in Europe would help spread equal rights at home, and, often, their causes overlapped. Strong links were forged. And since the Dodgers had no great Jewish player (Sandy Koufax was eleven years old), Robinson became the hero of choice for a second ethnic group. He, too, knew persecution. He, too, knew suffering.

At 1574 Fiftieth Street in the Borough Park section of Brooklyn, Henry Foner's family invoked Robinson's name that year in their Passover Seder. As the youngest at the table, Henry asked the traditional question, "Why is this night different from all other nights?" and went on to answer it himself. This night was different, he said, because Jackie Robinson had ascended to the major leagues, to baseball's promised land.

"When Robinson came among us," author Pete Hamill wrote years later, "you saw what he meant in the stands of Ebbets Field, where we saw the games with free tickets from the Police Athletic League. In 1946, the crowds were almost all white. A year later, the African-Americans, after too long a time, finally joined the other Brooklyn tribes in the stands. Jews and Irishmen and Italians and blacks all roared together for the team. This was seven years before *Brown vs. Board of Education,* ten years before anyone in New York ever heard of Martin Luther King. Robinson's arrival as the first black player in the major leagues added another dimension to being a Dodger fan, although as kids we could not name it. That dimension was moral. It was about right and wrong. 'This is America, godammit,' my father said. We became the most American place in the whole country."

One evening that spring, the Robinsons decided to have dinner at the Orange Blossom Inn on Ralph Avenue. They brought the baby. The Orange Blossom was a new restaurant, opened after the war by an army cook, Willie Moore, who was eager to show he could whip up more than hash and beans. Moore dressed his waitresses in orange uniforms with green and white trim, and he alternated three sets of tablecloths — orange, green, and white — depending on his mood and which ones were cleanest. He served fried chicken and brisket and thick steaks, everything with a southern accent. When the Robinsons sat down to eat that night, word spread through the neighborhood, and Dodger fans started flocking to Ralph Avenue, squeezing into the restaurant and lining up on the sidewalk for a chance to meet the neighborhood's seldom-seen star.

Soon the waitresses couldn't move between the tables. Moore invited the Robinsons to come back the next night and promised to shut the restaurant for two hours so they could eat in peace. The Robinsons accepted his offer. After that, Moore would occasionally send food free of charge to the Robinsons' apartment. He would arrange the provisions carefully on his finest plates, and then he would look around for someone to bring it over to 526 MacDonough. Clarence L. Irving, twenty-three at the time, was one of the regulars at the Orange Blossom. He liked to drink coffee in the back of the restaurant and drop nickels in the jukebox, killing time between work and chasing girls. When Moore asked for a volunteer, Irving's hand shot up. He said nothing to Robinson upon delivering the food. He sought no tip. He was proud to have played the tiniest of parts in the great athlete's success.

"You have to remember something," recalled Irving. "Brooklyn was ready for Robinson. What I mean by that is this: It probably couldn't have happened any place else on earth. Most of the people who came to Brooklyn, their parents came from the South or they came from Europe. Everybody wanted to be Americans, and they were a little too busy to really hate anybody. . . . You can say Jackie Robinson integrated baseball, but you've also got to say it was the people of Brooklyn who were ready to do that."

FOURTEEN:
A REAL GONE GUY

In early June, Branch Rickey tried again to trade Dixie Walker. This time, an outfield wall got in the way.

The Dodgers were playing the Pirates on a cool, cloudy Wednesday night at sold-out Ebbets Field. The Bums were leading, 7–2, top of the sixth, bases empty, when Culley Rikard of the Pirates sent a fly ball deep to center. Pete Reiser turned his back to home plate and started running. Most men would have played the carom, but not Reiser. Still fast as a jackrabbit at twenty-eight, and accustomed by now to running on a tender ankle, Pistol Pete thought he had a chance to make the catch. He almost always thought he had a chance. As he neared the center-field wall, fans started screaming, trying to warn him. They'd seen this act before. If Reiser heard them, though, he didn't listen — and he wouldn't remember later.

313

Ebbets Field had no warning track on its outfield. Man, ball, and wall came together simultaneously. Ball met glove. Man met wall. Down went man.

Gene Hermanski, the left-fielder, was the first to reach his fallen teammate. He didn't notice the blood leaking from Reiser's head, not right away. What he noticed was the ball, which had rolled out of Reiser's glove and into the grass between Reiser's body and the wall. Quickly, Hermanski tucked the ball back in Reiser's glove and raised his teammate's arm to show the umpire. The ump, running across the outfield, called Rikard out. Only then did attention turn to the outfielder's condition.

"Hell, fellas," Reiser said, as if apologizing for his recklessness, as his teammates gathered around. Shortly thereafter, he blacked out. It was the fourth time he'd done battle with a concrete barrier, and, not surprisingly, the fourth time he'd lost. In the Dodger dressing room, two priests and a doctor stood by his side. Reiser's condition appeared so dire that one of the priests administered last rites. But the patient quickly rebounded, and by the time an ambulance arrived, he felt well enough to ask for a cigarette.

"What happened?" he asked, as he took a

puff and tried to smile.

That week, Rickey had been working out a deal to send Walker to Pittsburgh. Some reports said the Dodgers would get Jim Russell, a switch-hitting outfielder who had played well during the war years but whose numbers had steadily dropped ever since. Others said the trade was for Nick "Jumbo" Strincevich, a right-handed pitcher who had won ten and lost fifteen the year before. Whether it was for Russell or Strincevich, Rickey reportedly had settled on the trade until Reiser hit the wall. With one of his best hitters out of the lineup, possibly for a long stretch, the boss had to think again about his plans. He also had to think about investing in some rubber padding for the outfield walls, or a warning track. Eventually, though, he decided it would be cheaper to ask Reiser to wear a helmet.

The Dodgers enjoyed a long home stand to start the month of June, and played pretty well, winning seven of eleven. Pee Wee Reese finally started to hit. Spider Jorgensen came back from his injury and helped make up for the loss of Reiser's bat. The rookie Duke Snider filled in for Reiser and showed some promise. The clubhouse was relaxed. "How 'ya doin', Pete?" the men would ask when they walked past Reiser's empty locker in what became a running joke. The pitching improved, too, although not enough. There were no stars among the starters, and that meant the hard-throwing reliever Hugh Casey, no sure thing, was called on too often to bail the team out. The Dodgers weren't playing great baseball, but in a well-balanced league, they were doing enough to hang around. The most impressive thing about the home stand was the attendance, with an average of almost twenty-six thousand fans turning out for each game.

Wendell Smith explained the big crowds in verse:

Jackie's nimble,
Jackie's quick,
Jackie's making
The turnstiles click

Smith had it right. The Dodgers did not have a great home-run hitter. They were not in first place. Their biggest celebrity, Leo Durocher, was out in California chopping down trees. The only explanation for their popularity, the newsman said, was Robinson. Brooklyn's fans were a sophisticated bunch well tuned to the subtleties of human drama. Black fans were coming out to cheer Robinson, which was simple enough and not unexpected. There may have been some white fans scared off by the presence of all those new black spectators, but there were nevertheless plenty still eager to see the Dodgers and Robinson play. Before each game, white kids stood on the sidewalks around Ebbets Field selling pins that read "I'm Rooting for Jackie Robinson." After each game, Robinson would have to dash from the stadium to the subway to avoid the mobs of autograph hunters. He hadn't won over all his teammates yet, and he hadn't persuaded the fans in St. Louis and Cincinnati that integration was here to stay, but in Brooklyn he was doing fine.

Dodger fans of a certain age, looking back at the glory days of Brooklyn baseball, tend to describe Ebbets as a field of dreams, a place where the stands were always packed, the spectators eternally friendly, where raucous fans shouted out with joy, where cowbells clanged and marching bands oompahed deliriously, a place of pure baseball magic. It wasn't always so. Ebbets Field was a gem, to be sure. In a crowded city of concrete and brick, it startled fans with its humble beauty. Fans who had only listened to games on radio or watched on black-and-white TVs were shocked when they walked through a congested neighborhood into the cool, dark shadows of the ballpark's tunnels, and then emerged to see the brilliant green diamond shining before them. But the romanticists tend to forget that many of those fans also emerged to see a lot of empty seats. In the 1930s, the team attracted an average of only eighty-five hundred fans per game, which meant that nearly three out of four seats were vacant. Attendance improved after the war, but by 1947 there was already a sense that the Brooklyn way of life, characterized as much as anything by the Ebbets Field experience, was breaking up. Black families were moving in and white families were looking for a way out, looking in particular toward Long Island. Soon, a massive push toward suburbia would be underway. The values associated with life in Brooklyn, where you knew your neighbors, saw the same people every day at the bus stop, ran a line of credit at the neighborhood butcher shop, and met friends at Ebbets Field for an afternoon game and tried not to drink so much beer that you spoiled your dinner, would seem quaint, replaced by a growing sense of materialism, by a quest for an American dream that meant a two-car garage, a backyard with a swimming pool, and the occasional drive on the highway to some massive ballpark surrounded by a parking lot.

Nineteen-forty-seven marked the zenith for Ebbets Field. Black and white fans would fade as Brooklyn's middle class dissipated. Never again would so many gather to cheer their Bums. Ten years later, the team would pack up and move to Los Angeles, leaving fans bitter and betrayed, as if a hole had been carved in the borough's heart. For decades fans would nurture a sweetening collection of shared memories — almost enough of them to offset the hurt. But the truth, difficult for many to accept, is that Brooklyn left the Dodgers long before the Dodgers left Brooklyn. It began in 1947. Jackie Robinson packed Ebbets Field like never before, but his arrival signaled a cultural shift that foretold the destruction of Brooklyn's lyrical little ballpark.

On June 5, in front of 27,000 fans, Robinson homered, singled twice and stole his eighth base of the year, leading the team to a win over the Pirates. Five days later, when he homered again, the public address announcer informed the crowd that Robinson's family was sitting behind home plate, and the crowd rose to give Rachel and Jack Jr. a special cheer. The day after that, playing before a crowd of 18,000, including 700 orphans, 5,000 schoolboys, and 2,000 Ladies Day "fanettes," all of them admitted free of charge, Robinson went 4-for-4, with two singles, a double, and a triple, raising his average to .301.

Dick Young of the *Daily News* said the excellent performance was a sign that the pressure on Robinson was easing. The *Brooklyn Eagle* said the first baseman was "in the charmed circle to stay." Fans, black and white, were learning to recognize his tics — the way he held his bat high and wiped his hands on his pants between pitches, the way he seemed to swing down on the ball, as if to pound it into submission. Robinson's steady play was keeping the Dodgers in the pennant hunt, and it even earned him his first endorsement opportunity. Bond Bread, which used many of New York's top athletes in its newspaper ads, reportedly offered him five hundred dollars to pose for pictures that would run in some of the city's newspapers. But Robinson had promised Branch Rickey he would not make any endorsements, not just yet anyway.

On June 12, the Dodgers left town for their second road trip of the season, beginning this time in St. Louis. If there were any signs of resentment among the Cardinals for the way the media had handled the story of their alleged strike, none showed. In fact, Wendell Smith outdid himself in congratulating the Cardinals on their kindness toward Robinson. "The St. Louis Cardinals aren't only good ballplayers," he began his story from St. Louis, "but they're good guys as well." He continued: "It was as though they were trying to show him they aren't the villains they appeared to be earlier in the season."

Smith reported that the Cards went out of their way to make chit-chat. Eddie Dyer, the team's manager and an insurance salesman in the off-season, was serving as the first-base coach, where he had a lot of time for small talk. Dyer told Robinson that he'd seen him play once with the Monarchs and he'd been impressed even then. After Robinson banged a solid single to center, Dyer greeted him the next inning with his congratulations. He pointed to the big crowd of black people in the bleachers and said, "Boy, if you'd hit a home run today those people out there would go crazy."

In another game, when Robinson slid into

second on a close play, he and Marty Marion got tangled up. "Did I spike you, Jackie?" the shortstop asked. Robinson said no. "I got new spikes on and they'd cut pretty deep," Marion said. "I'm glad I didn't."

Joe "Ducky" Medwick, the Cards' veteran outfielder, took Robinson aside to offer him advice at one point in the series. "Listen, Robinson," Medwick said, "you're a much better hitter than you appear to be. 'Course, you're doing alright, but you could be doing better. You're too tight up there at the plate. For goodness' sakes, loosen up and hit that ball. If you do, you'll burn up this league, Jack."

Smith noted that Musial and Garagiola were friendly, too. Of course, the Cards might have been in a benevolent mood with Robinson because they were tearing the rest of the Dodgers limb from limb. St. Louis swept the four-game series, outscoring Brooklyn, 31–8. Robinson, writing in his column, said that the four games sent a clear message that the Cards remained the team to beat in the National League. Most of the writers covering the Dodgers agreed. One of them, apparently without irony, compared the four-game sweep to the collapse of the Roman empire. For the Dodgers, the only highlight was a ground ball by Carl Furillo that somehow rolled up the sleeve of shortstop Marty Marion and got lost in his shirt. Not even old Burt Shotton had seen that trick before.

"Shotton's team as now constituted isn't a pennant contender," Harold Burr wrote in the *Brooklyn Eagle.* "The youth movement in Brooklyn has backfired badly and must be abandoned temporarily." The youth movement, however, had largely been brought on by injuries. Not only was Reiser out, but Walker was missing time with a sprained wrist and Bruce Edwards was on the bench nursing a bruised throwing hand. Their replacements, Cookie Lavagetto, Duke Snider, and back-up catcher Gil Hodges ("just a boy who doesn't know what a curveball is," according to Branch Rickey), were not getting the job done. At one point, when Snider complained about being made to bunt when he preferred to swing away, Shotton sent him back to Montreal for a taste of the minors. It was an important moment for the team. It sent the signal that Shotton, for all his patience and calm, was not to be trifled with.

Reiser was not yet ready to play, but he had recovered enough to travel with the team. "I ache all over and now I'm having those dizzy spells I had in '42 all over again," he said. Nevertheless, Reiser decided to skip an appointment to see his doctor in Baltimore and stay with the team as it headed for Chicago. One day in Chicago he felt well enough to shag fly balls in the outfield before the game. The sight doubtless gave his teammates hope that Reiser would soon return — until, unbelievably, he collided with one of those teammates and knocked himself silly again.

With the lineup depleted, Robinson became more aggressive. Maybe he didn't know that the Cubs and Dodgers had bad blood, or maybe he did and didn't care. A year earlier, the two teams had brawled viciously. Cubs shortstop Lennie Merullo got a bad black eye when Stanky grabbed him in a bear hug and Reese punched him in the face. The next day, before the game, Merullo approached Reese and challenged him to go at it again, threatening to break his neck in a fair fight. While Merullo was making his threats, Dixie Walker snuck up behind and threw a punch to the shortstop's head, connecting solidly. Merullo chased him, tackled him, and punched him in the face, knocking out one tooth and breaking another. New York City police officers were assigned to sit in the dugouts during the game to prevent further incidents.

A year later, tempers remained sore, and, now, Robinson wasn't helping. In the second game, he went from first to third on a sacrifice bunt and then scampered home when the catcher threw the ball into the outfield. It was the sort of play, equal parts speed and guts, for which he was developing a reputation.

The next day, with the Dodgers down 1–0 in the sixth, Robinson opened with a walk and began hopping around at first base, taking a big lead, trying to distract the Cubs' pitcher Johnny Schmitz, who had been mowing the Dodgers down with ease before surrendering the walk. Each time Schmitz prepared to throw, Robinson skittered farther from the bag. Three times Schmitz threw over there trying to catch him. When Schmitz finally did deliver a pitch, it "didn't have much strength," according to the *Daily News,* and Reese ripped it for a game-tying triple. The *News* said Robinson deserved half the credit for Reese's drive. The *Times* said Robinson's antics were a "great annoyance," and "Schmitz obviously was hampered."

In the next inning, Schmitz still seemed rattled. He walked a batter. The catcher,

Clyde McCullough, threw late to second base on a sacrifice bunt. The close play sparked a sharp argument between short-stop Merullo and the umpire at second. Then Robinson singled to load the bases, "which made the Cubs feel madder," wrote Dick Young, "because anything Robby does of a commendatory nature burns up the Confederate opposition."

In the ninth, with the score at 5–1 in favor of the Dodgers, Robinson stole second and went in standing up. Now Merullo was ready to explode. He may have been justified in his anger, to an extent, since Robinson had little reason to swipe the base with his team leading by four runs in the ninth. Before the next pitch, the Cubs' pitcher threw to second, trying to catch Robinson off the bag. Merullo came in from behind, grabbed the throw, and slapped a tag hard on Robinson. "I was on the bag, but I kind of leaned forward to put the tag on him," he recalled years later. "I tagged him once in the face. Then his legs flew up and hit me in the shoulder and I tagged him again. He got up with fire in his eyes. He was mad. He could've eaten me up if he wanted to. He just gave me that look, like, 'I'll take care of you later.' I didn't say anything to him. . . . We were all told to avoid any possible reaction because it was a black boy playing for the first time. . . . I was very, very conscious of it. All of us ballplayers were conscious of it. They were going to be stepping on him at first base, swinging their arms out and trying to knock the ball out of his hands. They did that to everyone, but not the same way. You had to be careful. You could not start a riot."

Merullo, already on the Dodger enemy list, came very close to sparking another fight. In the dugout, the Dodgers rose from the bench and began cursing the Cubs' shortstop, warning him that he'd pay for mistreating Robinson.

Years later, Merullo said he had no problem with Robinson, no problem with black players in the major leagues, no problem at all. He hated everyone who wore Dodger blue, he said; that was all.

On June 24, in Pittsburgh, the Dodgers and Pirates were tied, 2–2, in the fifth before another massive crowd. Branch Rickey removed his coat as he watched his team play, feeling good about the way his misfits were hanging in there, and no doubt delighted that there was no powerhouse team emerging in the National League. One of Rickey's castoffs, Fritz Ostermueller, the pitcher who had hit Robinson on his last trip to Pittsburgh, was on the mound again for the Pirates. Ostermueller was known around the league as "Old Folks," not so much for his age, which was thirty-nine, as for the slow, labored manner in which he pitched. He rocked back and forth, bent himself at the waist "like a Mohammaden on his prayer rug," as *The Sporting News* said, rotated his left arm like a windmill, and only then undertook the critical but necessary action of actually throwing.

After giving up a two-run homer to Pee Wee Reese in the second inning, Ostermueller shut down the Dodgers on one hit. Then, in the fifth, Al Gionfriddo worked a walk and Robinson followed with a grounder to third. Gionfriddo was out at second, but Robinson, hustling to avoid a double play, reached first on the fielder's choice.

Ostermueller had told his teammates before the game that he wasn't going to let Robinson take advantage of his slow delivery. He was going to watch him like a hawk. As Robinson crept away from first, taking his lead, Ostermueller looked at Robinson and Robinson looked back. But before Robinson had a chance to try swiping second, Furillo singled. Robinson went all the way to third.

Walker stepped up to the plate next. As Ostermueller went into his windup, Robinson danced down the third-base line, trying to distract the old pitcher, hoping he would balk, or perhaps throw one to the backstop. Robinson's instincts for base-running were superb, but he was also an intelligent player who understood the game's subtleties. Now he recognized that he had a slow-moving lefty on the mound and that the slow-moving lefty had a lot to worry about: runner on first, runner on third, dangerous hitter at the plate, close game . . .

The first pitch was a ball. So was the second. On the third pitch, a called strike, Furillo took off and swiped second base. The Pirates could have walked Walker to load the bases and set up the force play but decided not to. As Ostermueller went into his elaborate windup yet again, he might have paid less attention to the runners. Now that Furillo was on second, there was no chance of a double steal. Even if he walked the batter, it wouldn't hurt him all that much.

When Ostermueller threw, Robinson began running, head down, arms pumping, dirt flying behind him. This time, he didn't stop. He ran straight down the line toward the plate. At some point, he peeked at the catcher to see where he was set up and where the ball was headed. He prepared to throw his body into a slide. From the dugout and the grandstand, it dawned on people in a sudden flash what was happening. Robinson was stealing home!

The ball thwacked into Dixie Howell's mitt as Robinson slid toward the plate. The catcher grabbed the ball with both hands and pivoted in Robinson's direction, trying to make the tag. Too late. Robinson's foot was wedged under Howell's mitt. Robinson had his first steal of the plate. He'd also scored the go-ahead run, which would prove to be the game-winner.

The crowd roared. Branch Rickey leaned back and laughed as "the boy he had emancipated streaked for the plate and made it with a long slide," the *Brooklyn Eagle* reported.

In the years to come, the steal of home would become Robinson's calling card. He would pull off the trick nineteen times in his career, enough to put him in the top ten on the all-time list, though well behind Ty Cobb's record of fifty-four. But for Robinson, it wasn't the quantity that counted so much as the style.

Buddy Johnson and Count Basie paid tribute to Robinson's steals of home in their hit song, recorded in 1949:

> Did you see Jackie Robinson hit that ball?
> Did he hit it? Yeah, and that ain't all.
> He stole home.
> Yes, yes, Jackie's real gone.
> Did you see Jackie Robinson hit that ball?
> Did he hit it? Yeah, and that ain't all.
> He stole home.
> Yes, yes, Jackie's real gone.
> Jackie is a real gone guy.

The play meant a great deal to Robinson, and even more to his fans. It spoke of both the fearlessness with which he carried himself and the fear he inspired. In the ninety-foot race to home Robinson put himself forth as both a team player and an individual, an insider and an outsider, a man playing by the rules yet boldly bending them to his will. While Branch Rickey had curbed Robinson's natural aggressiveness with the gag order, he couldn't curb Robinson's killer instinct on the field, and nothing symbolized that instinct better than his brazen thefts. The steal of home was his special weapon, the switchblade in his pocket.

Wendell Smith made no mention of Robinson's accommodations on the team's second long road trip. It would appear that most, if not all, of the hotels had begun welcoming the entire Dodger team. Teammates who were interviewed years later would recall Robinson coming and going from the hotels and reading newspapers in the lobbies. They remembered Robinson's presence during card games played on hotel room beds. But they failed to recollect meals shared, which probably meant that Robinson continued to dine alone, or with Smith. The hotels were admitting him now, but in all likelihood they had made it clear that they still preferred not to have him in their restaurants.

Allan Roth was the team's newly hired statistician, a fanatic where baseball's numerology was concerned, and fairly passionate about racism and anti-Semitism, too. Just thirty-four years old and Jewish, Roth, too, was a rookie and an outsider among the Dodgers. While packing neckties at his uncle's factory in Montreal a few years earlier, Roth had begun analyzing patterns in baseball statistics. He became fanatical about the hobby, developing methods to determine how well a certain hitter matched up against lefties and righties, how well he hit in day games compared to night, whether he hit better on weekdays or weekends, and much more. Long before the notion became widely accepted, Roth concluded that on-base percentage mattered more than batting average, and he made a believer of Branch Rickey, who hired him as baseball's first full-time numbers cruncher. Roth attended every Dodger game in 1947, charting every pitch and noting in his ledgers whether it was a fastball or curve, high and inside, low and outside, or down the middle, where it was hit, and who fielded it. He sat just left of the Dodger dugout and passed index cards to Burt Shotton throughout each game, alerting him to matchups that might prove helpful to the Dodgers. Shotton became a believer. In later years, Roth would tell his family about his encounters with Robinson in 1947. Roth kept no personal diary, recording only baseball statistics as the season went along. But as best his family could tell from his stories, his friendship with Robinson, like that of all others with the team who knew the rookie in 1947, did not go deep.

Rickey was so pleased by now with his first baseman's progress, on and off the field, that he was beginning to consider the next stage of his experiment. To properly integrate baseball, there would have to be more black players. He'd known that much all along. But he wanted to make sure that other teams integrated their ranks, too. In fact, in a rare display of selflessness, he had recently passed up on a couple of terrific Negro-league prospects in the hopes that other teams would snap them up.

"I think that the other clubs are going to have Negro players in a year or so," he told the *Brooklyn Eagle.* "One of our scouts just the other day was investigating one of the colored stars. The boy confessed to him that he had already received an offer from a big league club. I don't think too many could make good in the National or American [leagues]. We have one — Roy Campanella, the catcher with Montreal. Why, in the not too distant future I look for the thing to take its natural course! The signing of a Negro won't create any more comment than the signing of a white boy." Rickey said another team had asked him to pass along the names of any high-quality Negro players "who would not fit into our plans."

He went on to praise his first baseman, saying, "In all my years in baseball I can't recall a player coming into the big leagues and making good in a new position without any previous experience there. And that's just what Robinson has done. Don't forget he'd never played first base in his life before we handed him a mitt in Havana."

The *New York Post* said the high opinion of Robinson was fast becoming unanimous, as he carried the team almost singlehandedly through this injury-plagued stretch. The *Post* also noted that even in the Cincinnati press box, "where bigotry runs high, they are finally conceding that he's quite a ballplayer."

None other than Ben Chapman, Robinson's loudest attacker, went on the record with praise, saying, "He is a major leaguer in every respect. He can run, he can hit, he is fast, he is quick with the ball. And his fine base running keeps the other team in an uproar. Furthermore, I want to congratulate the colored race for their particularly fine actions at baseball games in which Robinson has participated."

If Robinson was feeling more secure, he wasn't saying. Wendell Smith reported yet again that the integration of the team was going smoothly. "Robinson is definitely now one of the Dodgers," he wrote on June 28. "He is 'one of the boys' and treated that way by his teammates. No one on the team seems to resent his presence any more, and Jackie seems to have won them over simply by being himself."

The day after Smith's report, newspaper reporters everywhere noted another sign of racial progress, this one coming at the closing session of the thirty-eighth Annual Conference of the National Association for the Advancement of Colored People. More than ten thousand people gathered before the steps of the Lincoln Memorial in Washington to hear President Truman deliver a speech on civil rights. It was the first time a U.S. president had ever addressed the NAACP. Eleanor Roosevelt was on hand, too. "It is my deep conviction," Truman said, "that we have reached a turning point in the long history of our country's efforts to guarantee freedom and equality to all our citizens. Recent events in the United States and abroad have made us realize that it is more important today than ever before to ensure that all Americans enjoy these rights. When I say all Americans, I mean all Americans." The nation could not afford to wait another decade to resolve the problem, Truman said. A month later, he took action, issuing one order intended to end segregation in the military and another designed to eliminate discrimination in federal hiring. Four months after that, Truman's commission on civil rights issued a report called *To Secure These Rights.* The report presented a stark portrait of a country still very much troubled by racial bias, covering everything from lynch mobs to the imprisonment of Japanese-American citizens during the war. But a brief section intended to celebrate signs of progress made several references to the integration of major-league baseball, and, in particular, to the hope offered by "the presence of a Negro player on the Brooklyn Dodgers."

As the baseball season stretched its legs and loped into summer, that Negro player seemed to be making genuine progress with his teammates. Even Walker, a dedicated student of the game, was heard in the locker room giving Robinson tips on improving his swing. But none of that was happening as a result of Robinson's "being himself," as Smith had suggested. On the contrary, it was happening because Robinson was going to great pains not to be himself. Robinson's instinct was to engage Walker on the subject of his racist beliefs. If he'd had his way, he would have argued with Walker, humiliated him even, until the white southerner lashed out in anger or admitted the error of his ways. But he didn't. He remained quiet among his teammates, by and large. He could be funny when he wanted to, but his sense of humor was a lot like a Hugh Casey

337

curveball: It only worked because he used it so seldom.

"Say, Jackie," Carl Furillo said one day during batting practice. "I'm gonna catch you. I'm gonna get hot and pass you up." He was referring to his batting average, which had fallen below that of Robinson.

"Good," Robinson said dryly. "We need hitters on this ballclub."

"I'm gonna pass up that Walker, too," Furillo continued. "Just watch me go!"

"Fine," Robinson answered. "Then we'll have three of us hitting over .300 and we can sure use that."

"You said it!" Furillo chimed.

Robinson grinned. "But you're not going to do it standing here talking about it all day, Carl," he said.

Furillo's mouth opened but no words came out.

To offer proof for his theory that Robinson had won acceptance, Smith told the story of a golf outing that took place in Danville, Illinois, before a night-time exhibition game. Robinson and Smith teed off behind a foursome of Pee Wee Reese, Rex Barney, team secretary Harold Parrott, and *Times* reporter Roscoe McGowan. After about four holes, Robinson and Smith caught up to the quartet, whereupon Reese

338

invited the two men to join their group. Throughout the game, Smith wrote, Reese and Barney "joked and kidded with Jackie and he did the same with them. They were three baseball players and without actually saying it to each other, they admitted that each had something in common." Robinson knew what the men had in common. It was a uniform, and not much more. Smith looked ever at the sunny side, even though the white men in the press corps didn't treat him any better than the players treated Robinson. They came to him when they wanted access to Robinson, but they never approached the story the way Smith would have liked, never adopted integration as a cause, as he thought they should have.

But if Smith nonetheless managed to let the insults and disappointments slide, Robinson remained hypersensitive. He must have wondered why Reese and Barney had preferred the company of a middle-aged newspaper reporter and the team secretary in the first place. Robinson was an avid golfer, and a good one, yet no one on the team had invited him to play. Nor, it seems, had anyone invited him to a movie, or a restaurant, or to go for a stroll. The people around him thought Robinson was a pacifist, letting the insults fly past him. They tended to mistake his quiet anger for acquiescence.

Years later, Reese, Bragan, Lavagetto, and many others on the team would describe how much Robinson's friendship had meant to them, how they had felt empathy throughout his struggle, and how they had learned from him the true meaning of courage. Robinson, they would say, made them better men. But they made the claims only after Robinson had established himself as a winner, and only after it had become fashionable to support civil rights. In 1947, when he needed them most, Robinson had no true friends, not among the Dodgers, anyway. Smith had it right elsewhere in his column when he wrote that Robinson "makes his living playing baseball and the first base bag is to him what a work bench is to a carpenter. That is where he labors and turns out a product. When the day is done he goes his way, and the others who work beside him go theirs. The next day is the same thing all over again. He does his work and they do theirs."

From Pittsburgh, the Dodgers went home. A road trip that had started poorly ended pretty well. Winning seven and losing five, the Dodgers climbed into second place, half a game behind the Braves, who were led by two of the best pitchers in the league, Warren Spahn and Johnny Sain. (After Spahn and Sain, as the saying went, the Braves would pray for rain.)

It had been ten weeks since Robinson's first game in the big leagues, when Sain had handled him with curveball after curveball and when a black man in the white and blue uniform struck almost everyone as a strange sight. Now, as he prepared to face the right-hander again, Robinson was batting around .300, best among everyday players on the team. He ranked among the league leaders in runs scored. He'd struck out only a dozen times, and drawn twenty-seven walks. His defense had been solid, too, with only four errors. The season's midpoint approached, and a strong case could be made that Robinson was the Dodgers' most valuable player.

This time, in the first inning against Sain, Robinson slapped a single to center and scored. Sain won the next two contests, inducing a ground-out and a pop-out. By the time Robinson came to bat in the eighth, the game was tied, Si Johnson on in relief of Sain. Robinson smashed a bullet down the left-field line for a double, no slide required, and when Dixie Walker knocked him home with a single, the Dodgers were winners. Better yet, they were in first place.

The *St. Louis Post-Dispatch,* noting Robinson's success, printed a cartoon showing the Dodger first baseman dressed as a tap dancer, holding a bat as if it were a walking stick and shuffling up a flight of stairs. "Bo Jangles of the Diamond," the headline read. Others were not so patronizing. "The time has come," wrote the Associated Press on June 27, "to recognize Jackie Robinson . . . as a major league ballplayer who has come through under extreme pressure to become an important factor in the Dodger's rise to the National League lead." On July 4, he ran his hitting streak to twenty-one straight games.

In addition to all his hits, walks, and sacrifice bunts, he'd been hit by pitches seven times. Rookies often took some lumps, but Robinson seemed to be getting more than his share. No player in either league had been hit more often. That pitchers were throwing intentionally at Robinson, aiming to intimidate if not injure, was never in doubt. But more interesting was the fact that six of the seven plunks had come in April and May. By June, the indoctrination had more or less ended. When Robinson failed to react, opponents saw no further reason to provoke him.

"Like plastics and penicillin," wrote one commentator, "it seems like Jackie is here to stay."

FIFTEEN:
A GOOD THING FOR EVERYBODY

Sooner or later, all the Negro-league ballplayers noticed the white men in the grandstands. The parks were mostly empty that summer, as the fans who once rooted for the Newark Eagles or the New York Cubans or the Homestead Grays shifted their attention to Jackie Robinson and the Dodgers. So when the white scouts in their rumpled suits plunked themselves down in the good seats behind home plate and started taking notes, everyone with a bat or glove snapped to attention. They ran out their pop flies, took the extra base when they could, and slid a little more ferociously into second to break up double plays.

Who would be next? On buses during road trips, on the field during batting practice, even in the dugout during games, that was the question the black ballplayers asked. Was Ol' Satchel too old? Would the Dodgers promote Roy Campanella from

Montreal? Was Monte Irvin of the Newark Eagles ready to make the leap? And how many big-league clubs were prepared to take on black players? Only one or two? All of them? How many jobs were the men fighting for, exactly?

Reporters at some of the white papers seemed to think the Boston Red Sox might be the next team to step up. Others said Cleveland, or Pittsburgh, and some reporters even suggested that Ben Chapman had been thoroughly cured of his prejudice and that his Phillies were ready to sign Reese "Goose" Tatum, who played baseball for the Indianapolis Clowns and basketball for the Harlem Globetrotters. No one expected much movement from the ball clubs in the circuit's most southern cities: St. Louis, Cincinnati, and Washington, D.C. Still, the consensus among writers seemed to be that every team, or nearly every one, would be integrated inside a couple of years.

So the scouts scribbled their notes and wired their reports back to the home offices. Older black ballplayers like Oscar Charleston, believed by many to be one of the best ever to play the game, found work as scouts thanks to their long-running associations with the Negro leagues. But most of the work remained in the hands of the white men who had been trawling the sandlots and schoolyards in search of white players for so long. Suddenly these men — skilled with stopwatch and scorecard, not psychology — were being asked to conduct interviews and evaluate the character of the black men they were evaluating. Bias remained, and team owners worried far more about the personalities of their prospective black players than they did about the white ones. It was one thing to find a black man who could play the game, the thought went, and quite another to find one who could handle the sort of challenges that had greeted Robinson.

It was a thrilling time to be a Negro-league player, and a frightening one, too. Gone was the world they had known and in which they had thrived. For some, the new world would offer undreamed-of opportunities and unimaginable wealth and fame. For many more, it would mean the end of their careers in baseball. It almost certainly augured the end of one of the longest-running and most popular black-owned businesses in the country.

"We were delighted that Jackie had gotten the chance," said Monte Irvin. "We knew what it meant. It was going to make it easier for the rest of us to follow. We weren't jealous. A little envious, maybe." Irvin had more reason than most to be envious. Had a poll been taken in 1945, most black ballplayers in the country probably would have selected Irvin as the black man most likely to succeed in the majors. "Monte was our best young ballplayer at the time," the Negro-league legend Cool Papa Bell said. Branch Rickey knew all about Irvin, too. He had met Irvin at about the same time he first met Robinson, in 1945. On paper, Irvin did indeed look like the better candidate to break baseball's color line. Like Robinson, he'd played with white boys in high school, had been to college, and had served his country in the war. Like Robinson, he didn't drink or run around. On the question of baseball experience, Irvin, having already established himself as a big star with the Newark Eagles, had Robinson beat hands down. He was a can't-miss prospect, as the scouts said, with a gorgeous swing, a strong arm, and terrific speed. But Irvin, like a lot of black men who had fought in the war, had suffered an injury not directly connected with bombs or bullets.

The army had assigned Irvin to a battalion of black engineers trained to build and destroy. Be it a road, bridge, mess tent, or latrine, Irvin and his men could set it up fast and take it down faster. The battalion spent more than a year and a half in Europe, touring England, Belgium, and France. But the men never saw action and never got to do the work for which they'd been trained. Instead, they followed a battalion of white engineers, cleaning up after them. Their biggest battle, it turned out, was to maintain their own dignity.

"We were like janitors," Irvin recalled years later. "I was disgusted. Here we were, sacrificing, and we were being treated like we weren't even human. Our own [white] soldiers seemed to resent the fact that we were in the army. . . . There was a lot of trouble with our own soldiers, a lot of name-calling. . . . You couldn't go here, you couldn't do that. Here we were, fighting to make the world safe, and we were treated like second-class citizens. . . . It affected me. . . . It affected me mentally and physically."

Irvin would have preferred combat. He would have preferred anything that would have lifted him from the doldrums of indentured servitude. Yet it was not to be, and after the war, the despair lingered like a long rain delay. When he met Branch Rickey in 1945 to talk about joining the Dodgers, Irvin could tell that Rickey seemed interested. Yet the ballplayer himself mustered only mild enthusiasm. He didn't feel like getting back to baseball, didn't feel like doing much of anything. So off he went to Puerto Rico, hoping to work himself back into shape with some Negro-league teams. There he played with little pressure and few expectations, away from white men in uniforms. He joined the Eagles in 1946, feeling somewhat better, hitting the ball on the button, and helping that team win the World Series of the Negro leagues. But even then, he said, he didn't have "the enthusiasm and the love for the game I once had." If a championship and a batting average of around .380 couldn't shake his apathy, he wondered, what would?

In 1947, he signed on for another season with the Eagles. But by now everything was different. As Irvin listened to Red Barber on the radio and snuck over to Ebbets Field to see a black man compete with and against whites, he felt a spark. Perhaps he hadn't been cut out to be the first man. Perhaps he'd merely been a victim of bad luck and bad timing. No matter now. Robinson had done the hard part. Providing reinforcement was all that anyone would ask now of Irvin, and he was more than ready to offer it. "We said to ourselves, 'If Jackie can do it, we can do it,' " he recalled. "It made us want to succeed that much more."

It might have been Irvin, and it might have been Roy Campanella. Had Robinson been overlooked, or had he failed, or fallen to injury, or succumbed to his rage in Montreal while on trial there, Campanella might well have been next on Branch Rickey's list. He would not have been a bad choice. Campanella first attracted the attention of professional black teams around his hometown of Philadelphia when he was a mere fourteen years old. He was a hefty, strong-armed, hard-hitting kid, the son of a white father and a black mother. At sixteen, and still hefty, he dropped out of school and turned pro. Campy, as everyone called him, was a sweetheart, and even as he began traveling with the Baltimore Elite Giants, sometimes catching four games a day, living on hot dogs and pop, learning to shoot craps, listening to the old men tell tales, the hardships of the road did not spoil his gentle personality.

Competing with grown men never was a problem for the teenager. His talents were man-sized long before he'd reached his full height of five-feet-eight. Before he was eighteen he had played in Puerto Rico,

Mexico, Cuba, Venezuela, and in so many small American towns that he never bothered trying to count or remember them. He played year round. Wherever there was a game and a team in need of a catcher, that's where you'd find him, shin-guards on, ready to go. His parents didn't mind. "They pay our boy good, real good," his mother once said. "Would he be better off as a porter — a shipping clerk, or perhaps work in a fruit and vegetable store?"

Before long, he was the second-best catcher in the Negro leagues, the best, by universal decree, being Josh Gibson. Gibson was six-feet-two, 230 pounds, all chest and arms, a baseball-hitting machine said to have belted more than eight hundred homers over the course of his career, and said to have hit them for greater distance than anyone alive, including Babe Ruth. No one had ever doubted Gibson was good enough for the big leagues. The interesting question is why so many big-league owners resisted the temptation to make Gibson the game's first black player, particularly in the 1930s and early 1940s, when he was in his prime, or in the war years, when talent was in such short supply that the St. Louis Browns played the one-armed Pete Gray in left field. Kenesaw Mountain Landis, the old goat who ran the game, might have objected. But wasn't there one owner willing to take on Landis and take a chance on a man of such stupendous talent? There was not. And while racism no doubt played a role in the outcome, Gibson did, too. The great black slugger was an emotional disaster, given to depression and fits of rage. He drank heavily and partook liberally of drugs. The black press did its best to present the image of Gibson as a star, ignoring his trips to mental hospitals, but there was a good reason why Wendell Smith and other writers never pushed for Gibson's promotion. On the field, the man could handle anything. Off, he was a lost soul. On January 20, 1947, less than three months before Robinson's first game with the Dodgers, Gibson died, apparently from a stroke. He was thirty-five.

Campanella was no Gibson. He lived cleanly, loved his wife, and stayed far from trouble. His only madness was for the game. And he was young enough yet, at twenty-five, not to have been torn up by life on the road in the Negro leagues. Other men grew weary after a couple of months bumping from town to town, but Campy loved it all. On October 17, 1945, about six weeks after Rickey's first meeting with Robinson, the catcher received his own summons to appear at 215 Montague Street in Brooklyn. The boss held forth for four hours. "Mr. Rickey certainly was a man with the words," Campanella said of his visit. "I wasn't sure I had understood everything he said."

A week later, Campanella discovered just how much he had failed to understand. He and several other black ballplayers were at the Woodside Hotel, one of Harlem's popular gathering places, and the inspiration for Count Basie's huge 1938 hit, "Jumpin' at the Woodside," when Campy ran into Jackie Robinson. The men had never met. All Campanella knew about Robinson was that he murdered inside pitches, a fact he had filed away for future use. Robinson invited Campanella to his room for a game of gin rummy, half a cent a point. Campy lit a cigar as Jackie dealt the first hand.

"I hear you went over to see Mr. Rickey last week," Robinson said.

"Yeah, that's right," Campanella answered, surprised, for he had told no one. "How did you know?"

"I was over there myself. What happened with you?"

"Nothing much," said Campanella. "We talked, or rather Mr. Rickey did. Man, he's the talkingest man I ever did see."

"Did you sign?" Robinson asked.

Campanella said he didn't, because he didn't want to take a pay cut to play for the Brown Dodgers, a team that didn't even exist.

Robinson got so excited that he revealed a secret of his own. He told Campanella that he'd signed a contract to play for Brooklyn's top minor-league team and he was going to Montreal the next day for the official announcement.

Campanella sat dumbstruck, realizing suddenly his terrible mistake. His cigar gone cold, Campy continued sucking and pulling at it, replaying in his mind Rickey's monologue. It occurred to him only then that Rickey had never mentioned the Brown Dodgers. Had the Dodger boss been offering him the same thing he'd offered Robinson: a shot at the big leagues? Had he blown his chance?

A few months later, in March 1946, Campanella heard again from Rickey, and this time the boss made his intentions clear, offering a contract to play in the Dodgers' minor-league system. Campanella signed.

After adding Campanella and pitcher Don Newcombe, Rickey continued shopping. He liked Monte Irvin and Larry Doby, both of the Newark Eagles. He liked Sammy Gee, an infielder, who was fresh out of high school in Detroit. He liked Dan Bankhead, a hard-throwing pitcher for the Memphis Red Sox. The issue now for Brooklyn's boss was whether to buy every good black player available or let some of the other teams in on the action. Did he want to field a team with three or four black players while the rest of the league remained entirely white, or let Robinson fly solo for a little while longer and see if integration would catch on elsewhere? As usual, the great pragmatist wanted to have it both ways. So, with Campanella and Newcombe already on board, he waited.

But not for long.

Bill Veeck (rhymes with "wreck," as he famously titled his autobiography) took over the Cleveland Indians in 1946, shortly after Rickey had signed Robinson to play for the Royals. Instantly, Veeck had a lot of ideas for how to rejuvenate the Cleveland franchise. It was Veeck, as an employee of the Cubs in 1937, who thought of planting ivy on the outfield wall at Wrigley Field. It was Veeck a few years later, at the age of twenty-seven, who bought a bankrupt minor-league team in Milwaukee and turned it into a sensation by offering fans fireworks shows,

355

free beer, and morning games for swing-shift workers. He made a trip to the ballpark more like a trip to the circus, ensuring that fans would be entertained whether the home team won or lost. Once he proved his point, Veeck sold the team for a nice profit and moved on, his thoughts turning to more ambitious schemes.

In 1943, he supposedly organized backers in a plan to buy the down-in-the-dumps Philadelphia Phillies, who over the past decade had never finished better than seventh place. Veeck's transformation plan for the Phils included a secret weapon: Negro-leaguers. He wasn't sure how many of them he would need, and he was not planning to establish a quota system, but he was certain that he wanted to integrate the team. "With Satchel Paige, Roy Campanella, Luke Easter, Monte Irvin, and countless others in action and available," he wrote in his autobiography, "I had not the slightest doubt that in 1944, a war year, the Phils would have leaped from seventh place to the pennant."

For Veeck, it would have been a typical move — rushed, radical, and revolutionary. He was as much a social scientist as Rickey, even if their methods were entirely different. While Rickey proceeded cautiously,

Veeck didn't care if he blew up the laboratory. He smoked and drank and thought neckties had too much in common with nooses. He had a hole drilled in the bottom of his wooden leg so he could use it as an ashtray. He had little or nothing in common with the wealthy men who owned other big-league teams, and he loved tweaking them every chance he got. Turning to Negro-leaguers to restock the Phillies seemed like just the sort of thing he would do, although no one has ever been able to confirm Veeck's version of events. He claimed that he visited Commissioner Landis at his office in Chicago to tell him about his plans. "Judge Landis wasn't exactly shocked but he wasn't exactly overjoyed either," Veeck wrote. "His first reaction, in fact, was that I was kidding him."

Still, Veeck said he left the commissioner's office confident that the deal was done. By the time he got back to Philadelphia the next day, Landis had pulled the rug from under Veeck's ashtray and foot. The National League had taken control of the Phillies. Soon after that, the league sold the team to a lumber dealer for half of what Veeck had supposedly offered.

In 1946, with Landis dead, Veeck put together another deal, this time to buy the

Cleveland Indians. By then, Robinson had already been signed to play for the Dodgers' minor-league team in Montreal, and Veeck knew he wanted to be a part of the game's integration. So he moved quickly to hire a black public relations executive — Lena Horne's former husband, Louis Jones — and told him to start preparing Cleveland's black community for integrated baseball. "I moved slowly and carefully, perhaps even timidly," wrote Veeck. "It is usually overlooked, but if Jackie Robinson was the ideal man to break the color barrier, Brooklyn was also the ideal place. I wasn't that sure about Cleveland."

Veeck wanted someone like Robinson. He settled on Larry Doby, the hard-hitting second baseman for the Newark Eagles. Doby had attended college. He didn't smoke, swear, or drink. Of course, it didn't hurt that Doby had been hitting the hide off the baseball wherever he went. Midway through the 1947 season, after forty-two games with the Newark Eagles, Doby was batting .458 with fourteen home runs and thirty-five runs batted in. And he was only twenty-three years old.

The Indians were in fifth place in the American League, and going nowhere. Veeck was not inclined to wait. On July 1, he phoned Effa and Abe Manley, owners of the Eagles, and offered to pay ten thousand dollars for Doby, with another five-thousand-dollar payment to be made later if he stuck with the team. Effa Manley, who ran the team, had mixed feelings about the integration of the majors. She recognized that it was good for the black ballplayers and probably good for the country, even if it might prove disastrous for her championship team and the business of black baseball.

Veeck had not done as much preparation as Rickey. He had not let Doby spend a year in the minor leagues to acclimate. He had not given his first black ballplayer the benefit of a spring training camp to get to know his teammates and to get accustomed to big-league pitching. What's more, Doby, as a second baseman who could also play short, didn't fit into the Indians' lineup, where Joe Gordon was a star at second and Lou Boudreau, the team's player/manager, was planted firmly at short. Doby, like Robinson, would have to learn to play first base in order to see much action.

It was mid-June when Doby heard the Indians were coming after him. One of Veeck's men approached him and said arrangements would probably be completed within two or three weeks. Doby thought it was a joke. On July 3, when the deal was announced, Veeck told *The New York Times,* "I wanted to get the best of the available Negro boys while the grabbing was good. Why wait? Within ten years Negro players will be in regular service with big league teams. . . . The entrance of Negroes into the majors is not only inevitable — it is here." To another reporter, Veeck said, "I am operating under the belief that the war advanced us in regard to racial tolerance. I probably will catch hell for a while, but it is my hope it will work out."

Doby was a quiet man, strong and handsome. Born in South Carolina, at the age of fourteen he had moved to New Jersey, where he began attracting attention for his athletic talents. Now, less than a decade later, he told a reporter he didn't know whether he was "more surprised than excited, or more excited than surprised" at the opportunity presented him.

He played one more game with the Eagles, homering in his final at-bat on July 4. The next day, he was in a taxi with Veeck, on his way to Comiskey Park in Chicago, where he would join the Indians for a game against the White Sox. Doby wore a suit with a white shirt buttoned to the collar and no tie. He stuffed a white hankie in his jacket pocket. Veeck wore a white shirt, wide open at the neck, sleeves rolled all the way up to show off his biceps. Doby and Veeck held a press conference to answer questions for reporters and mug for photographers while Boudreau met with his players, warning them not to make any trouble for the new man. After the press conference, Doby walked into the clubhouse and put on an Indians uniform, CLEVELAND printed across the chest, a grotesque caricature of a Native American on the left sleeve, number 14 on the back.

With Boudreau at his side, the newest Indian walked around the clubhouse and said hello to his teammates. The team's two first basemen, Eddie Robinson and Les Fleming, reportedly avoided shaking hands. Otherwise, there were no problems.

Before the game, Doby stepped onto the rain-slicked field and threw a ball back and forth with Boudreau. When the action began, he took a seat at the end of the bench, the spot customarily reserved for rookies, and watched the White Sox jump to a 5–1 lead. In the seventh inning, with runners on first and third, Boudreau ordered Doby to grab a bat and pinch hit. Because of the rain earlier in the day, batting practice had been canceled. Doby hadn't even had a chance to check out the available equipment, much less take a few swings. As he took his cut at the first pitch from Earl Harrist, Doby seemed intent on entering the big leagues the same way he had left the Negro leagues twenty-four hours prior: with a home run. He swung like Babe Ruth, straight from the heels, and missed it by a mile. On the next pitch, he scorched a long foul ball. He let the next two go for balls, then swung at a pitch outside and fanned. The Chicago crowd applauded politely.

Doby returned to the bench. As yet, Veeck and Boudreau hadn't discussed what to do with their new player. Would he be a starter or strictly a pinch hitter? Would he play first base, second, short, or outfield? No one seemed to know. As the end of the game neared, two black men in jackets and ties joined Doby in the dugout. Their presence attracted the attention of the home-plate umpire, Bill Summers, who called timeout and asked Boudreau to explain. Boudreau said the men were Chicago police officers, sent to protect Doby. The ump let the cops stay.

After the game, when his teammates went to the downtown Del Prado Hotel, Doby was escorted to the DuSable Hotel on the

South Side.

In his *Courier* column the following week, Robinson offered advice for Doby, whom he referred to as a "grand guy and a very good ballplayer." Robinson warned that Doby would find tougher competition in the majors. In the Negro leagues, he noted, a hitter would feast from time to time on substandard pitching. Not so in the majors. "I hope Doby won't try so hard that he'll tighten up and lose some of his effectiveness at the plate," Robinson wrote. "I guess it's the tension that does that." He went on to thank the owners of Negro-league teams for giving up their best players to the majors. "The signing of Doby by Cleveland is a good thing for everybody," he wrote. "It's good for all baseball; it's good for Negro baseball and it's even good for me. I'm glad to know another Negro player is in the majors. I'm no longer in there by myself. I no longer have the feeling that if I don't make good it will kill the chances of other Negro players. Larry is up here with me in the big leagues now. We'll both do all we can to make it easier for someone else. We'll try to act and play in such a way that the other owners will sign Negro players and be glad to have them."

In his column two weeks later, Robinson

made a pitch for Sam Jethroe, center-fielder for the all-black Cleveland Buckeyes, who had joined him in Boston for a big-league audition a few years earlier. "I think he would make good if given the opportunity," Robinson said. Rumors, meanwhile, were flying: The Yankees were preparing to take Dan Bankhead, the Indians were after Jethroe, the Pirates were close to signing Irvin . . . and on it went.

The notion that black ballplayers might suddenly descend on teams through the majors, as exciting to Robinson as it was to many of the younger men in the Negro leagues, proved too much for some to take. Pete Norton of the *Tampa Tribune* warned that big-league baseball might be in for trouble come spring training if a lot of teams traveled across the Mason-Dixon Line with black players in tow. "Custom in the South . . ." he wrote, "has always banned mixed sports contests. This action has been taken to avoid unpleasant incidents, and has been found, over a period of 82 years, to be the sensible way to eliminate any possible trouble."

In *The Sporting News* that same week, an editorial writer quoted an unnamed ballplayer, reportedly an all-star, saying he had no objection to playing alongside a Negro:

"I know we are going to have Negroes on all clubs, with the possible exception of the Senators, Cardinals and Browns. I feel that if the majors fight this movement, they will be placed in a very uncomfortable position. However, the Negroes have their own league. Is it going to open up to white players? Another thing. The Negroes holler 'discrimination.' Well, Robinson moves right into the National League after one year in the AAA minors, and Doby gets a job in the American League without previous schooling in white baseball. I fought my way through the minors for five years. I rode buses all night for three of those five years, so that I could get a chance in the majors. If we are to have Negroes in the majors, let them go through the long preparation the white player is forced to undergo. Let us not discriminate against the white player because he is white."

Two weeks after Doby joined the Indians, the St. Louis Browns joined the action, signing the black players Willard Brown and Henry Thompson. They also purchased a thirty-day option on Negro-leaguer Lorenzo Davis. Suddenly, black ballplayers were popping up everywhere.

It should have been shocking news that

two black men — and possibly a third — were set to play in the nation's southernmost big-league city. Instead, the announcement went largely unnoticed. In New York the *Daily News* devoted three paragraphs to the story, the *Post* gave it two, and the *Times* wrapped it into a six-paragraph story about the latest Browns loss, a 16–2 shellacking by the Philadelphia Athletics. The *St. Louis Post-Dispatch* awarded the news six paragraphs, describing the two players as "capable," and injecting a note of skepticism. The story noted that Browns owner Richard Muckerman was not on hand for the announcement but left a note saying the players had been signed only because he thought they would help the team, not as a cheap trick to boost attendance. No one was buying it, but, then again, no one cared much, either. While it's tempting to chalk up the blasé response to growing racial harmony and the widespread acceptance of Jackie Robinson, it probably had more to do with the fact that no one cared about anything where the St. Louis Browns were concerned.

The Browns were baseball's garbage heap, an assemblage of trash and spare parts tossed aside or untouched by other teams. They were so far and so consistently out of the running in the American League that it was possible at times to forget they were playing at all. St. Louis fans often wished they weren't. In 1935, while compiling a 65–87 record and finishing in seventh place, the team drew only 80,922 fans the entire season. The Yankees, by way of comparison, packed 74,747 fans into their home stadium for one game in May of 1947. But who wanted to buy a ticket to misery? In 1939, the Brownies finished 43–111, leaving the team an astonishing 64½ games out of first place. Only when the war began and every team found its talent supply depleted did the team finally manage to compete. In 1944, to nearly everyone's surprise, the team captured the American League pennant. The next year, though, they reverted to form, and by 1947 they were back in last place with a record of 28–50.

"A bunch of bums," said Bob Dillinger, the Browns' third baseman, recalling his teammates in 1947. For one game in July, shortly before the announcement that Thompson and Brown would join the team, only 478 fans showed up at Sportsman's Park for a Browns game against the Washington Senators. Shirley Povich, stuck with the job of covering the action for the *Washington Post,* noted that the Senators' take from the game's receipts wouldn't be enough to pay the team's laundry bill.

Thompson and Brown had been playing with the Kansas City Monarchs before getting the call to join the Browns. Tom Baird, a white man who co-owned the Monarchs, was still angry that he'd lost Jackie Robinson to the Dodgers without compensation from Branch Rickey and that Rickey had more or less ignored his complaint. When the Browns agreed to pay five thousand dollars for Thompson and Brown, with more to come if they lasted a month with the team, Baird made sure to tell the press that this was the way he expected business to be done in the future if white teams expected to continue using his Monarchs as an orchard for the growth and development of black talent.

Brown and Thompson expressed excitement about their promotions, setting aside whatever doubts they might have felt at joining major-league baseball's worst team. Had the opportunity come along a year or two later, they might have been more selective. They might have turned their backs on the Browns and waited for better offers, but that wasn't an option yet. On July 17, less than two weeks after Doby's debut, Thompson was penciled in as the starting second baseman and the seventh batter in the lineup against the Philadelphia Athletics. He popped out on a foul ball in the second inning, lined out to right in the fourth, popped out on another foul in the seventh, and grounded out to second in the ninth. The Browns committed four errors, including one by Thompson, in a 16–2 loss. And the worst news of all was that a mere thirty-six hundred people paid to see the game. Brown remained on the bench.

The next day, with six thousand fans on hand, Thompson played while Brown rode the pine once again. Muddy Ruel, the team's manager, had Ray Coleman (a .259 hitter), Jeff Heath (.251), and Paul "Peanuts" Lehner (.248) in the outfield. They were not exactly terrorizing opponents, and yet Ruel decided he had no room in the lineup for Brown, and he made it known that he had no intention of discussing his decision.

Not until June 20, against the Red Sox, did Brown get a chance to start in right field. With Thompson at second and Brown in right, the Browns became the first team to put two black men on the field at the same time. In the first half of a doubleheader, Thompson went hitless. Brown managed only a single. Still, the Browns topped the Red Sox, 4–3. In the second game that afternoon, Thompson had two hits, Brown had none, and the Brownies won again, 7–6, giving the team its first sweep of a doubleheader in fourteen tries. The team now had a winning record, three wins against two losses, since integrating its lineup.

In St. Louis, fans were unmoved. Attendance remained woeful, and Ruel continued to play Thompson and Brown only sparingly. On July 23, Brown banged four hits against the Yankees, leading the Browns to an 8–2 win in front of a big crowd in the Bronx. On August 13, the Browns were trailing the Tigers 5–3 and had one man on base when Brown was sent in to pinch hit. Using a bat borrowed from teammate Jeff Heath, Brown blasted the ball to deep center, and then sped around the bases for a game-tying, inside-the-park homer. It was the first home run ever hit by a black man in the American League, yet the bat was not destined for the Hall of Fame in Cooperstown, New York. When Brown returned to the dugout, Heath grabbed the piece of lumber he had loaned the black slugger and smashed it to pieces, making sure no one would ever use it again.

Ten days later, Brown and Thompson both were gone, sent back to the Monarchs in time for the Browns to avoid paying for a full season of their services. A spokesman for the team said the players had failed to reach major-league standards. Brown, hitting .179, had not done much to win a spot on the roster. But Thompson had been batting .256, better than the team average of .241, with a .341 on-base percentage, better than the team's .318. His five errors as a second baseman were cause for concern, although not so unusual for a rookie. Replacing Thompson was Johnny Berardino, who would go on to finish the season with a .261 average and a measly 20 RBIs. (He had better luck as an actor, landing the part of Dr. Steve Hardy on TV's *General Hospital* in 1963, and keeping it more than thirty years.)

Had the Browns been the least bit interested in Thompson, or in integration for that matter, they might have sent their young, black infielder to the minor leagues for some grooming. Perhaps if St. Louis fans had shown more support for the team's black players, Muckerman would have considered making a greater investment in Thompson. As it turned out, Thompson got another chance in 1949 with the New York

371

Giants, and he proved that he belonged in the majors. He went on to hit .267 with 129 home runs in nine big-league seasons, and played in two World Series.

Brown, however, never again appeared in the major leagues. He finished the season in Kansas City with a .336 average, and went on to hit .374 the following year, and .371 the year after that. In 2006, he was inducted into the Baseball Hall of Fame. He never had anything good to say about his big-league tour. "The Browns couldn't beat the Monarchs no kind of way, only if we was asleep," he recalled. "That's the truth. They didn't have nothing."

In Cleveland, meanwhile, Larry Doby was struggling almost as much as Brown had been. Though the Indians were not in the running for the American League pennant, and though manager Lou Boudreau seemed enthusiastic about his newest player, Doby nevertheless got very little playing time.

On July 6, Doby's second day with the team, Boudreau sent him out to play first base in the second half of a doubleheader. Doby had never played first and didn't own a first baseman's mitt. He tried to borrow one from the team's regular first baseman, Eddie Robinson, but Robinson refused to hand it over. He said he had no problem playing with a black man; he simply didn't want to lend a glove to anyone who might cost him his job. He admitted, though, that he and his teammates were unsure how to treat Doby. "We were apprehensive," he said. "You didn't know exactly how it was going to go." Robinson eventually relented, handing his glove to the team's traveling secretary, Spud Goldstein, who passed it along.

Doby drove in a run with an infield single in his first game as a first baseman, but after that he watched three games in a row from the bench. His next five appearances were as a pinch hitter. Over the rest of the season, he appeared in only twenty-nine games, usually as a pinch hitter, and managed only five hits in thirty-two at-bats, striking out eleven times. "Doby wasn't prepared," said Al Rosen, who was also a rookie with the Indians in 1947. "Pinch hitting is not a very pleasant experience for a young player. You're just up there swinging. For an older player, it's another story because you know the pitchers and what they throw."

Years later, when analyzing the results of his experiment, Bill Veeck called Doby "a complete bust" in his rookie season. The ballplayer "had never come face-to-face with prejudice until he became a big leaguer," he wrote. Had he come along a few years later, when the pressures were less, said Veeck, Doby might have become one of the game's all-time greats. On the other hand, if Veeck had assigned Doby to the minors and prepared his team better for its experiment in integration, the results might have been different. Even so, Doby would return in 1948 and have a much better season. As a full-time outfielder that year he hit .301 and helped the Indians win the World Series. After eleven more seasons, he retired with a .283 batting average and 253 home runs. In 1998 he was elected to the Baseball Hall of Fame.

Black Americans had developed many strong businesses in response to segregation, taking what they were given and making the best of it. There were black hospitals, black schools, black charities, black motion picture companies, black churches, black newspapers, black bus lines, black taxicab fleets. Though most of these businesses and institutions were sources of pride, they were also seen as somehow inferior, reminders that black Americans had not yet been accepted as equals in their own country. Integration, many hoped, would bring equality, dignity, and opportunity.

Later, those feelings would change. Frustration would settle in, subtly at first, and then with force. Many black Americans would come to resent the fact that white people were setting the terms for integration and proceeding at a less-than-urgent pace. They would complain that when white Hollywood producers hired black actors to attract black audiences, they tended to cast them as butlers and maids. But by the time many black Americans recognized what was happening, it was too late. Now, as black baseball fans attached themselves to the Brooklyn Dodgers, they also became familiar with the pleasures of the big-league game, with the voice of Red Barber, with daily box scores in the newspaper, with the sweet swing of Stan Musial. As a result, the Negro leagues suffered an identity crisis. Should the black leagues try to compete with white leagues, or give up and serve as de facto farm teams? Should they try to hang on by embracing segregation, or accept what even some owners considered the greater good of integration?

"There is considerable apprehension within the ranks of Negro baseball these days," Wendell Smith wrote. "Owners of teams in the Negro American and Negro

National Leagues are concerned because they fear that Organized Baseball is going to take their stars and subsequently kill Negro baseball altogether. . . . They contend they have felt the effects of Robinson's drawing power already this season." Smith tried again to be an optimist. If the Negro-league owners did a better job of promotion and presented games in a more "dignified and business-like manner," fans would remain loyal, he said.

The black newspaper writers were nearly unanimous in their support for integration, and so were the owners of Negro-league teams, even though Jim Crow was essential to the success of both their industries. The few voices crying out for the protection and preservation of black baseball tended to be whites, including Calvin Griffith, owner of the Washington Senators, who wrote that white baseball had "no right to destroy" the Negro leagues. He continued: "Your two [Negro] leagues have established a splendid reputation and now have the support and respect of the colored people all over this country as well as the decent white people. . . . Anything that is worthwhile is worth fighting for so you folks should leave not a stone unturned to protect the existence of your two established Negro leagues. Don't let anybody tear it down." But the black press accused Griffith of dishonesty, saying his kind words for the Negro leagues were a clever way of disguising his opposition to integration. They noted that Griffith, known as "The Old Fox," collected a fair bit of money from Negro-league teams who paid rent to use Griffith Stadium.

Various proposals were floated to save the Negro leagues, estimated at the time as a $2-million-a-year business. Some suggested the leagues should start recruiting white players. Others said the leagues should become part of white baseball's farm system. But most people believed Negro baseball was worth sacrificing on behalf of integration.

As one letter to the editor of the *Chicago Defender* said:

The protest of the Negro baseballers is as selfish as any plantation owner of slavery-bound men in the days prior to the Civil War. Their own interest is above that of their nation. This is an appeal to all Negroes to avoid this, for their freedom means freedom to all men, and courage to men of other lands. Segregate yourselves and others will do no better.

Attendance was slipping wherever Negro-league teams played ball in 1947, and it was slipping at a particularly alarming rate in the Northeast, where fans had the greatest opportunity to see Robinson. At Yankee Stadium, attendance for black baseball games dropped from 158,000 in 1946 to 63,000 in 1947. In Newark, the number of paying customers fell from 120,000 to 57,000.

The speed of the collapse was stunning, and so was the response of team owners in the Negro leagues. To offset their losses, owners of black teams began cutting some of their veteran players and hiring younger talent. Operating budgets were stretched thinner than ever, and the quality of competition slipped. In July, a mere thirty-eight hundred fans turned out to see the Baltimore Elite Giants play the Newark Eagles on a sunny Sunday afternoon in Baltimore — and that was the largest crowd the Elite Giants had drawn in more than two months. The picture was coming into focus, and it was gloomy.

The Negro leagues enjoyed one last hurrah in 1947, at the East-West All-Star game, played on July 27, 1947, at Comiskey Park in Chicago. Fans buzzed over the game for weeks in advance, and tickets sold out quickly.

The East-West game, which began in 1933, was inspired by the first big-league All-Star game, which had been held earlier the same summer. The Negro-league version was sponsored by the *Pittsburgh Courier* and the *Chicago Defender,* and readers chose the starting players by clipping ballots from their newspapers and mailing them in. The East-West game was bigger than the Negro Leagues World Series. For players, there was no greater honor than being elected.

On the day of the game in 1947, enormous crowds packed the streets around Comiskey Park. Chicago's new mayor, Martin H. Kennelly, threw out the first pitch. Big-league scouts came out to watch, and the black papers were saying that at least three or four all-stars would likely wind up in the big leagues. Charles Graham, owner of the San Francisco Seals, one of the top teams in the all-white Pacific Coast League, attended the game and told a reporter he was prepared to integrate his team. "We'll hire any Negro player who really can help us," he said. There were plenty of talented men to choose from, including Orestes "Minnie" Minoso of the New York Cubans. Minoso recalled feeling extra pressure, knowing the scouts were watching, and knowing that Jackie Robinson had flung open the door. "You doubled your ambition," he said. "You worked harder."

By game time, 48,112 paying customers filled Comiskey Park. The West beat the East, 5–2. Dan Bankhead, the hard-throwing righty, got the win after giving up one run in three innings of work. Less than a month later, Bankhead would be in the majors, signed by Branch Rickey to help boost the Dodgers' bedraggled pitching corps. Minoso would follow soon after, as would his fellow all-stars Monte Irvin and Sam Jethroe. Never again would such a crowd gather to see all-black teams play ball.

SIXTEEN:
THE POISON PEN

As summer rounded second and headed for third, everything was going Robinson's way. Yet he was not the sort of man to celebrate his success or to attempt to cash in on it, at least not yet. He did not buy new suits or treat his wife to lavish nights on the town. He did not demand a better locker. Nor did he pressure Branch Rickey to renegotiate his salary. He made no effort to charm the men in the press box. In fact, he still wasn't even sure whether to call the newspapermen by their first names, as the rest of his teammates did without hesitation. "Hello, how are you?" Robinson would say, and leave it at that.

On July 18, when the Cardinals came to town, Ebbets Field was filled to capacity. The return of the Cards might have prompted some members of the press to revisit the story of the alleged player strike or to assess how much progress Robinson had made since the early part of the season. But no one did. The Dodgers were leading the race for the National League pennant, but the Cards, Giants, and Braves all were close behind. That was the big story at game time.

In the first inning, Robinson reached on a fielder's choice and scored. In the third inning, he drove in a run with a single. In the seventh, he lined his sixth home run of the season into the seats beyond left field. It was the first time all season he'd driven in three runs in a game. For seven innings, Ralph Branca threw a perfect game, twenty-one batters up, twenty-one down. In the eighth, Enos Slaughter bounced a single between Robinson and Stanky for the Cardinals' only hit. After the game, the long-armed, big-nosed Branca was all smiles, and the mood in the clubhouse was effervescent. "You'd have thought the Dodgers had just clinched the pennant . . . ," Dick Young wrote.

The next day, rain splattered the ballpark, making puddles in the outfield. The bad weather compelled some fans to stay home. Only 15,685 passed through the turnstiles. But even that small crowd was enough to put the Dodgers past the one-million mark for home attendance in 1947. Though their park was puny, they were drawing more fans than any other team in the league. What's more, they were becoming popular across the country, even in cities where big-league baseball was not played. Thirteen radio stations around the country, as far as Miami and San Diego, picked up coverage of the second game of their series with the Cardinals. With the Yankees running away with the American League, fans turned to Brooklyn for their fill of baseball drama. What's more, black fans around the country had made the Dodgers their team of choice.

"I live in a small all negro town," a woman named Bernice Franklin of Tyronza, Arkansas, wrote to Robinson. "We go to Memphis for all our amusements, but there is no greater thrill than a broadcast of the Dodgers' ball game. . . . I own and operate a rural general store, and right now the farmers are gathering for your game."

If they happened to be listening to his game on July 19, they heard a lot of sloppy baseball. Robinson misplayed a throw in the first inning, helping the Cards get two quick runs. He made up for it, however, in the bottom half of the inning by lining a sizzling double down the left-field line. He went to third on a sacrifice fly and watched Dixie Walker draw a walk. Howie Pollet, a lefty, was on the mound for the Cards. As he went into his windup, Walker and Robinson attempted one of the game's most daring and thrilling maneuvers, the double steal of second and home. As Pollet threw, Walker took off for second. When the catcher, Del Rice, threw down to second, Robinson dashed for home. Red Schoendienst, the second baseman, saw Robinson going and decided to let Walker take second. He wanted to nail Robinson at home. So he stepped in front of second base to catch Rice's throw and, with his body moving toward the plate, threw it back to Rice. Rice leaped to grab the high throw as Robinson slid under his feet. By the time the catcher landed, Robinson was brushing home plate with his right leg. Umpire Beans Reardon spread his arms like airplane wings to signal safe. Robinson, with an assist from Walker, had his second steal of home. He added a single and a run batted in that afternoon, raising his batting average to .312. Still, the Dodgers lost, 7–5.

The third and deciding game of the series was one of the season's strangest. The Cardinals took a 2–0 lead in the second inning and held it until the ninth. In the top of the ninth, with two outs, Ron Northey hit a long fly ball to deepest center field. The ball hit the top of the concrete wall, bounced high in the air, and plopped back down onto the outfield grass. The umpire waved his arm to signal a home run, and Northey slowed from a sprint to a trot. Dixie Walker, meanwhile, ran over from right field, picked up the ball, and threw it back to the infield, where Stanky caught it and threw home. Northey saw the ball coming and began running hard again, not sure if he'd hit a home run or not. The throw beat him to the plate and Northey was called out. A rumpus followed, with Eddie Dyer complaining that his team had been robbed. If not for the ump's signal, he said, Northey would have run all the way and beaten the throw.

The extra run mattered, because the Dodgers rallied for three in the bottom of the ninth. Reiser doubled, Walker doubled, Reese singled, Eddie Miksis singled, and the Dodgers hustled off the field, laughing.

After the game, Dyer and the Cardinals lodged a protest with Ford Frick. Five days later, Frick overturned the result of the game, giving Northey the home run and ordering the teams to replay the game. But in a sense, the victory had already gone to the Dodgers. They believed they had won the series, and for five days the newspapers all showed that their lead over the Cards had grown by a game. They were beginning to believe that they had luck on their side this time.

A day after the conclusion of their series with the Cardinals, the Dodgers took off on another long road trip. For all the reporters who had so far failed to update their readers on the progress of Branch Rickey's great experiment in integration, here was another opportunity. There were no great controversies to write about, and Robinson had nothing but time to sit and chat as the team's train rolled out of New York. Yet no one interviewed him.

Most of the ballplayers were on good terms with the men who wrote about them. They were not quite friends, but they were friendly. On occasion, a writer and his wife might go out for dinner or to the theater with a ballplayer and his wife. But the writers knew they would never join the inner circle. They accepted their status just as they accepted the unwritten rule that prevented them from writing about the private lives of the men they chronicled every day. As a result of that rule, newspaper readers in 1947 had no clue that pitcher Kirby Higbe's trade to Pittsburgh had been hastened

386

by hard drinking, carousing, and his malicious attitude toward Robinson. Nor did they have any hint that Hugh Casey, the overworked relief pitcher, drank and caroused just as much as Higbe did, and that he, too, had treated Robinson harshly in spring training. Only Dixie Walker had been fingered as an enemy of Robinson, but once the season got underway and it became clear that Walker and Robinson would have to coexist, the sportswriters never again mentioned the rift or explored its effect on the team.

They accentuated the positive in large part because they were conditioned to do so. The Dodgers were their meal ticket, not to mention their hotel ticket and their train ticket. The team picked up the full tab for the writers' travel expenses and plied them with lots of free booze on top of that. There was no contract stipulating that the journalists would treat the team kindly in exchange for services rendered, but the quid pro quo was clear: Don't bite the hand that pours your cocktails.

Most of the reporters covering the Dodgers were old-timers, men who'd been around since the days of Ruth and Gehrig. Baseball beats were cherished prizes, and reporters did not let go of them easily. But one young man who had broken into the ranks was beginning to change the way the old men approached the game. He was Dick Young of the *Daily News.* He came along at about the same time as Jackie Robinson, and while his contributions were more subtle, he, too, was something of a revolutionary. If anyone covering the Dodgers was equipped to pierce the fog and produce a story that went beyond balls and strikes, it was Young.

New York City had dozens of newspapers in 1947. It had papers for Italians, Jews, Germans, blacks, and Chinese. It had papers for Bronxites, Brooklynites, and Staten Islanders, for Republicans, Democrats, communists, working stiffs, and bluebloods. It had morning papers and afternoon papers. It had tabloids and broadsheets. A man stopping at his favorite newsstand might pick up *Il Progresso* and the *Post,* or maybe the *Jewish Daily Forward* and the *Times.* But there was only one newspaper that appealed to all corners of the city and every sort of person. There was only one paper that came close to claiming universal appeal, and that was Dick Young's *Daily News.* With a circulation of 2.4 million on weekdays and 4.7 million on Sundays, the *News* was far and away the best-read newspaper in the country. It was also one of the most fun. The saucy tabloid had grown up with Babe Ruth. The *News* recognized before most of its competitors that baseball players, covered in news ink, could become bigger-than-life heroes. It recognized, too, that sports went beyond politics, race, or religion. It united the city like nothing else and therefore sold papers like nothing else. The paper's blue-collar readers may have hated the *News'* Truman-bashing editorials, but they couldn't live without its sports section.

The *News* was the only New York City newspaper to pay its reporters' expenses on the road, in order to establish their independence and objectivity. Young was the paper's rising star. He was a city kid, born in Washington Heights, and full of New York's distinctive brand of arrogance. When he was very young, his parents divorced, and his father lit out for California. Young stayed in New York. Like Robinson, he was raised single-handedly by his mother, and, like Robinson, was taught to be ambitious, if not always polite. Though he wanted to go to college, he lacked the money. That was 1936, "the asshole of the Depression," as he called it, and he settled instead for the Civilian Conservation Corps, where he helped build a beach on Upper Cayuga Lake in upstate New York. One day his mother clipped an item from the *Daily News* and sent it to him. It said the newspaper would pay fifteen dollars a week to college graduates who wanted to be copyboys. The paper was swamped by applicants. Young wrote three times to the paper's managing editor, but he was rejected three times because he didn't have a college degree. On his fourth try, he was offered a job as a messenger, a job even lower in rank than copyboy. He took it.

Once the *Daily News* let him through the front door, Young knew what to do. He began sending wisecracks and tidbits to Jimmy Powers, the sports editor and columnist, who used them without giving the kid credit. Once, Young wrote a whole column on stickball and Powers ran it word for word under his own byline. Young didn't mind. He was collecting markers. Soon he got married and had a child. When some of the young copyboys got drafted, jobs opened up, and Young (deferred from military service because he had a family) began inching his way up the ladder of the sports department. In 1946, when the Dodgers beat writer left the paper to go to work for

Branch Rickey (not an uncommon occurrence), Young got his big break.

Before Young, the locker room had always been considered sacred, a place where ballplayers could be themselves, where they could say and do as they pleased without fear of reading about their behavior in the papers. Reporters watched the game, filed their stories, then joined the ballplayers for dinner at the hotel. Young changed that. He went into the clubhouse for interviews after the game. While that might seem like a modest reform, it proved groundbreaking. Suddenly, ballplayers were discussing in detail their hits and errors. Suddenly, they had voices. Suddenly, they were expected to be people, not just players, with opinions, feelings, and personalities.

Young wasn't afraid to offend the players, either. He drank with them at night, and while doing so picked up small details that enlivened his stories. He also added a bit of editorial comment to his stories, letting readers know when he thought someone had pulled a boneheaded play or no longer belonged in the majors. And he was never afraid to show his face in the clubhouse even after he'd written something inflammatory. The athletes were doing their jobs, he was doing his, and he expected everyone to be grown up about it. It didn't always work out like that. When Young described pitcher Clem Labine as gutless, Labine challenged the writer to a fight, offering to tie one hand behind his back. Young fled. "The ballplayers called him Poison Pen," recalled Jack Lang, who covered the Dodgers that year for the *Long Island Press*, "because he didn't hold back."

The differences between a Dick Young game story and another reporter's were subtle, but readers in the 1940s were connoisseurs of news ink. They appreciated Young's snappy verbs, his concise summary of key plays, and his perfect instinct for where a particular contest had turned. His stories conveyed a self-awareness and a dry sense of humor. After one game in which the Dodgers suffered a brutal defeat, he began by writing, "This story belongs on page three with the rest of the axe murders." After another game, he wrote: "Waldon Westlake, which is a baseball player and not a Summer resort, spent a good part of the afternoon clearing things up at Ebbets Field yesterday. In the first frame, he cleared the bases with a double."

A few years later, writers following in Young's footsteps would take his approach several steps further, becoming more snide, more confrontational, and more interested in showing off their stylish writing than in describing for readers what actually happened in the ballgames they watched. Not Young. "I'm not a writer, I'm a reporter," he used to say. In truth he was both. He covered his beat with dogged determination, but he also wrote with panache. Yet, somehow, day after day in the summer of 1947, he muffed what should have been the biggest and best story of his career. The road trip in July was but one example.

In 1946, the Dodgers had played less than smashingly away from Ebbets Field, finishing with a record of 40–38 on the road. Through the first half of the 1947 season, they were playing even worse on the road, with a record of 17–21. Given that the second half of their schedule was heavily weighted with away games, the pattern did not bode well for their pennant hopes. Yet on this road trip, the team played brilliantly, and no player was more brilliant than Robinson.

On July 22 in Cincinnati, the Dodgers and Reds were tied at one in the sixth inning when Robinson knocked a triple off the fence in left. After that, pitcher Red Lively of the Reds fell apart, and the Dodgers rolled to an easy win. The headline in the

Daily News went not to Robinson, however, but to Branca, who notched his sixteenth win of the season. The next day, Robinson singled, doubled, and scored a run in a 5–2 victory, but Young decided to make pitcher Hank Behrman the focus of his story. And so it went for twelve days and nights, as the team put together a thirteen-game winning streak. Robinson in that stretch scored sixteen runs (a whopping 21 percent of the team's total), banged thirteen hits, walked nine times, and hit two home runs, yet his name never appeared in a *Daily News* headline or in the first paragraph of a story. Some of this had to do with his style of play. He was the grease, not the gear, that made the team work. Some of it had to do with his personality, too. He never sought the spotlight. Nor was he an outgoing figure in the clubhouse.

While on the road in July, Young did find time to bang out a couple of feature stories, one of them about the contenders in the National League for the Rookie of the Year award. Even then, he managed to slight Robinson, rating his teammate Spider Jorgensen as the top candidate. "His legs are agile, his hands sure, and his bat has been cracking a crisp .300 or thereabouts all season," Young wrote of Jorgensen. As for

Robinson, he continued, "The Negro star's batting average is more than adequate [it was also a crisp .300 or thereabouts, although Young didn't mention it], but he is still learning his way around first base."

Did Young really believe Jorgensen was more valuable than Robinson to the Dodgers, or was some other factor at work? Many years later, Robinson said in an unpublished interview with Carl Rowan, his biographer, that he always felt Young was a bigot. A few years later, when writing about Roberto Clemente, Young developed a habit of quoting the slugger in phonetic English: "Eef I have my good arm, thee ball gets there a leetle quicker than he gets there." Others who knew the reporter said that while Young was ornery and opinionated, and never took much of a liking to Robinson, it was nonetheless a mistake to attribute his combativeness to racism. These two stubborn men, with more in common than they may have cared to admit, did not hit it off. "I am positive," Robinson said once, "that Dick wrote the way he did because he didn't particularly like me."

Young never revealed his feelings, but all season long he avoided writing meaningfully about Robinson. In his piece on Opening Day, he mentioned the rookie's bunting and base-running, but not his color. He explained the decision later by saying the first baseman hadn't done anything to merit special attention in his first game, which is like saying Neil Armstrong did nothing but plant a flag and collect rocks when he landed on the moon. In May, when the story broke that some of the Cardinals were threatening to sit out rather than play against Robinson, *Daily News* readers must have been stunned to see that Young didn't provide his version of events. Instead, they read a wire service account. When police said they were investigating death threats against Robinson, one of Young's colleagues, Hy Turkin, covered the story. The next day, in a big Sunday feature, Young weighed in with a long article on Pete Reiser's tendency to collide with outfield walls and the various merits and demerits of the cinder warning tracks that some teams were laying at the edges of their outfields.

He kept his eye on the action and, by and large, tried to treat Robinson the same way he treated the other Dodgers. In this case, unfortunately, that constituted a huge failure. History doesn't tell us what Young was thinking, only what he did, and he clearly didn't do enough, even by the standards of the 1940s, when sports writing seldom delved deeply into social commentary. He was too smart a baseball man not to know that Robinson was a better player than Jorgensen, and it seems too great a coincidence that he missed every important racially themed story over the course of the season. Whether the cause was racism or simple stubbornness, Young, for all his intelligence and for all his skills as a reporter, wasn't able to see past the events on the baseball diamond and make sense of them for his readers.

Fortunately, the events on the diamond were compelling. The Dodgers, though utterly exhausted and quite banged up, finished their road trip with twelve wins against six losses and a four-game lead over the Cardinals in the race for the pennant. The Giants and Braves were not far behind, but Brooklyn was in firm control, with a long stretch of home games ahead. Meanwhile, over in the American League, the Yankees were cruising to the pennant. If everything fell into place, New York City would have a subway series, Brooklyn versus the Bronx, the puttering, sputtering, underpaid Bums versus the high-powered, high-priced Yanks.

For Young, that was the whole story.

SEVENTEEN: THE UNBEATABLE YANKS

The 1947 Yankees had less muscle and less mystique than earlier editions. Outside of DiMaggio, the team possessed no stars of serious luminosity, and even DiMaggio was not playing with his usual shine. The war had left him weak and frail, like certain European countries, and suddenly vulnerable.

He'd had his worst season in 1946, hitting .290, with twenty-five home runs, as the Yankees finished in third place, a whopping seventeen games in back of the Red Sox. The doctors told DiMaggio he'd need surgery on his heel during the off-season, but the Yankee superstar kept putting it off, hoping the pain would go away. Some wondered if he would ever be the DiMaggio of old. The outlook was so bleak that Larry MacPhail, the Yankees' boss, offered DiMaggio to the woeful Washington Senators in a trade for Mickey Vernon. And if that weren't enough of a blow to DiMaggio's psyche, this must have been: The Senators declined.

DiMaggio was thirty-two years old. Even with his bad heel and his bad season in 1946, he remained baseball personified: calm and elegant, perhaps a little dull at times, and yet capable of moments of surpassing beauty. He was not only the game's greatest hero, but also one of America's biggest celebrities, bigger than many a movie star. The man had more hit songs written in his honor than some big-leaguers had hits. "Joltin' Joe DiMaggio" memorialized his fifty-six-game hitting streak ("Who started baseball's famous streak/That's got us all aglow?/He's just a man and not a freak/Joltin' Joe DiMaggio"). Soon to come was another tribute, this one by Woody Guthrie ("Joe Deemaggyoe done it again!/Joe Deemaggyoe done it again!/Clackin' that bat, Gone with the wind!/Joe Deemaggyoe done it again!").

Just now the great DiMaggio felt compelled to prove his greatness once again. It wasn't enough for him to play, or even to play well. He had to display the grace that had made him a legend and re-establish the Yankees as champions before his aura would be restored. Before the war, he had been baseball's finest center-fielder, capable of covering more ground more gracefully than anyone. Yet the heel injury jolted Joe in the worst way, shaking his confidence as it had seldom been shaken. At the same time, Ted Williams had staked his own claim to the title of baseball's top player, a circumstance that irked his pinstriped majesty. DiMaggio seldom boasted, yet he made clear that he had no love for Williams. When a sportswriter asked him once what he thought of Boston's slugging outfielder, DiMaggio replied, "Greatest left-handed hitter I've ever seen." When the writer pressed him, asking what he thought of Williams as an all-around player, DiMaggio repeated, "Greatest left-handed hitter I've ever seen."

The Yankees in '47, with a gimpy DiMaggio, looked like they might fare even more poorly than they had in '46. Tommy Henrich and Charlie Keller struggled at times with injuries. Larry Berra, referred to sometimes as Yogi, proved such a great liability as a catcher that the Yankees tried him in right field. Branch Rickey had once declared Berra too clumsy and slow to make it in the majors, despite his booming bat, and the rookie had not yet done much to prove that assessment wrong. Then there was George McQuinn, an aging refugee from the St. Louis Browns at first base; Snuffy Stirnweiss, a weak hitter, at second; Billy Johnson, shaky at bat and in the field, at third; and little Phil Rizzuto, a slick fielder but light on the lumber, at short. Looking over the team's marginal roster made DiMaggio all the more eager to get back to work. Five days into the season, defying doctors' orders, he told manager Bucky Harris he was ready to go.

In his first game, DiMaggio was steamrolled by Berra while chasing a fly ball in right-center. Yankee fans held their breath as the golden child slowly picked himself up from the grass. The Yanks started sluggishly, playing .500 ball, more or less, through April and May, as DiMaggio worked his way back into shape.

Harris was in his first year as manager of the team. He was a good man — calm, relaxed, and eternally patient. He'd started managing at the age of twenty-seven, leading the Washington Senators to their only world championship in 1924, followed by a pennant in 1925, but he had hopped from team to team ever since, with limited success. Harris had no trouble with his players — they loved him — but he had his hands full dealing with Larry MacPhail, the team's president, referred to in the newspapers as the red-headed wildman. MacPhail liked to have his hands on everything and his name in all the papers. He'd been making trouble all season, mostly for his former team, the Dodgers. First, he'd hired away two of Brooklyn's coaches. Then, by some accounts, he had gone after Durocher. When his attempt to lure the Dodger manager failed, MacPhail raised the stakes, filing complaints with the commissioner that eventually led to Durocher's suspension. MacPhail had once been Rickey's protégé. Now, the men were bitter rivals. MacPhail was everything Rickey wasn't — a drinker, a showboat, and, most notably, an opponent of baseball's integration.

Back in the summer of 1946, when Robinson had been playing in Montreal and Rickey plotting his strategy for introducing the majors' first black man, MacPhail had done his part to postpone the arrival. As chairman of baseball's new joint steering committee, he had been assigned to present a report to owners on the key issues facing the game. Tom Yawkey of the Red Sox, Sam Breadon of the Cards, and Phil Wrigley of the Cubs joined him on the committee. The "Race Question," as MacPhail put it, was one of their top concerns.

The question, as MacPhail defined it,

wasn't how to get black players into the game; it was how to defend the game against charges of discrimination coming from "political and social-minded drum beaters" who singled out baseball "because it offers a good publicity medium." He wrote that the supply of black talent was thin, in part because Negro-league players didn't receive proper training in the game's fundamentals. Integration of the major leagues, he continued, would harm Negro-league owners, put hundreds of black ballplayers out of work, and take money from the white team owners who rented their ballparks to the Negro-league teams. He saw a lot of problems and few benefits. And he threw in a subtle shot at Rickey. "Your Committee does not desire to question the motives of any organization or individual who is sincerely opposed to segregation or who believes that such a policy is detrimental in the best interest of Professional Baseball," he wrote. But, "The individual action of any one club may exert tremendous pressures on the whole structure of Professional Baseball, and could conceivably result in lessening the value of several Major League franchises."

With Kenesaw Mountain Landis out of the way, dead since 1944, some expected the path to integration to open up in a hurry. Jackie Robinson had already been signed to a minor-league deal, and at least a few owners had expressed interest in following Rickey's lead. In the end, MacPhail couldn't stop the Dodgers from taking on a black player, but he nevertheless had no intention of integrating the Yankees. To MacPhail, the Yankees were baseball's elite. They were morally as well as athletically superior. They didn't need black players, and they didn't want any more black fans than they already had. For years to come, the Yankee front office had a standard answer when asked when the team would sign its first black player: Not until they found a black man worthy of wearing pinstripes.

Branch Rickey wasn't the only one with reason to be angry at MacPhail. The Yankee players weren't all that keen on the boss, who had fired or forced the resignation of three managers in 1946, including the legendary Joe McCarthy. But the players' biggest gripe concerned what the newsmen referred to as MacPhail's Flying Circus. MacPhail loved planes, and he loved flying his players around anywhere they might help the team earn money. To make it possible for the Yankees to fly off in unplanned directions as the need arose, he tried to eliminate train travel as much as possible. But in baseball, traditions die hard, and many in the clubhouse began to complain that they missed the clackety old trains and the leisurely card games and bull sessions they allowed. Some of the men were scared of spending so much time in the air. Others didn't care for the hours wasted in airports waiting for bad weather to clear. Some began skipping the flights and arranging their own train travel. They also began skipping some of the charity events and dinners MacPhail asked them to attend. A dark mood, unusual for the mighty, first-class-all-the-way Yanks, descended on the team. MacPhail eventually gave in and allowed the players to go back to the rails, but he reminded them that they were still contractually bound to participate in promotions for the team.

One day in May, MacPhail sent a newsreel crew on the field before a game to take pictures of the Yankees as they posed with a group of soldiers. But the crew arrived late, after DiMaggio had begun his batting practice, and he and the other Yankees told the cameramen to get lost. MacPhail flipped. He issued a memo reminding his players of their obligations. He fined two players fifty bucks each and slapped DiMaggio for a hundred.

It proved a critical moment for the team. Fans all over the country backed DiMaggio in the dispute. In Buffalo, the Butler-Mitchell Boys Club collected $1.03 in pennies and mailed them to MacPhail to help pay the star's fine. It was just a first installment, they said. The Yankee clubhouse could have turned into a snake pit. Everyone on the team looked to DiMaggio to see how he would respond. The sportswriters waited, too, knowing the story would get bigger and juicier if DiMaggio squawked. But he didn't say a word. It was about that time he went on his first real tear of the season, hitting four game-winning homers in two weeks, and the Yankees started climbing toward first place.

Berra, out in right field, learned to let DiMaggio have all the running room he needed. Spec Shea, the rookie pitcher, discovered that if he could make opposing batters hit balls in the air, his center-fielder would always find a way to catch them. "It would be goin' over the shortstop's head, I'd say to myself: 'Get goin', Joe,' " he later told writer Richard Ben Cramer. "And I'd turn around and there'd be that big gazelle. Boy, he took them big strides, you know.

And when he'd catch it, he'd catch it just so easy. There was nothin' to it." But if Shea crossed his center-fielder, he'd hear about it. If he tried to pitch a man inside and went outside instead, DiMaggio would wind up leaning the wrong way, and then he would look foolish because he wouldn't get a good jump on the ball. DiMaggio hated being made to look foolish. Shea would catch hell. "And I'd say, 'Well, the ball got away from me,' " he recalled. " 'It shouldn't get away from you!' " DiMaggio would snap. " 'You're in the major leagues now. You're here. And this is where you gotta do these things perfect.' "

DiMaggio expected perfection from those deemed worthy of playing at his side. Perhaps the best and most important example in 1947 was Joe Page. Page was a pitcher with a great arm and a lousy head. He threw hard and hoped for the best, never knowing where the ball would go. If home plate were a moving target, he might have been the best pitcher in the league. He was certain that his teammates distrusted and disliked him, certain that his big-league days were numbered. He was demoted to the bullpen in 1947, but he got a promotion of another kind, becoming the road roommate to DiMaggio. Suddenly, Page found a focus for his frequently flustered mind. He became DiMaggio's shadow. He even started dressing like his roommate. He still went out to clubs. He still drank. But he wasn't such an ugly drunk anymore. He began gaining confidence, picked up almost by osmosis, courtesy of the Great DiMag.

One evening in May against the Red Sox, Bucky Harris called on Page in the third inning. There were 74,747 fans at Yankee Stadium that night, one of the biggest crowds ever to see a game anywhere. Bodies were packed three and four deep in the aisles. The Yankees were already trailing, 3–1, when Page came in. The bases were loaded with nobody out. Page threw three straight balls to Rudy York, then came back to strike him out. He followed with a strikeout of Bobby Doerr and got Eddie Pellagrini on an easy fly ball. He pitched the rest of the game without giving up a run as the Yanks came from behind for a 9–3 win. Had Page failed that day, had he thrown one more ball to York, reported the *New York Post,* he likely would have been out of a job, put on a bus bound for some minor-league town. Instead, he turned his season around, as did the Yankees.

Beginning on June 29, the Yanks went on the greatest streak ever seen in the American

League, winning nineteen straight, a record that would stand for a quarter-century. Pitching was the key to the run, as Yankee opponents scored little better than two runs per game over that span. When the streak ended in the middle of July, the pennant race was finished. In the middle of September they clinched the American League title.

Yet looking back, it was not clear how they had done it. Only DiMaggio and McQuinn would finish the season with averages better than .300, and DiMaggio's twenty homers were tops for the team. Tommy Henrich came through with a lot of big hits, and Berra and Charlie Keller supplied some pop off the bench. Rizzuto bunted well and played wonderful defense, and Billy Johnson enjoyed the best season of his career. Still, there was nothing terribly frightening about this lineup.

Likewise, the pitching was good, but not great. Allie Reynolds, who would finish the season at 19–8, with a 3.20 earned run average, was the team's ace. Reynolds, known as "The Chief," was probably the best athlete on the team, although he wasn't always in the best shape, and he hadn't yet learned some of the finer points of pitching. Reynolds was now discovering, as everyone in DiMaggio's world did, that expectations in the Bronx were higher than elsewhere. Throwing hard — and Reynolds threw very hard — was no longer enough. So he concentrated a little more and pitched a little better. In addition to Reynolds, Shea was having a great season, but he was a rookie, and rookies often tire at season's end. Spud Chandler, also terrific at times in 1947, turned forty in September and appeared to be winding down.

It was the newly invigorated Joe Page who carried the Yankees. Page appeared in fifty-six games, and forty-four times he remained in the game until it was finished, piling up 141 innings of work. It was a heavy load for a hard-throwing relief pitcher, but the more he pitched, the more his confidence soared. In 1946, he'd been error-prone and wild. Now, he went an entire season without making an error. He struck out 116 batters, walked only seventy-two, and permitted a mere thirty-nine earned runs.

Pitching wins championships, the saying goes. Thanks to Page — and thanks, indirectly, to DiMaggio — the Yanks had pitching. Once again, the Bronx Bombers were brimming with confidence as they marched toward the World Series.

EIGHTEEN: DIXIE WALKER'S DILEMMA

In July, reporter Clif Keane of the *Boston Daily* overheard a conversation between Dixie Walker and Jackie Robinson in the Dodger clubhouse. Walker was on the training table, having his shoulder rubbed, when Robinson ambled in and sat down nearby. Walker was the first to speak.

"You're improving a lot," the Alabaman said, according to Keane's transcript. "But there are a couple of things I might suggest to help you."

"I'd like to hear them," Robinson answered.

"Well, you're trying to pull the ball to left all the time."

On this score, Walker was right. Robinson had not yet mastered the art of hitting to the opposite field. A remarkable number of his batted balls went to the left side. Had it not been for his terrific bunting ability, teams probably would have shifted their

411

infielders from the right side to the left in the same way they shifted in the opposite direction for Ted Williams. Walker asked if Robinson had noticed a certain at-bat a night earlier. Robinson had been on second base after a double hit off Boston's Si Johnson. Walker, a left-handed batter, wanted to pull the ball to right field. That way, even if he hit a ground ball to second or a long fly to right, Robinson would have a chance to take the extra base. Walker got two good pitches from Johnson, called strikes, but they weren't where he wanted them. He was waiting for one on the inside part of the plate. He finally got what he was looking for and laced a single into right field. Robinson scored from second.

"It was the right kind of baseball," Walker said. "You want to think of that when you bat."

"Yes, I was wondering about those pitches when you let them go," said Robinson, who had a fine view of the strike zone from second base during Walker's at-bat.

The men went on talking nuts-and-bolts baseball for ten minutes.

Later, when Walker had gone, Keane approached Robinson.

"Then all this talk of bitterness isn't true?" the writer asked.

"It certainly is not," Robinson said. "I get all kinds of help from these fellows. I wouldn't be anywhere without it."

A few days later, a West Coast columnist, picking up on Keane's story, described Walker as Robinson's "best friend and chief adviser among the Dodgers." Rachel Robinson clipped the article and penciled the following comment in the margins: "Some sports writers fall for anything."

Years later, Robinson said that Walker was the only man on the team with whom he had no relationship whatsoever in 1947. It's possible that Keane invented the conversation between the two men, although it seems unlikely given that he reported the interaction immediately after the game and that no one challenged it at the time. What's more likely is that Robinson had so few encounters with Walker that he forgot about this one (and perhaps others) as the years went by. It was easy — and not just for Robinson, but for many writers — to make Walker the unvarnished villain and to omit evidence to the contrary. The relationship may well have remained frosty all season long, as Robinson suggested years after the fact, yet it's clear that Walker had accepted his black teammate, at least to an extent. From the start of the season to its finish he never criticized Robinson publicly for mistakes on the field. He never publicly questioned the right of black ballplayers to compete in the major leagues. And as far as anyone could tell, he never again spoke of organized protest. Faced with a dilemma, he decided to set aside his anger and play ball, which is all Robinson had asked in the first place.

Back in the spring, reporters had said Robinson would have a hard time surviving in the big leagues without Leo Durocher to stick up for him. They'd also said the Dodgers would never win without their fiery old manager directing the show. By now, however, the writers and players both were beginning to appreciate the understated charms of Burt Shotton. No one on the team was going to run through a brick wall for the new skipper (unless it was Pete Reiser, who never needed an excuse), but Old Barney was so gentle-natured and caring that it was almost impossible to dislike him. Not that the players didn't complain at times. There was a faint sense in the clubhouse that Shotton might be missing a few tricks, that he didn't strategize quite as carefully as Durocher had, that he wasn't always thinking ahead about how the action on the field might unfold. Some said he was hapless when it came to handling pitchers. Others simply considered the old man a sourpuss who tut-tutted and sighed dismissively when his players behaved immaturely. What was the point of playing baseball for a living, they wondered, if not to behave immaturely? But such concerns were trivial so long as the Dodgers kept winning.

"You fellas can win the pennant in spite of me," he'd told them at the start of the season, with typical honesty. "Don't be afraid of me as manager. I cannot possibly hurt you." Now they knew what he meant.

The better the Dodgers played in 1947, the more Shotton tried to shrink from the spotlight. "Put Burt on a bench in Central Park, give him a bag of peanuts for vagrant pigeons," wrote the *Brooklyn Eagle,* and he'd pass for the statesman and financier Bernard Baruch. But as the team began its march toward the pennant, Shotton would not be able to remain anonymous for long. Durocher, after eight years with the Dodgers, knew that managing a baseball team required two distinct sets of skills — managing the action on the field and managing the men at the center of that action. Durocher was especially good at getting the most out of each man on his roster. He understood that a manager closing in on a pennant needs to fine-tune his lineup. He has to rest certain players and test others. He has to help define players' roles so they'll know when and how they'll be expected to perform. He has to get the team to play with a combination of urgency and calm. He has to build confidence among those who have played poorly and award playing time to the bit players who might be asked to pinch hit or pitch in relief under the spotlight of the World Series. For Shotton, there were specific concerns to be addressed as well. He needed to nurse Pete Reiser back to health, keep Walker from breaking down, and figure out how to restore Hugh Casey to the form that had made him so effective in 1946.

The Dodgers, for all their success through July, remained an imperfect team, with weak pitching and not a single power hitter. Branca had emerged as a bona fide ace. Joe Hatten, in only his second year, was pitching almost as sharply as Branca, although he seemed to falter when facing the league's most talented teams. And Harry Taylor, fresh up from the minors, mixed a smoking fastball with a beguiling curve to give the team yet another reliable starter. Great defense — especially by Reese and Stanky

— helped calm the younger pitchers. In 1947, the average shortstop and second baseman in the league combined to make 9.85 outs per game. Reese and Stanky combined to make 10.41 outs per game. For the Dodger pitchers, that difference was huge because it meant they didn't need strikeouts to escape trouble. Pee Wee and the Brat were behind them, gobbling up balls that other players would never have reached.

But the two players most critical to the Dodgers' success were Robinson and Walker. Robinson by now ranked among the league's leaders in hits and runs scored, and he was tops in stolen bases. He was electricity. He made things go. Hitters throughout the Dodger lineup were getting better pitches when Robinson got on base. Walker, in particular, was having one of his finest seasons even as he approached his thirty-seventh birthday. Playing every day on creaky knees, he was no longer a great outfielder, but he remained a cunning hitter. Statistically, the most interesting thing about Walker's season was his on-base percentage, which would increase from .391 to .415 between 1946 and 1947. He and Reiser, the two men hitting behind Robinson, were both drawing more walks in 1947 than at any time in their respective careers. Walker grasped the game's nuances well enough to understand why. When Robinson got on base, pitchers got jumpy and made bad pitches. And when Robinson stole second, pitchers often walked the team's heavy hitters in order to set up a force play in the infield. That made it easier for Walker and others batting behind Robinson to drive in runs. With the end of his career fast approaching, Walker received a great gift from Robinson in 1947, a gift that would prove to be worth thousands of dollars the following winter when it came time to negotiate his next contract.

If Walker failed to appreciate all that Robinson had done for him in 1947, he was hardly alone. For his thirteenth birthday that summer, Myron Uhlberg received two tickets to see the Dodgers play at Ebbets Field. Myron had grown up a Dodgers fan the way some kids grow up farm boys or redheads: It had never seemed like a choice. The only thing different about Myron was that both his parents were deaf, which meant they found it difficult to follow the team and to cheer along with their son. When the Dodgers played important games, Myron would translate the Red Barber broadcasts into sign language for his parents, Louis and Sarah Uhlberg. Still, Myron felt he was missing something. He loved his father, but he longed to bond with him through baseball as so many of his friends did with their fathers.

The Uhlbergs lived in a third-floor apartment at 1648 West Ninth Street in Bensonhurst ("Bensonhoist," many residents called it). The only black people Myron ever saw were on the beach at Coney Island. But Louis Uhlberg took an unusually strong interest in Jackie Robinson in the summer of 1947. He felt a kinship with him because Louis, too, was an outcast, made to play without complaint by another society's rules. Jackie was called "nigger." Louis was called "dummy."

"It's not even baseball I'm interested in," he told his son, using sign language to explain why he decided to take his son to a game for the first time. "It's Jackie Robinson."

Myron was embarrassed at times by his father, who worked as a printer for the *Daily News.* But Myron, baseball glove in hand, felt no shame about stepping into Ebbets Field with his father one afternoon in July. Father and son walked through the marble rotunda, under the enormous chandelier, and out toward the bright green diamond, which was the most perfect thing Myron had ever seen. They found their seats on the first-base line. Myron was startled at first by the number of black people in the stands, particularly along the left-field line and in the bleachers. He had never seen so many in one place. Everyone at the ballpark dressed well — the men all in hats; the women in dresses. But the black men and women seemed even better dressed than the white. Myron asked his father why. His father said it was for the same reason that he dressed better than the other printers at work, and why his mother put on a nice dress to go to the supermarket. They had to overcome expectations.

The game began, and Myron soaked in its details: Robinson's dark skin contrasting with his white uniform; his dour expression; his roundhouse swing; his odd stride, which seemed to Myron slightly effeminate. As he watched, the boy came to think that his father wasn't following the action all that well. Nothing in the *Daily News* or in the sign-language evocations of Red Barber's broadcasts had prepared Louis for the action on the field. There were so many subtle movements, so many vivid sights. When Jackie Robinson came to bat, Myron used sign language to tell his father that most of the fans were cheering, but that there were a few hecklers, too. When his father asked what the hecklers were saying, Myron spelled out the word "coon."

That's when Louis Uhlberg got up from his seat and started shouting. Whenever he tried to speak, Louis's words were a jumble, as if his tongue and mouth were on opposite teams. Now Jackie came out as "Ah-gee!" Over and over he shouted: "Ah-Gee! Ah-Gee!"

Even by ballpark standards he was very loud. Nearby fans stared. Myron looked at his shoes. But over time, Myron got used to his father's shouting. And over even more time, Myron discovered that his father taught him an important lesson that afternoon. "It's not fair that hearing people discriminate against me just because I'm deaf," Louis Uhlberg told his son once. "It doesn't matter to me, though. I show them every day I am as good as they are." Many years later, Myron decided to write a children's book about his day at the ballpark. He called it *Dad, Jackie and Me.*

Robinson had maintained all summer that his success depended on his ability to play ball. If he hadn't played well enough, he knew, he would have wound up on the bench, like Larry Doby, playing only on occasion, and he would have remained largely invisible to the American public. Formally, the integration of the big leagues would have been achieved, yet in practice not much would have changed. By hanging on to his spot in the starting lineup, Robinson assured that people would see him every day, and that meant people would confront the reality of integration, not just the concept. Each time he played, tens of thousands came together to witness and participate in the reshaping of America. Sometimes the effects were as loud and clear as the roar of a crowd. At other times, however, they were so subtle as to go unnoticed until many years later.

On July 29 in St. Louis, he stepped to the plate for the 451st time as a big-leaguer. As he dug his right foot into the dirt beside home plate, thrust out his chest, and cocked his bat in anticipation of the first pitch, a smattering of racist cries fell around him. He ignored it, as usual.

It wasn't surprising, really, especially at Sportsman's Park, where black and white spectators had been segregated until 1944, that a few cranks in the cheap seats would holler angrily at baseball's leading black man. The surprising thing was what happened next. Slowly at first, then with a sudden burst, men and women began to stand and applaud for Robinson. Black fans started the spontaneous display of support, but white ones soon joined in, and the cheering and whistling grew louder and louder until it rolled across the crowded grandstand, squashing the voices of those who'd been booing a few seconds earlier. Robinson hit a routine fly to center field and returned to the dugout.

At another point in the same game, a couple of white men with standing-room-only tickets wandered into Section B of the grandstand, hoping to find a place to sit, and complained loudly that it seemed a shame to see so many good seats occupied by black men and women. That would never happen back in Tennessee, one of the men announced. A white man seated in the section looked up and said that if the Tennesseans missed home so much they should start walking in that direction. The Dodgers cruised to an easy win that day behind Harry Taylor's three-hit shutout, widening their lead over the Cardinals to an imposing eight games. Robinson's personal triumphs, however, were entirely symbolic: He went 0-for-5.

The next day, the Dodgers and Cardinals

played before another sellout crowd at Sportsman's Park. It may have been the best game of the season. It was certainly the wildest. And it went a long way toward convincing the Dodgers that luck was truly on their side for a change.

The Dodgers jumped to a 10–0 lead through four innings. It looked like Branca would coast to his seventeenth win of the season. But in the sixth inning, with two men out, the scorching sun sapped his strength, and he gave up four runs. Hank Behrman came on to pitch and held the Cardinals scoreless until the ninth. Again, it looked like a game the Dodgers couldn't lose. When Behrman got two outs to start the inning, fans all through the grandstand started making for the exits. But then the Cardinals managed four softly hit singles in a row. Hugh Casey came on in relief of Behrman and, as had been his habit of late, he made things worse. A pair of solid singles by Marty Marion and Del Wilber tied the score.

Down by ten, the Cardinals had fought back to tie it up. But in the top of the tenth, the Dodgers answered right back, regaining the lead with a Hermanski double and a Reese single. In the bottom of the tenth, Clyde King got three quick outs to secure the victory. The next day, with Branch Rickey watching the action, Brooklyn completed the three-game sweep. They were out in front of the National League pack now by ten games.

"But anyhow," the poet Langston Hughes wrote in his newspaper column, "this summer of our Lord 1947, the Dodgers are doing right well with Jackie Robinson at first. . . . And maybe if the Dodgers win the pennant, a hundred years from now history will still be grinning."

NINETEEN: THE FOOTSTEPS OF ENOS "COUNTRY" SLAUGHTER

Lawrence Douglas Wilder lived in Richmond, Virginia, in a two-story frame house with chickens, geese, and homing pigeons in the yard. He was poor, but poverty felt to him like a mild affliction. His family always had food on the table and flowers in the vases. If his parents had any trouble keeping the family housed and clothed, Doug, as everyone called him, didn't notice. In the summer of 1947, the St. Louis Cardinals were his biggest worry.

He was a huge fan. When he heard that some of the men who worked and loitered in the neighborhood barber shop were planning a trip to see the Cards and Dodgers play at Ebbets Field, he invited himself along. The others going were grown men who might have had good reason not to take along a kid, but Doug was persuasive — "the arguingest little man I ever saw," as one barbershop patron later recalled. Those powers of persuasion would take him a long way. In 1990, he would stand in front of the Virginia state capitol building and take the oath of office as governor, the first black man in America elected governor of a state. But at this moment, at age sixteen, he was low man on the barber pole. His arguments won him a seat in the car — the middle seat in the back of Dick Reid's shiny black Buick. The four men and the teenager departed early in the evening on a Tuesday, August 19, for the 330-mile drive to New York City.

Doug Wilder was the grandson of slaves, the seventh of eight children, named (with allowances for spelling) after the black poet Paul Laurence Dunbar and the nineteenth-century political figure Frederick Douglass. His father sold policies for Southern Aid Insurance, the nation's oldest black-owned insurance company. His mother raised the children. Black families in Richmond had their own schools, churches, rest rooms, drinking fountains, libraries, and playgrounds. Yet Doug had not given much thought to segregation — to how it would limit his options for college, how it would affect the friends he made, or how it might restrict his career opportunities. The other men in the car were making the trip to see

Robinson — to be witnesses to history — but Doug was interested only in watching his beloved Cardinals claw their way back into the pennant race. The Buick rolled into Harlem at daybreak, past Sugar Ray Robinson's famous night club, where the boxer's fuchsia-colored Cadillac sat spectacularly by the curb. "Wow!" said the kid in the backseat. After a stop for breakfast, it was on to Brooklyn.

Just when the Dodgers thought they had locked up the pennant, the Cardinals went on a terrific run, closing the gap. Their sluggers Enos "Country" Slaughter and Stan Musial were slugging again. The pitching remained shaky, but not as shaky as it had been earlier. The Cardinals came to Brooklyn saying they needed to win at least three of four, and Shotton agreed. "They have to beat us," he reminded everyone before the doubleheader that opened the series. "We don't have to beat them."

In the first game, the Cards sent Howie Pollet to the mound. They'd been resting the lefty for almost two weeks, hoping he'd be strong. But Pollet may have rested too much, because he had trouble with his control. His first three pitches were fastballs — high and outside, low and outside, high and outside. When Stanky finally saw a fastball on the inside half of the plate, he smacked it deep to left, about as deep as he was capable of smacking one. If not for a spectacular catch by Slaughter, who threw his body at the unpadded left-field wall to make the grab, Stanky probably would have had a triple. Robinson stepped next to the plate and hit a high fastball where even Slaughter couldn't catch it: into the left-field bleachers, for his ninth homer of the season. Later in the first inning Bruce Edwards's triple drove in the second run. The Cardinals came back with two runs in the second and two more in the third. In the fifth, Pollet once again lost connection with the strike zone, walking Stanky and Robinson to open the inning. The Dodgers scored five runs and cruised to the win.

The only other highlight came in the seventh inning, when the Cardinals put a man on base with one out and summoned Joe "Ducky" Medwick to pinch hit. Medwick, the gruff former Dodger, grounded to short and ran hard to first, trying to beat out the double play. He did beat the throw, but he also stepped hard on Robinson's left foot in the process. All season long, Robinson had struggled with his footwork around first base. Opponents complained that if he didn't learn to keep his foot off the middle of the bag he was going to get hurt. He was lucky this time to escape injury, and no one accused Medwick of trying to hurt the Dodger first baseman.

The Dodgers won the second game that night. The next day, though, the Cardinals clobbered Joe Hatten. Now they needed to win the final game of the series, played on Wednesday, August 20, if they wanted to get out of Brooklyn in no worse shape than they'd arrived. Each team sent its best pitcher to the mound: Harry "The Cat" Brecheen for the Cardinals, and big Ralph Branca for the Dodgers. Branca was throwing more innings than any Dodger, striking out more batters, and winning more games, on his way to becoming only the eighth player in the twentieth century to win twenty games by age twenty-one. If it had not been for Jackie Robinson's domination of Dodger news, Branca might have been the toast of New York City in 1947. He was young, smart, funny, tough . . . and seemingly cursed with bad luck.

Leo Durocher had picked Branca to start the opening game of the playoff series with the Cardinals in 1946. It was the first time in the history of the major leagues that a playoff had been needed to settle the pennant. A dozen photographers and fifty writers covered that game at Sportsman's Park, an entire nation watching, waiting to see which team would represent the National League in the first postwar World Series. Branca lasted less than three innings, undone by little more than bloop hits and walks, as the Dodgers lost it, 4–2. Ever since, Branca had been pitching like a man hell-bent on redemption, going deep into games, offering his service as a relief pitcher between starts, giving himself over entirely to the cause of getting another chance. He paid no attention to the long-term risks attached to such a heavy workload.

After a forty-five-minute delay for rain, Branca came out throwing gas, roughly one curve for every three fastballs, just enough slow stuff to keep the Cardinal batters guessing. The Dodgers scored first when Robinson ripped at a curveball and sent it flying for a double off the wall in left, scoring Stanky. Through seven innings, Branca threw no-hit ball. It was the second time in five weeks that he had held the Cards hitless for seven innings or more. While the big righty had a habit of throwing unhittable stuff for seven or eight innings, he also had a habit of getting clobbered in the late innings when his velocity slipped. The problem was that he relied almost entirely on his

431

fastball, and when he lost a few miles per hour on his pitches, or when batters got used to seeing him and began better timing their swings, he got in trouble. Still, reporters blamed the trouble not on his arm, despite the fact he was pitching a ridiculous number of innings, but on his head. "He just thinks too much," wrote Dick Young, "and when he thinks he presses." Branca may have been thinking too much when he finally gave up a hit to Whitey Kurowski in the seventh, but he got out of the inning with no further damage and went into the bottom of the ninth inning with a 2–0 lead. At last, when Branca walked two men and fell behind on a third, Burt Shotton signaled for Hugh Casey to enter in relief. Once again, Casey failed to close the deal. Ron Northey singled on a ground ball past the mound to drive in a run. Then Kurowski bounced a high grounder to Jorgensen, who misplayed the ball and let the tying run score. To extra innings they went.

As the game approached the three-hour mark and shadows covered the field, Doug Wilder and the barbershop quartet from Virginia remained firmly planted in their seats along the first-base line. Wilder was pleased to see so many black men and women around them, their voices rising in joyful noise — "Hit da ball, Jackie boy! Hit da ball!" — every time Robinson stepped to the plate. He was equally pleased to see that the white men and women seemed unbothered by their black neighbors. The Virginians' seats were so good they could hear the ballplayers cursing and see the hard lines of exertion drawn on their faces when they ran. Doug hoped to watch the Cardinals complete their comeback. The men from the barbershop didn't care who won so long as Robinson did something special. No one suggested leaving early to get started on the drive home.

In the top of the eleventh, with one out and Musial on first, up stepped Enos Slaughter. A native of North Carolina, Slaughter was one of the toughest men in baseball, and in this year of ups and downs for the Cardinals, he'd been one of their few reliable hitters. Slaughter played the way Stanky did — running hard on every play, chasing after every fly ball until it touched down, no matter how far out of reach it appeared to be. He'd become famous in the 1946 World Series when, after badly injuring his elbow in the fifth game, he stayed in the lineup for games six and seven. In the final game of the Series with the score tied, he led off the eighth inning with a single, broke for second on the next pitch, and kept running until he scored on a hit by Harry Walker. The play, which wound up winning the Series for the Cards, became known as the Mad Dash, and cemented Slaughter's reputation as one of the game's all-time greatest hustlers.

Now, with the chance to be a hero again, Slaughter took a big swing on a low fastball, hitting it sharply to first base. Routine play. Robinson fielded it, turned to second to see if he had a chance to throw out Musial, and thought better of it. He squeezed the ball and hustled toward first to get the sure out. Stepping on the bag, Robinson turned back toward the infield to make sure Musial had no intention of trying for third. But just as he turned, he felt a searing pain shoot through the back of his right foot, just above the heel. Slaughter, coming down the line hard and fast, had gashed him with his spikes. Robinson hopped in the air, grabbed the back of his ankle, and hopped some more before calling timeout. Slaughter put his head down and ran to the dugout.

The Medwick spiking a couple of days earlier had raised no ire, but to many in the press box and in the crowd of twenty-six thousand, it seemed plain that Slaughter had spiked Robinson intentionally. That's how Doug Wilder saw it. "I was shocked," he recalled, "because Slaughter was one of my heroes. . . . My heart sank." And that's how Robinson saw it, too. "What else could it have been?" Robinson asked immediately after the game, adding some foul language the newspapers couldn't repeat to say what he thought of the Cardinal slugger. "I had my right foot on the inside of the bag after taking his ground ball. He had plenty of room."

Doc Wender treated the lower part of Robinson's calf for slight contusions. "Jackie was lucky he wasn't maimed," the trainer said. "I can't understand how one ball player can deliberately do that to another one. He might have severed Robinson's Achilles' tendon and finished his baseball career." Harold Parrott, the team secretary, walked into the Cardinal clubhouse after the game to tell the visitors what he thought of Slaughter's conduct. Some of the men in the press box felt that Slaughter had stepped purposely on Robinson's foot. The only real question was whether he'd done it out of racial bias or pure competitive passion. Some suggested that Slaughter knew the Dodgers had no backup at first base and that his team's pennant chances would be helped by getting Robinson out of the lineup.

Robinson stayed in the game after the spiking. In the top of the twelfth, Kurowski slammed Hugh Casey's first pitch into the left-field stands for a homer, putting the Cards ahead by a run. Robinson led off the bottom of the inning with a sharp single to center and went to second on a sacrifice by Reiser. As he danced off second, hopping around now not so much in pain as in anticipation, Robinson must have been eager to exact his revenge. He may have been a bit too eager, in fact. George Munger spun from the pitcher's rubber and threw quickly to Marty Marion, who snuck in from behind and slapped the tag on Robinson for the second out of the inning. One play later, the game was over. Robinson was not quite the goat, but his blunder was a significant one.

Doug Wilder should have been happy. His trip from Richmond to Brooklyn had been everything he'd dreamed. His team had won a thrilling game. Yet something — he couldn't say just what — troubled him as he squeezed into the backseat of the car for the ride home.

"It took me the better part of the season for what really took place to visit with me,"

436

he recently recalled. "You know, you saw something here that was unusual. First of all you saw the acceptance of Robinson by the Brooklyn fans. Everybody there was terribly upset with the spiking. You saw the determination of Slaughter to spike him. He really went out of his way to do it, you could see. It just left me deflated for two reasons. One, to see this done to Robinson, and also to see it done by my team. I never got over that. Just amazing. I recognized later what he was going through. . . . I started thinking, taunts are one thing, epithets are another, but physical harm, intentional. . . . That, possibly, was Robinson's greatest moment, in showing how he would rise over and over to be the person he was. It wasn't an athletic thing, it was a human thing. 'I will show you I can rise over and above.' It's not a matter of forgiving you for doing it. It's a matter of saying, 'No matter, not withstanding what you did, it doesn't prevent me from being the man I am.'

"It was a tremendous lesson."

After splitting the four-game series with the Cards, the Dodgers went on a nice run, taking three in a row from the Reds, two of three from the Pirates, one of two from the

Cubs, and then three in a row from the Giants. The end of their passage was in sight.

Way back in April, few of baseball's cognoscenti had given them a chance. Even as the season unfurled, skeptics remained. The Dodgers didn't hit as well as the Cardinals or pitch as well as the Giants. In fact, the 1947 Dodgers in most departments appeared to be worse than the 1946 team that had settled for second place. Spider Jorgensen was an improvement over the platoon that had manned third base in 1946, but Jorgensen's batting average, on-base percentage, slugging average, and fielding percentage were all almost identical to the league averages. He was hardly the difference between second place and first. And the team's core players — Reese, Reiser, Walker, and Stanky — played no better in '47 than they had in '46. In fact, their numbers on the whole slipped slightly. The team's pitchers were worse in '47, too, allowing about one hundred more runs than they had the year prior. How did they do it?

Jackie Robinson would finish his rookie year with a .297 batting average, twelve home runs, and forty-eight runs batted in. His .427 slugging percentage (total bases divided by at-bats) ranked third among the team's regulars. His 125 runs scored were second-best in the National League — and far and away best among the Dodgers. His twenty-nine stolen bases and twenty-eight sacrifice bunts were tops in the league. Fourteen times he had bunted for hits, and, though no records were kept on bunted hits, that, too, was almost certainly a league-leading quantity. Only four times, reported *The Sporting News,* had he bunted and failed to either advance a runner or reach base safely. Robinson led the Dodgers in games played (151), at-bats (590), hits (175), total bases (252), doubles (tied with Walker at thirty-one), and home runs (tied with Reese at twelve). He was also hit by pitches nine times, which was more than anyone on the team. In recent years, the statistician Bill James has developed a useful statistic called Runs Created to measure how much a player contributed to his team's offense. The formula is:

$$(\text{Hits} + \text{Walks}) \times (\text{Total Bases}) / (\text{Plate Appearances})$$

Robinson and Walker tied for the team's lead with ninety-four runs created. Ed Stevens and Howie Schultz, who had shared the first-base job in 1946, created only sixty-six runs combined that year. Thus Robin-

439

son gave the Dodgers at least twenty-eight more runs than they'd had the year before from the first-base position. The true number of runs Robinson delivered was certainly higher, but it would require a statistical formula of much greater sophistication to account for the sacrifice bunts, the stolen bases, and the general frazzling of pitchers' nerves that occurred whenever Robinson stepped on the diamond. But one sure measure of Robinson's impact can be seen in the performance of his teammate Pete Reiser, who usually batted behind Robinson in the Dodger lineup. As Robinson made pitchers edgy, Reiser stood at the plate ready to take advantage. Before 1947, he drew walks in only about 9 percent of all his trips to the plate. But in 1947, he increased that number to almost 15 percent. In 1946, he had hit only .277, with a .361 on-base average. In 1947, getting more fastballs thanks to Robinson, he hit .309, with a career-best .415 on-base average, despite complaints of suffering vertigo on and off after his collision with the outfield wall.

A lot changed between 1946 and 1947. The Dodgers got a new manager, a new third baseman, and some new part-time outfielders. They lost a couple of pitchers and added a couple. Such variables make it impossible to measure the impact of a single player. But Dixie Walker, who had his biases, to be sure, offered this assessment: "No other player on this club with the possible exception of Bruce Edwards has done more to put the Dodgers up in the race than Robinson has. He is everything Branch Rickey said he was when he came up from Montreal."

As Branch Rickey began fine-tuning his roster for the World Series, pitching remained the priority. Late in August, he made an intriguing move, paying fifteen thousand dollars to the Memphis Red Sox of the Negro American League for Dan Bankhead. The lanky right-hander could do it all, the newspapers reported. He threw a scorching fastball, hit the ball hard and often, and ran with fantastic speed. Though he had been preaching for several years now that black ballplayers needed time in the minors to get acclimated, Rickey suddenly changed his mind and sent Bankhead directly to the Dodgers, making him the majors' first black pitcher.

In America, few achievements confer more glory than reaching the big leagues. Survey a hundred high-reaching men and it's a good bet that ninety or so will tell you they dreamed of being big-leaguers before they ever gave a thought to being senators, college presidents, or brain surgeons. In the Bankhead family of Empire, Alabama, no one was imaginative enough to dream of making the majors, but it was practically a given that the males in the family would play professionally in the Negro leagues when they weren't mining coal. When Dan joined the Dodgers, his brothers Sam, Garnett, and Fred were all firmly planted in the Negro leagues, and brother Joe was preparing to start his career. Sammy Bankhead was the most talented of the brood, and had he been born a couple of years earlier (he was thirty-one in 1947), he might have been the brother chosen first. Sam could field any position on the diamond. He had a great arm, good speed, and decent power. Playing mostly as a shortstop, he developed a reputation as a leader who made everyone on the diamond play more sharply. He would have been a valuable asset to any number of big-league teams, even if only as a utility player, but he missed out, just barely. Some say Sammy Bankhead became the inspiration for Troy Maxson, the tragic hero of *Fences,* August Wilson's devastating play about a former Negro-league player. Like Maxson, Sammy Bankhead retired

442

from baseball to become a garbage collector. He would look back on his career with both pride and a pulsing feeling of resentment at the fame and fortune he'd been denied. If Robinson represented the ultimate manifestation of the American baseball dream and Sammy Bankhead its dark underbelly, brother Dan fell somewhere in between. He was the second-most-talented athlete in his family, the fifth black man chosen to play in the majors, and, at that moment, the lowest-rated member of the Brooklyn Dodger pitching staff. But at least he had been given a chance.

"Call me if I can help you about anything," Robinson told his new teammate — and his new roommate for road trips — on the day they met at Branch Rickey's office.

"I guess I'll be calling you tonight," Bankhead replied.

Some writers had warned that violence might erupt if a black pitcher threw too far inside and hit a white batter. Given Bankhead's great fastball and his occasional control problems, it was far from a hypothetical matter. But the next day, when Bankhead plunked Wally Westlake of the Pirates, Westlake didn't say a word. "It was as though he had been hit by Joe Gluttz," wrote Dick Young. "No precipitous incident.

No fuss. No nothing." Unfortunately for Bankhead, "no nothing" also described the quality of his pitching that afternoon and for much of the remainder of the season. The righty surrendered ten hits in three and a third innings as the Dodgers suffered a blowout loss. It was one of the most brutal debuts anyone had seen in a long time. Only one thing made the afternoon less than a total disaster. In the second inning, facing Fritz Ostermueller, Bankhead belted a two-run homer to left, making him only the twenty-first player in the history of the game to homer on his first trip to the plate as a big-leaguer.

"It was just one of those days," he said after the game. If nothing else, he had already mastered the big-league cliché.

Before issuing World Series tickets, the Dodgers had to make one more trip to St. Louis. Only a Cardinal sweep of the three-game series would delay an order to the print shop, and even then the delay would likely be temporary. Back in Brooklyn, fans were so excited about this chance to finish off the Cards that hundreds gathered at Ebbets Field to stare out at an empty ball field and listen to Red Barber and his partner, Connie Desmond, broadcast the action over

444

the public address system. It was as if they'd all come out to worship.

In the first game in St. Louis, played on the evening of September 11, Robinson was stepped on yet again. This time Joe Garagiola wielded the spikes. In the bottom of the second inning, with a man on first, the Cardinal catcher swung at the first pitch, a fastball up and away, producing a routine ground ball to short. Garagiola ran hard to first, trying to stay out of the double play, and caught a piece of Robinson's foot on the bag. The press made no mention of whether Robinson's foot was in the middle of the base or safely by its side. Neither did the reporters speculate this time whether there was intent to harm, an odd omission given the recent dustup over Slaughter. Robinson's shoe was torn, but he suffered no injury.

The next inning, Robinson came to the plate with two outs and two men on, the Cardinals leading 2–0. Before the first pitch, he turned and said something to the catcher about their contact the inning prior. Garagiola was a tough kid from an Italian section of St. Louis known as Dago Hill, twenty-one years old, still trying to prove he could make it in the big leagues, and he liked to run his mouth. Robinson made him nervous. Whenever the Dodgers' speedster got on base, Garagiola called fastball after fastball, looking for easy pitches to handle, never mind that his pitchers were more likely to get knocked around. "He made all catchers nervous," Garagiola said of Robinson in an interview decades later. "A lot of games I wished I could have bought a ticket instead of being where I was."

This was one of those games. Garagiola may have made a crack about Robinson's color. Robinson said he did, Garagiola said he didn't. Whatever was said, both men became incensed. Garagiola rose from his crouch to more effectively tell Robinson how he felt. Robinson stepped in Garagiola's direction in order to offer a rebuttal. Quickly, the umpire, Beans Reardon, stepped between them. While Reardon and Garagiola went at it, Robinson stepped back and clapped his hands. He appeared to laugh. That only made Garagiola angrier. For a moment, it looked like the men might fight. Clyde Sukeforth, the Brooklyn coach, rushed from the dugout to pull Robinson away. Finally, everyone cooled off and the game resumed. Robinson swung at a belt-high fastball and popped out to Garagiola to end the inning.

The fracas with the Cardinal catcher had

two effects. In the short-term, it made an angry man of Robinson — never a good thing for Dodger opponents. In his next trip to the plate, Robinson said nothing to the catcher. He stepped into the box, worked the count full, and then swung at another belt-high fastball. This time he banged it deep into the left-field seats to tie the score. As Robinson crossed the plate, Eddie Stanky, who did not believe in showing up opponents by celebrating on the field, allowed himself a rare display of emotion. He grabbed Robinson's hand and gave it a vigorous shake, then let go and slapped his teammate's back.

At that very moment, back in New York, forty-five hundred fans were watching a Negro-league doubleheader at the Polo Grounds, New York Cubans versus Newark Eagles. Suddenly, at a moment of no import in the game, the crowd began to buzz, and then roar. Men stood and danced in the aisles. "I bet Robinson just a hit a home run," someone in the press box said. A minute later, news of Robinson's blast came across the wire service ticker. Robinson's fans at the Polo Grounds had heard it first on their portable radios.

The long-term consequences of the Garagiola-Robinson spat were less predict-

447

able, and beyond the imagination of anyone involved. In 1984, a Chinese-born American named Bette Bao Lord published a slender book of fiction intended for young readers. She called it *In the Year of the Boar and Jackie Robinson.* The autobiographical story describes Shirley Temple Wong's passage from China to America, and her adjustment to life in Brooklyn in 1947. Shirley doesn't know English and makes few friends — until she discovers Jackie Robinson and baseball, and learns that America really is the land of opportunity. If Robinson can find acceptance among the Dodgers, Shirley decides, then she can manage to fit in at Public School Number 8. A staple of elementary-school classrooms, *In the Year of the Boar and Jackie Robinson* has been read by countless hundreds of thousands of children. The book, which singles out Garagiola for his attack on Robinson, has haunted the former ballplayer since its first publication, establishing him as a bigot in the minds of a generation that never saw him play and never heard his enchanting television and radio broadcasts. When Garagiola's grandchildren read the book, they were stunned, asking him, "Was that you, Papa?" Why had he hated Jackie Robinson, they wanted to know.

"Look," he said recently, his voice breaking at times, "Jackie was a firebrand. Even in '47, he was a competitor. You're fighting for the pennant, and who cares what color he is. . . . He said something to me. I said, 'Why don't you just hit!' And then here comes Sukeforth. I've lived with this thing unfairly. It was a little bit of jockeying to break his concentration, that's all. . . . It wasn't even an argument. . . . You just don't know the grief and aggravation this has caused."

The Dodgers went on to win the game, and two of three in the series. Robinson went 6-for-13 with three walks and a stolen base in the three games. Again and again, he made life miserable for the Cards. In the final game, the Cardinals were threatening with two out in the eighth inning. Robinson chased after a twisting foul pop. When he reached the lip of the Dodger dugout, no more room to run, he hurled his body down the steps and stabbed at the ball with his glove. As Robinson leaped, so did his teammate Branca, leaving his seat on the bench. The ball plopped into Robinson's glove just as Branca reached Robinson. Branca threw his arms around Robinson's waist and tackled him on the infield grass, preventing what might have been a nasty tumble onto

449

the concrete floor of the dugout.

As the Dodgers jogged off the field, they rushed around to congratulate Robinson on one of the season's great catches, and to praise Branca for another. No one was more impressed with Branca's grab than Robinson. Six months earlier, he wasn't sure anyone would have cared enough to break his fall.

The rest of the road trip, through Cincinnati and Pittsburgh, felt like a coronation tour. "Hail to Those Dodger Bums!" the *Post* declared in its headline of September 15. Dick Young wrote that Robinson's clutch play down the stretch had wiped out the "last bit of passive but ever-apparent resentment" some teammates showed toward the black ballplayer. "With each valuable contribution by Jackie, in almost every money game on this decisive Western swing," the writer continued, "the barrier of precedent dwindled and the warmth of acceptance grew to the point, where, today, it can be at last honestly said: Robinson is a member."

The trip brought one more accolade: *The Sporting News,* baseball's bible, named Robinson the recipient of its second Rookie of the Year award. The newspaper, which earlier in the season had only grudgingly accepted integration, now bragged of its progressive approach. "In selecting the outstanding rookie of 1947," wrote J. G. Taylor Spink, *The Sporting News* sifted and weighed only stark baseball values. That Jack Roosevelt Robinson might have had more obstacles than his first-year competitors, and that he perhaps had a harder fight to gain even major league recognition, was no concern of this publication." Even so, the newspaper did not quite attain a perfect state of colorblindness: "He's 'Ebony Ty Cobb' on Base Paths," read the second deck of the story's headline.

Meanwhile, *Time* magazine began putting together a cover story on Robinson. Brooklyn fans made plans for "Jackie Robinson Day" at Ebbets Field, with gifts that would include a new Cadillac sedan, a television console so heavy it required four men to carry, a portable radio, a gold pen and pencil set, a gold watch from Tiffany, an electric broiler, a set of cutlery, and a check for $168 to help defray the taxes on all the gifts. Plans were being made for a Jackie Robinson movie and a Jackie Robinson vaudeville show. Off-season banquets honoring the athlete were in preparation across the country, organizers hoping that if the trophies and accolades were large enough the great man might be induced to appear in person. On top of all else, the Harlem Globetrotters extended an offer of ten thousand dollars for Robinson to play with the team in the off-season.

"It's been a long time since we've had one man in the league who has an upsetting effect on every infield whenever he gets on base," said Charlie Grimm, manager of the Cubs. "Robinson makes 'em all squirm. After all, he takes such a good lead that you got to make a play for him. You've got to try and pick him off. He sets up the play himself and there's no choice but to make him take back a step or two." Grimm compared the Dodger rookie to Johnny Leonard Roosevelt Martin, better known as "Pepper" during his playing days with the Cardinals in the 1930s, another fellow who "just loved to get on base for the confusion it would create."

All the attention and accolades coming Robinson's way were nice, wrote Jimmy Powers in his newspaper column, but what Robinson really deserved was a bigger payday from the Dodgers. If Branch Rickey loved his first baseman as much as he claimed, Powers wrote, the boss would nullify his $5,000 contract and write a new one for $25,000. Even then, Robinson would be a bargain. By Powers's estimate, the Dodger rookie had sold at least $100,000 in tickets.

In 1947, the Dodgers pulled 1.8 million fans into their snug little park, more than any team in the history of the National League had attracted to that point. On the road, they drew even more — almost 1.9 million, which was also a record for the league. Yet while Powers and many others assumed that the bulk of the credit belonged to Robinson, it's not entirely clear they were right. Big crowds followed Robinson everywhere he went in 1947, but they also showed up in the places he didn't. As researcher Henry Fetter has noted, while attendance for Dodger games both home and away increased 10 percent from 1946 to 1947, attendance for National League games not involving the Dodgers increased 19 percent. It's possible that Robinson brought new waves of fans to the game and that those fans embraced all the action, not just Dodger games, but there was probably more to it than that. What likely happened is that the strong economy gave fans extra spending money, and they chose to splurge on baseball because it was not too great an indulgence, well within the working man's budget, and because the National League

453

had a lot of evenly matched teams in 1947, which meant fans in almost every city held out hope long into the summer that the home team might win a pennant. And there was one more thing: Baseball made people feel good. It connected them with simpler times, and now, with Robinson on the scene, it also offered them reassurance that the country was capable of adapting to the changing world.

Even so, Robinson's rookie year marked the start of a steady slide for Brooklyn baseball. No matter how well the Dodgers played in the years ahead, never again would the team approach the level of popularity it enjoyed in 1947. Brooklynites were loading their cars and moving to Long Island. They would always love Dem Bums, but in the years ahead they were much more likely to love them from out in da burbs. Then came television, and suddenly fans had one more reason not to go back to Brooklyn. Nineteen-forty-seven would long be remembered as a season of beginnings, but it was a season of endings, too.

It was Friday morning, September 19, when the Dodger train sighed to a stop on Track Thirteen at Pennsylvania Station, half an hour late. Three thousand fans were there to greet the team. "Our Bums will make bums of the Yankees," read the banner held aloft by one of the flock. The Dodger Symphony was there, blowing horns and rattling drums. Brooklyn borough president John Cashmore took advantage of the moment to announce that the following Friday, September 26, would be Brooklyn Dodger Day, with a big parade, a pep rally on the steps of Borough Hall, and gifts for all of the team's players and coaches. The Dodgers were home. Brooklyn was all set to celebrate its first pennant since 1941.

"There's no use going across the East River today to look for Brooklyn," Arch Murray of the *Post* wrote. "It isn't there. It's floating dreamily on a puffy, pink cloud, somewhere just this side of Paradise. Flatbush is reeling in mass delirium. Canarsie is acting like on an opium jag. The Gowanus is flowing with milk and honey. Because Next Year finally came."

As the Dodgers stepped down onto the train platform along Track Thirteen, some of the less recognizable players mixed with the crowd and escaped, their hats pulled over their faces. Not Robinson. As he walked toward a phone booth, eager to call his wife, some five hundred people — most of them men, most of them white — moved with him. He took off running, got to the phone booth ahead of the crowd, and slammed shut the accordion door. When he finished his call, half a dozen policemen rescued him, forming a circle, and, like the front line of the UCLA football team, clearing a path. Robinson took off for the IND subway line, where several pursuing fans begged for the privilege of paying his five-cent fare. At last, he reached his train and climbed aboard. And, still, dozens of giddy admirers trailed him. They squeezed into his subway car, their destination of little matter, happy enough just to be along for the ride.

Robinson didn't mind. The Dodgers were winners. He was going home to his wife and son.

"I'm tickled silly," he said.

TWENTY:
SHADOW DANCING

Robinson had no trouble sleeping now. The early-season anxiety that had caused him to gnash his teeth and toss in bed had passed. He drifted off every night to the whisper of Jack Jr.'s short breaths and woke most mornings to the same pleasing sound. As he waited for the World Series to begin, Robinson, for the first time all year, seemed to relax. When the Dodgers paraded through Brooklyn, he rode in a convertible, waving to the crowds lined up along Flatbush Avenue and Fulton Street and smiling confidently. When the motorcade reached Borough Hall, only the two most popular men on the team — Robinson and Walker — were invited to address the enormous gathering, estimated at more than one hundred thousand. Robinson smiled again, assured the fans that the Dodgers would beat the Yankees, and quickly stepped away from the microphone.

Mallie Robinson flew in from Los Angeles to watch her son play in the World Series. So did Rachel's mother, Zellee Isum. Neither woman had seen Robinson play big-league ball, neither had been to New York, and neither had been on an airplane. They held hands as they soared east. Also arriving in time for the Series were Jackie's sister, Willa Mae; his brother Mack, the former Olympian; five of Mack's friends; and Jackie's former pastor and mentor, the Reverend Karl Downs. Jackie and Rachel had no room for guests in their apartment, so the mothers stayed with Florence and Lacy Covington in their big brownstone on Stuyvesant Avenue, a short walk from their children and their grandson.

At last, Jackie and Rachel had babysitters — a sudden abundance of them, in fact — and they took advantage. The Dodger players and their wives organized a couple of parties before the start of the World Series. Though the Robinsons had been excluded from the team's social events earlier in the season, they were invited now. The rest of the Dodgers couldn't ignore them anymore, and Jack and Rachel felt enough a part of the group that they wanted to share the celebrations.

Rachel Robinson had not grown up in the

world of athletics. All of it was new to her. Now she was watching top athletes at the peak of their games, poised at what promised for some to be a defining moment. The intensity of the emotions fascinated her. Significant money rested on the outcome of the competition. The winners of the Series would get about $5,800 each, the losers $4,000. For men making $5,000 or so a year, it might mean the difference between an apartment and a house, between living with one's parents and moving out, between working at a gas station and owning one. But it was more than the money that electrified the air at these Dodger parties and at practices leading up to the competition with the Yankees. For the players, there was a sense that they were each about to do something bigger than they'd ever done, something that would mark them for life and forever link each one of them to the others.

Hotels all over the city were booked solid as men and women from around the country funneled into New York. For black fans, Harlem's Hotel Theresa became the hub. Fay Young of the *Chicago Defender,* prowling in search of stories, jotted down the names of 134 prominent black out-of-towners who'd arrived at the hotel in time for the first game. There were Negro-league baseball executives from Chicago, a doctor from Mississippi, an attorney from Detroit, a college president from Florida, a police detective from St. Louis, and on went his list. Eighteen Cadillacs were parked outside the hotel, Young reported, nine bearing southern plates. Not since the heyday of Joe Louis had the Theresa seen such action. Scalpers were getting $30 or more for tickets with a face value of $6 each, and $10 for standing-room tickets originally priced at $4 each — "all to see this great boy Robinson in action."

In the black newspapers, the contest between the Dodgers and Yankees was often described as a contest between Jackie Robinson and the Yankees, which sounded a lot like David and Goliath. Given the scale of the mismatch, such a description was not entirely unfair. The Yankees were the most intimidating team in baseball, especially come October. The mere sight of the Bronx Bombers in their pinstriped uniforms trotting out onto the grass at jam-packed Yankee Stadium frightened opposing teams, putting them at a disadvantage before the first pitch.

Shotton warned his Dodgers before the

Series not to buy into the Yankee hype. Ruth, Gehrig, and Combs would not be suiting up, he assured his players, only Joe DiMaggio and an assorted cast of supporting characters named Stirnweiss, Lindell, and McQuinn. These Yanks were solid, but Old Barney saw no reason to get worked up. "Why, we could put on the Yankee shirts ourselves," he said.

All season long the Dodgers had defied expectations. They'd beaten the Cardinals, picked by the experts as baseball's next dynasty. They'd fought off the Giants, the most powerful home-run-hitting team in history to that point. They'd acquitted themselves nicely against the Braves' great hurlers Spahn and Sain. And on top of everything else, they'd served as lab rats in a sociological experiment unlike anything the game had ever seen — and lived to tell about it. If ever a team deserved to be called champions, Shotton said, it was the Dodgers. He not only predicted victory, he very nearly assured it.

But almost every one of the writers analyzing the Series seemed certain the Yankees would make quick work of the Brooklynites. "The New York Yankees should win the World Series from the Dodgers in five games," wrote Rud Rennie of the *Herald*

461

Tribune. "With luck and good pitching, they may win in four straight and get it over with." The newspapermen were hard-pressed to find even one category in which the Dodgers had an edge, although some of them did mention that the Dodgers were good at drawing walks — in other words, standing there and not swinging the bat.

Brooklyn's biggest weakness by far, as it had been all season, was pitching. Branca was the staff ace, but he was a fastball pitcher whose fastball was good, not great, and he had a reputation for losing his composure at critical moments in big games. What's more, the twenty-one-year-old righty had shown signs of tiring at season's end. The writers said he was the sort of pitcher a disciplined team like the Yankees would destroy. Then there was little Vic Lombardi, who had neither an overpowering fastball nor a dangerous curve and got by instead on cute stuff, trying to outsmart opponents. The Yankees were an experienced bunch, and not easily outsmarted. Dodger pitcher Joe Hatten was another question mark. Though he won seventeen games, he left everyone scratching their heads about how he'd done it. He had no great arm and no great guile. That left Hank Behrman (sent from Brooklyn to Pittsburgh

462

in an early-season trade but returned to the Dodgers as damaged goods, his throwing arm apparently shot), Clyde King, and Rex Barney to tame the Yanks. No doubt the Dodgers would rely heavily on their reliever Hugh Casey. But Casey, after a brilliant year in 1946, had struggled through much of 1947 and complained of fatigue down the stretch. Also, no one knew how he would respond upon revisiting his most traumatic baseball moment, a calamitous loss to the Yanks in game four of the 1941 Series.

To the Yankees, Robinson represented the wild card. Reese might slap a lot of base hits and perhaps steal a base or two. Dixie Walker might bang a few doubles off the wall. But only Robinson could take over a game, so the players and managers spent a great deal of time talking among themselves about how to contain him. "Only one thing remains to make 1947 the most memorable year in Jackie Robinson's life," wrote Leonard Cohen of the *Post*. "If he can help the Dodgers win the World Series from the Yankees next week, his cup of happiness will be filled to overflowing." Pitchers were reminded that the Dodgers' flashy rookie was much more destructive on the bases than at the plate. When Robinson danced on the base paths, pitchers lost their composure and nervous catchers called for a steady diet of fastballs. And a steady diet of fastballs made even Spider Jorgensen look like Ted Williams. Whatever you do, the Yankee pitchers were urged, don't walk Robinson. Make him hit his way on base. Don't put a loaded gun in the enemy's hand.

The Yanks had an experienced pitching staff, with Allie Reynolds their top starter and the brilliant Joe Page working in relief. Though their pitchers tended to walk batters and give up a few home runs, on the whole they were not easily unnerved. The thing that worried them most was the man to whom they threw: Yogi Berra, the sweet, daffy catcher. Berra was a short, barrel-shaped kid of twenty-two years, who swung at pitches way out of the strike zone and somehow banged them with gigantic force. He was a St. Louis native who had grown up with Joe Garagiola, his best friend. While the Yanks expected Berra to be a star, they were still trying to figure out where to play him. Catching seemed too complicated for him. They tried him in the outfield, but he showed an almost laughably poor ability to chase down fly balls. Berra knew it, too. He also knew that he had the great DiMaggio, who covered more ground than Rand Mc-Nally, next to him in center field. DiMaggio sensed the rookie's reluctance and took command, ranging farther and farther into the rookie's turf, until Berra learned that the most important part of his job was to stay out of DiMaggio's way lest the team's star trip over him and break a leg. But Berra's outfield adventures had come when one or another of the Yanks' regular outfielders had been hurt. Now, Tommy Henrich and Johnny Lindell were healthy, which meant Berra would have to catch if he hoped to play. Robinson intended to test him immediately.

It was a cool, sunny day that looked every bit like summer and yet felt unmistakably like fall. A sharp wind blew, forcing turned collars and tucked chins. When the first pitch of the World Series was thrown at one-thirty in the afternoon on September 30 — a called strike from Spec Shea to Eddie Stanky — it was seen by more people than any event in history. There were 73,365 fans packed into Yankee Stadium, the biggest paying crowd ever to see a World Series game, and another 25,000 or so watching from nearby rooftops. But even that enormous audience was minuscule compared to the one watching on television. In 1946, NBC had run coaxial cables between New

York, Washington, D.C., Philadelphia, and Schenectady, New York, thus establishing the nation's first primitive television network. The network was now getting its first important test. There were an estimated fifty thousand television sets in use in metropolitan New York on September 1, 1947, about 15 percent of them in bars. Across the four wired cities, broadcasters estimated that 3.9 million people would watch the Series on television. That number may have been exaggerated by officials trying to show television's growing grip on the nation. An RCA 630 TS, with a ten-inch screen, was priced at about $375, putting it off-limits to many. Even so, there was no question that this World Series marked a momentous event in the industry's evolution.

For weeks leading up to the first game, newspaper ads trumpeted new model television sets — big wooden boxes with gray screens no bigger than a lunch box — as the best way to witness the world's most important events. "Thousands will see the World Series by PHILCO TELEVISION," boasted a big advertisement in the *New York Times.* "Winston Television Guarantees: A Front Row Seat at The World Series . . . with the new 1947 DuMont Teleset," read another ad. Bars all over New York hurriedly installed new sets. One watering hole in Flatbush made headlines by installing two — one for Dodger fans, one for Yankee fans. At the Park Avenue Theatre, where *Frieda* was showing on the big screen, a little screen was set up in the lobby so fans could step out during the movie to check the baseball action. When Judge Samuel S. Liebowitz heard that jurors in his Kings County courtroom were threatening to walk out on the trial of a cabdriver accused of rape because they didn't want to miss the first game, he called a recess, sent a member of his staff to buy a television set, and set it up in his library for all but the defendant to watch. When President Truman was asked by reporters if he'd have time to attend a game, he said no, but he would try to catch a few innings on television. A few days later, Truman issued the first televised presidential address from the White House, asking Americans to give up eating meat on Tuesdays and to eliminate eggs and poultry on Thursdays in order to conserve the world's food supply and help save the starving millions in Europe. The president said nothing about whether World Series hot dog sales should be curtailed.

So the big event began with a called strike from Shea to Stanky, then a routine fly ball to left, followed by another first: the sight of a black man stepping to the plate in a World Series game. Twenty-two men worked the cameras, microphones, and cables around Yankee Stadium, and now the entire crew turned its attention to capturing Robinson's image. New, more powerful camera lenses brought the game closer to television viewers than ever — closer even than the view afforded from box seats. For the first time, personalities and emotions went on electronic display. For the first time, a player's intensity, his anxiety, or his glee could be discerned by viewers. It was, unquestionably, the start of something big.

"To the individual before a television screen," wrote R. W. Stewart of *The New York Times* that fall, "a beaten pitcher is more than a stooped figure trudging off the mound; a base-line coach is something other than a gesticulating shape; no matter what player is being televised, he takes on a character beyond that visible from the stands. The added keenness of the cameras brings a viewer as far 'inside' baseball as a spectator can go." Long shadows cast by Yankee Stadium's walls and light stanchions bisected the infield, however, making much of the action difficult to discern on the small screen, despite the new camera lenses. Stewart, sensing the new medium's potential, wrote that "it would not be too far-fetched to believe that television might be brought into consideration in the construction of any future ball parks." But if the cameramen had difficulty working on this bright day of long shadows, they seemed to have no problem picking up Robinson, whose dark skin made him the most immediately recognizable man on the screen, even in the shade.

Seated in the grandstand for the game were Leo Durocher, Laraine Day, Johnny Mize, Ted Williams, Ty Cobb, Happy Chandler, Ford Frick, Danny Kaye, Herbert Hoover, New York governor Thomas E. Dewey, U.S. senator Irving Ives (who, as a member of the New York State Assembly, coauthored the Quinn-Ives Act, which helped push Branch Rickey to integrate the Dodgers), Mayor William O'Dwyer, John Foster Dulles, and Secretary of State George C. Marshall. But it was Babe Ruth, heavy coat buttoned to his neck, coughing into his hand between puffs on a big cigar, who drew the most attention.

Robinson had a smile on his face as he stepped to bat for the first time. Mallie Robinson strained to see her son, her view blocked partially by latecomers still settling into their seats. Robinson was an anxious hitter at times, swinging at so-so pitches, confident in his ability at least to foul them off. But today, despite the added pressure, he was patient. Five pitches went by, and he waved at none of them. On the sixth pitch, finally, he swung and hit a foul ball. On the seventh pitch, a chin-high fastball, he drew a walk, the first man on base in the '47 Series. As Robinson jogged to first, a reporter watching Mallie Robinson thought he saw her lips form the words, "Thank God."

In the days before the Series, even as the Yankees plotted their strategy on how to handle Robinson, Berra had repeatedly told reporters he wasn't worried. "I know all about Robinson from playing against him in 1946 when I was with the Newark club in the International League," the rookie catcher said. "Robinson never stole a base against me. He tried twice but each time I nabbed him. We know all about him. We know when he's going to run and when he's going to bunt."

To which Robinson had a response: "If I had an arm like that," he said, "I wouldn't talk about it."

The Dodger book on the Yankees said they could run on Berra. His arm was decent, despite Robinson's comment, but his mechanics were horrible. Some writers, half joking, said Berra hadn't made an accurate toss to second since throwing a ball from home plate into a barrel set up on the bag during a midseason stunt. Now, on Shea's second pitch, Robinson took off, kicking up clumps of dirt with every long, pigeon-toed stride. The pitch was high and outside, a good one for Berra to handle. He rose from his crouch, caught the ball, stepped, and threw, all with pretty good form and pretty good speed. Clearly, he'd been ready. But the throw from home to second is 127 feet and three and three-eighths inches. This time, Berra's throw fell about two feet short. It skipped into shortstop Phil Rizzuto's waiting glove a fraction of a second late. Robinson hooked his foot around the soft white bag as umpire Ed Rommel spread his arms to signal safe.

Now, as Shea worked on Reiser, Robinson hopped off second, eager to make more mischief. Reiser slapped a hard grounder back through the middle of the infield. Robinson had a perfect view. He must have thought the ball would get past Shea, or else he was going on contact, because he bolted for third before he could see where the ball was going. Shea, falling to his right, made a

471

great catch on one hop. He turned, saw Robinson headed for third, and cocked his arm to make the throw. Robinson, caught, slammed on the brakes, the entire weight of his body planted in his right foot. Without wasting a step, he reversed direction and began to head back toward second. Shea lowered his arm and ran right at Robinson, exactly as a pitcher is taught to do in a rundown such as this one. As Shea closed in, Robinson stopped again, and, like a halfback, faked with his head and shoulders, as if he were going to head for third again. Shea froze. Now Robinson had a little working room, and he used it to make a dash for second. Shea had seen enough. He tossed the ball to Rizzuto, who was standing on second base. As the ball flew over his head, Robinson reversed direction yet again, his lips spread, teeth clenched. As he caught the ball Rizzuto started chasing after Robinson. Robinson ran as fast as he could toward third. No time now for more trickery. Though momentum was in his favor, it took the shortstop seven full strides to catch up, and he slapped the tag on Robinson's rear end. By the time Rizzuto managed to stop and turn around, Reiser had dashed safely into second. Robinson had made a mistake by breaking for third on the ground ball, but he had redeemed himself by keeping the Yankees so busy with his "hithering and thithering," as one writer put it, that Reiser could advance into scoring position. When Dixie Walker punched a fly to short left and Johnny Lindell lost it in the sun, Reiser dashed home with the first run of the game. The Dodgers had the lead, and Robinson to thank for it.

In the top of the third, the score remained 1–0 in favor of the Dodgers when Robinson came to bat again, this time with two outs and none on. Shea was pitching well, but he wasn't overpowering anyone, and the Dodgers thought it was only a matter of time before they cracked him. Though he had finished the regular season with a record of 14–5 and a 3.07 earned run average, Shea was just a rookie. He'd been inconsistent over the course of the season, starting strongly, tiring in the summer's heat, as rookies so often do, and then finishing with a burst of strength. The right-hander threw a mean curve and a decent fastball, but Bucky Harris had probably chosen him to start the first game of the Series for another reason: The Dodgers had never seen him pitch. Once again, Robinson was patient. He worked the count full before drawing another walk, then jogged to first base and

473

began dancing in the shadows. Four times Shea threw to first base, trying to keep Robinson from getting a big lead. At least one of his throws was close enough to make Robinson belly-flop back to the bag. With each throw, Dodger fans cheered more loudly and Yankee fans grew more tense. Shea, in at least one writer's description, appeared to be flustered. As he stood atop the pitcher's mound, trying to decide whether to go after Robinson one more time or pitch at last to Reiser, he dropped the ball and watched as it landed in front of his foot and rolled down the mound. The umpire called a balk and awarded Robinson second base. Shea picked up the ball and slammed it angrily in his mitt.

From second base, Robinson began his routine all over again, taking a huge lead and trying to draw a throw. Shea obliged and unleashed a terrible peg. If it hadn't struck Robinson's foot, it might have rolled into the outfield. By now, Robinson's rooters at Yankee Stadium were delirious. Before a huge crowd, with millions watching on television and many millions more listening on the radio, he was putting on a dazzling show. "For the first time in my life," wrote Willard Townsend, a black union leader, describing how he felt watching Robinson torment the Yankees at that moment, "I really understood what was meant by the much used expression 'as American as apple pie and baseball.' " That wasn't just a baseball player out there, he wrote, it was "democratic promise" running the bases.

Through four innings, Robinson electrified the crowd, and Branca, the starting pitcher, held the Yankees without a hit. His fastball was humming. His curveball was sweeping in big, fat arcs. He seemed entirely untouchable until the fifth inning, when DiMaggio hit a ground ball deep in the hole between short and third. Reese made a nice play but threw too late to get the out. Suddenly, Branca's perfect game was gone, and so was his confidence. From the Yankee dugout, coach Charlie Dressen, formerly of the Dodgers, seized the opportunity and began heckling the pitcher. "You'll go wild!" he shouted. "You'll go wild!" Branca did. He walked the next batter on four pitches and hit the batter after him, loading the bases. Then, facing Johnny Lindell, he threw a sloppy curve that drifted too far over the plate. Lindell bashed it for a two-run double. Rizzuto came up next and drew a walk on five pitches, loading the bases yet again. Now Bobby Brown came on to pinch hit for Shea. When Branca threw two pitches out of the strike zone, Shotton had seen enough. Branca was finished. In came Hank Behrman. As Branca walked off the field and Behrman walked on, Robinson stood with hands on hips and lips pursed, his face a picture of sheer disgust.

Now Behrman, the pitcher who had been wanted by neither Brooklyn nor Pittsburgh and who had amassed a hideous earned run average of 6.25, found himself with a chance to make everyone forget about his dismal regular-season performance. In 1946, he'd come from nowhere to help pitch the Dodgers into playoff contention. But even with his terrific record that season, he'd never inspired much confidence among teammates or fans. Almost every player, even the marginal ones, was honored with a special day in that era. Fans would take up collections and buy cars and radios and watches for their heroes. But on Hank Behrman Day, fans came up with less than one hundred dollars. They bought him a savings bond, which Behrman dropped to the grass in disgust. Now, at last, he was being paid a compliment: With the opening game of the World Series on the line, he was Burt Shotton's first choice out of the bullpen.

Behrman, however, did not drape himself in glory. He completed the walk to Brown, forcing in a run, and gave up a two-run single to the clutch-hitting Tommy Henrich. By the time the inning ended, the Yankees had a 5–1 lead. In the sixth, with Joe Page now pitching, Robinson reached on a fielder's choice and later scored, but Page finished off the Dodgers by holding them scoreless over the final two innings.

After the game, Branca stormed around the locker room, cursing himself. "You don't think I was scared out there, do you?" he asked at one point, sounding like a man who was trying hard to convince himself.

Robinson, however, remained defiant. It had been a sloppy game, with a lot of misplayed balls in the outfield on both sides. Stripping off his uniform, he declared the outcome a moral victory for the Dodgers. "This is one defeat that gave us confidence," he told Dick Young. "We've heard so much about the 'Mighty Yanks' and they didn't show us a thing. Not a thing. We handed them the game."

The weather was cool again for game two, although the winds were less biting. Another big crowd filled Yankee Stadium. For the second day in a row, reporters noted that black fans were not out in great numbers, probably because tickets were so hard to come by, and because, at Yankee Stadium, so many tourists and business executives gobbled up seats with little concern over paying scalpers' prices. Burt Shotton showed up for the game in a new suit and a bright new bowtie. When asked if he intended for the new duds to change his team's luck, he responded with characteristic verbosity.

"Yes," he said.

In the first inning Robinson went down swinging against Allie Reynolds. He singled to left and drove in a run in the third inning. He doubled in the eighth inning. He was, of course, the first black player ever to do each of these things. Otherwise, the Dodgers had nothing to brag about. In fact, they looked like real bums, not the lovable kind. Pete Reiser, never the same after hitting the wall earlier in the season, tripped, fumbled, stumbled, and fell all afternoon in the outfield. Eddie Stanky dropped an easy throw at second on what might have been a double play. Robinson let a bunted ball roll under his glove and into right field (the official scorer generously decided not to charge him with an error). Relief pitchers Behrman and Rex Barney each threw costly wild pitches. When it was all over, the Yankees walked off with a 10–3 win.

Only once in the history of the World Series had a team overcome a two-games-to-none deficit. Now, as the competition moved to Ebbets Field, gamblers put the odds at six-to-one in favor of the Yankees. The headline of Red Smith's column read "Finis for Dodgers."

TWENTY-ONE:
"WE AREN'T AFRAID"

Ebbets Field held fewer than half as many fans as Yankee Stadium — roughly thirty-two thousand to seventy thousand. The celebrity lineup in the stands also fell off dramatically as the Series moved to Brooklyn. The actor Danny Kaye was on hand for game three, as was former heavyweight champ Gene Tunney, and the publisher Henry Luce. Ted Williams showed up at the ballpark, too, but he didn't have a ticket and couldn't talk his way past the turnstile boys so he repaired to a nearby tavern to watch the game on television. The Yankees got an even ruder reception upon arrival, their team bus pelted with eggs as it rolled down Flatbush Avenue. Bucky Harris announced that the mighty Yankees would henceforth travel by subway.

The *Brooklyn Eagle* tethered an eight-column headline to the top of its front page that read: "We Aren't Afraid."

It was a beautiful day, with pale blue skies and mild temperatures. Every seat was occupied, but Dodger fans were quieter than usual. Despite the *Eagle*'s proclamation, Dodger fans had begun to fear that the Yankees were simply too much for their team. For game three, both teams sent pitchers of uncertain ability to the mound. The Yankees tried Bobo Newsom, age forty, who had come up with the Dodgers in 1929 and subsequently pitched for the Cubs, Browns, Senators, Red Sox, Browns (again), Tigers, Senators (again), Dodgers (again), Browns (for the third time), Senators (for the third time), Athletics, Senators (for the fourth time), and now the Yankees. Newsom was a goofball, overweight and past his prime, but he'd been brilliant for the Tigers in the 1940 World Series and better than expected since joining the Yanks midseason. With a two-game lead, Harris could afford to take a chance. Shotton, however, could not. Unfortunately, every pitcher in the Dodger rotation represented a gamble. Shotton put his money on Joe Hatten, who won seventeen games in 1947, although all but one of the victories had come against teams with losing records. He was another one of those Dodgers, like Cookie Lavagetto or Eddie Miksis, who probably would have been

481

stuck in the minors if he'd been part of the Yankee organization. He owed his career in large part to Branch Rickey's bargain-hunting. This low-cost approach to team building worked fairly well most of the time — at least until the Dodgers had to face a powerhouse like the Yanks. Robinson admitted to feelings of gloom before the third game, but it helped to be back at Ebbets Field. In Brooklyn, the Dodgers believed, anything could happen.

After Stanky grounded out to the pitcher in the first inning, Robinson woke the cautiously quiet crowd, scorching the first pitch he saw from Newsom on a line drive to center field. By now, Berra had been benched. Even with a two-game lead in the Series, Harris couldn't stand watching Robinson humiliate his young catcher anymore. Sherm Lollar took over behind the plate, playing in only his fortieth big-league game. With Reiser batting, the count went to three balls and a strike before Robinson decided to test the new man behind the mask. He broke for second and slid in safely as Lollar's throw bounced through Rizzuto's legs. When Robinson saw the ball get away, he leaped to his feet and took a couple of steps toward third. Stirnweiss, backing up the play, grabbed the loose ball and flipped it to Rizzuto. Robinson tried to dive back to second, but Rizzuto dove, too, and tagged him out. When Reiser walked, he, too, tried to swipe second. This time Lollar rifled a perfect throw. Reiser was not only out, he tore a ligament in his ankle and eventually had to leave the game. The Dodgers were off to a rough start.

In the second inning, however, the team's offense exploded, and instantly changed the dynamic of the Series. After Walker grounded out, Hermanski walked, Edwards doubled, Reese singled, Jorgensen flew out to center, Hatten singled, and Stanky doubled. That was it for Newsom, who wasn't fooling anyone with his slow curves. In came Vic Raschi, a rookie right-hander with a blistering fastball. Robinson greeted him with a sharp single to right, sending Stanky to third. Furillo, replacing Reiser, smacked a double to score Stanky and Robinson. Walker grounded out to end the inning, but by then the Dodgers had a 6–0 lead and Ebbets Field was buzzing with laughter and loud voices.

Hatten took a 9–4 lead into the fifth inning, but when Lindell walked and DiMaggio homered to make it 9–6, Branca came on to pitch in relief. He escaped the fifth, but gave up a run on two doubles to open the sixth. Then he walked two batters to load the bases. Shotton decided to let Branca work his way out of the mess, and Branca did, getting Billy Johnson to pop to Stanky for the third out.

In the seventh, Berra, hitless so far in the Series, pinch hit for Lollar and creamed a fastball over the scoreboard in right, the first pinch-hit homer in World Series history. Just like that, the Yankees had pulled to within a run. A game that should have been a breeze suddenly turned tense. To protect his lead, Shotton went to one of the worst pitchers on his staff and yet the one he counted on most: big Hugh Casey. At last, Casey would get the chance to make amends for one of the game's most ignominious moments. It had happened back in 1941 — at about four-thirty in the afternoon on October 5, to be precise. The Yankees were ahead two games to one in the World Series, but the Dodgers were three outs away from tying it up. Going into the ninth inning, Brooklyn led by a run, 4–3. Casey, twenty-seven years old at the time, got two quick outs. One more and the Series would be even. Up to the plate stepped Tommy Henrich. Casey threw a ball, then two called strikes. Henrich fouled off the next pitch and watched two more balls float by. Full count. With all his pitches working beautifully that afternoon, Casey decided to throw a curve (or a spitball, as some have long contended). The pitch arrived low and inside, where it was almost impossible to hit and yet too good to lay off. Henrich swung and missed. For a glorious moment, it looked as if the game had ended, but the pitch was a little bit too low and inside for catcher Mickey Owen, who couldn't get his mitt around it. As the ball rolled behind Owen's right foot, Henrich ran to first, safe on a strikeout and a passed ball. The game continued, and Casey unraveled. DiMaggio singled, Charlie Keller doubled, and the Yankees piled on a couple of extra runs for good measure, winning the game 7–4, then taking the championship in five games. Owen and Casey never heard the end of it.

Now, leading off the eighth, Casey stared in again at Henrich. Henrich walked, and Lindell singled, and Dodger fans moaned as DiMaggio strolled to the plate. Casey could have pitched around DiMaggio and gone after McQuinn, the next batter, but that wasn't his style. Like the best of all bullpen stoppers, he was a gunslinger, and he remained a gunslinger despite his shaky start this day and despite his shaky history.

DiMaggio looked "bored and contemptuous" as he waited for the first pitch, according to Red Smith, who further noted that Ebbets Field was so quiet "you could hear a pretzel drop away off in Casey's saloon."

Casey bent a curve over the outside corner for strike one. He threw another curve wide for a ball. And then he zipped a fastball up and in. DiMaggio, expecting a curve, tried to check his swing but couldn't do it. He grounded into a double play. From there, Casey cruised. It was the longest game in World Series history to that point, exhausting fans through three hours and five minutes, and it ended with a desperately needed 9–8 win for the Dodgers.

In the fourth game, on October 3, Brooklyn's Harry Taylor pitched against the Yankees' Bill Bevens at Ebbets Field. Each team by now had severely drained its supply of starters. Had there been a day off in the World Series schedule, it's likely that neither of these men would have been given a chance. Taylor had a bum arm and Bevens had long-running difficulty throwing strikes. On a warm and lovely afternoon, fans settled in for what they expected to be another high-scoring contest.

If Dodger fans had their doubts about

Taylor, he moved quickly to confirm them. In the first inning he gave up two singles and a walk while getting nobody out. After eleven pitches, he was replaced by Hal Gregg, yet another pitcher of questionable talent. But baseball is a game of surprises, and Gregg supplied a nice one for Dodger fans. He pitched out of the jam created by Taylor, limiting the Yankees to one run in the first inning and another in the fourth.

Bevens started almost as badly as Taylor. He walked two Dodger batters in the first, one in the second, one in the third, two in the fifth, one in the sixth, and one in the seventh. Yet every time he got into trouble, the Yankees rescued him with brilliant defense. In the first inning, Stirnweiss scampered deep in the hole behind second base to take a hit away from Reese. In the third, Lindell made a spectacular tumbling dive in foul ground to get Robinson. In the fourth, DiMaggio hauled in a long drive off the bat of Hermanski. In the fifth, the Dodgers did scratch out a run on two walks, a sacrifice, and a ground-out, but Bevens escaped further damage by striking out Robinson to end the inning. In the eighth, Henrich leaped high against the scoreboard in right to take extra bases away from Hermanski again. And in the top of the ninth,

Lindell planted his rear end against the left-field fence to catch a long fly ball hit by Edwards. Somehow, amid all those walks and long flies, Bevens, owner of a miserable 7–13 record in 1947, had managed not to allow a single hit. The Yankees led by a score of 2–1. With two more outs, Floyd Clifford "Bill" Bevens would become the first man in history to pitch a World Series no-hitter. His approaching glory took fans by surprise. All afternoon he'd been on the brink of disaster. Now he was on the brink of immortality.

The next batter, Carl Furillo, drew a walk, the ninth of the day for the Dodgers. Al Gionfriddo ran for him. Gionfriddo was the extra man tossed into the deal on May 3 when Branch Rickey sent Kirby Higbe and four bit players to Pittsburgh for cash. At the time, the joke was that Gionfriddo, who worked as a firefighter in the off-season, was included only because Rickey wanted someone to carry his money from Pittsburgh to Brooklyn. He'd seen little action all year, but he hustled out to first base representing the potential tying run.

Bevens got Jorgenson to foul out. One out to go.

With pitcher Hugh Casey due to hit next, Shotton looked down his bench and spotted Reiser in uniform. Before the game, Reiser's foot hurt so badly he hadn't even taken batting practice. He'd spent much of the game in the whirlpool. Now he said he was ready to go. "All right, Pete," Shotton said.

The count to Reiser was three balls and a strike when Shotton took a huge gamble, signaling for Gionfriddo to try to steal second. Gionfriddo took off, but he stumbled and got a bad jump. As he dove headfirst for the bag, he expected the tag to hit him at any moment. But luckily for Gionfriddo and the Dodgers, Berra was catching again. His throw was horrible — too high and much too late. A good throw — even a mediocre one — probably would have had Gionfriddo. It would have sewn up not just the no-hitter but also, for all practical purposes, the World Series. Instead, the Dodgers survived. And now they had the tying run on second base.

Harris made the next move: He ordered Bevens to walk Reiser intentionally. By putting the winning run on base he violated one of baseball's fundamental commandments, but Harris thought his pitcher would have better luck with Stanky. Also, with a man on first, the Yankee infielders would be able to step on first, second, or third for the force play on a grounder.

Shotton countered by sending Eddie Miksis to run for the gimpy Reiser. Then he called Stanky back to the dugout, sending in the little-used Cookie Lavagetto as a pinch hitter. It was only the second time all year Shotton had sent in a pinch hitter for Stanky, and even some of the men in the Dodger dugout were taken aback. Earlier in the season, Stanky had broken up Ewell Blackwell's bid for a second consecutive no-hitter. Though he didn't have any power, he almost always made pitchers work hard to get him out, and given Bevens's wildness all day, Stanky at the very least seemed like a good bet to draw a walk. Lavagetto was a decent hitter, but he had managed only eighteen hits all season. It seemed incomprehensible that he would be Shotton's choice with so much on the line. And yet up walked Lavagetto, underweight and gimpy, bothered by chronic charley horses and a torn Achilles tendon.

The Yankees figured he could no longer catch up with fastballs, even ninth-inning fastballs from an exhausted man who had thrown 134 pitches on the afternoon. Bevens made up his mind he would pound him with nothing but hard stuff.

As he stepped to the plate, Lavagetto assumed one of the least-daunting stances in all of baseball, his body curved like a question mark, his head tilting listlessly toward home plate. Robinson stood in the dugout, waiting to see if he would have a chance to hit. In the stands, women clasped and unclasped their hands. Men edged forward in their seats, crossing and uncrossing their legs. Bevens threw a fastball up and in. Lavagetto swung and missed. The crowd released a collective sigh and went through the clasping and unclasping, the edging forward, the crossing and uncrossing all over again. Lavagetto collected himself. Robinson watched. Lavagetto knew that Bevens was going to throw nothing but fastballs, and he knew the pitcher would probably try to bust him up and in again, because that's where he always had the most trouble. Bevens inhaled, checked the runner at second, turned quickly back to the plate, and fired. It was another fastball, out over the plate. Lavagetto grimaced and swung. The shot flew high and far to right field. Henrich went back to the wall but couldn't get it. The ball bounded off the sign for Gem Single-Edged Razor Blades and ricocheted back onto the field. Henrich chased after it, bobbled, and threw . . . too late. Gionfriddo ran home. Miksis ran home. Lavagetto went to second. Robinson was among the first out of the dugout, hugging Lavagetto and punching him playfully on the side of the head. Then cops, ushers, hot dog vendors, and fans cascaded onto the field and mobbed him. With one hit, the Dodgers had a 3–2 win. Call it efficient or call it ugly; it didn't matter. The Series was tied.

"MIRACLE STRIKES FLATBUSH," declared the *Brooklyn Eagle*.

"Out of the mockery and ridicule of 'the worst World Series in history,' " Dick Young wrote, "the greatest ball game ever played was born yesterday."

Said Robinson in the locker room, apparently with a straight face: "We had it all the way. We just wanted to give 'em a thrill."

The Dodgers had looked horrible in the first four games; their inning-long offensive outburst in game three and Lavagetto's game-four lightning bolt were the only brief exceptions. Yet they stood now, incomprehensibly, perhaps even undeservedly, just two games from the championship.

In game five, they looked awful again, managing just four hits and one run against Spec Shea. Aaron Robinson, who had been in his manager's doghouse for reasons unclear, replaced Berra as catcher, and the

Dodgers never attempted a stolen base. Though their offense was anemic, the Dodgers kept the score close, and went into the bottom of the ninth trailing just 2–1. Then, when Bruce Edwards singled to open the frame, the crowd began to stomp and stir and buzz, much as it had the day before. Lombardi, running for Edwards, went to second on a sacrifice by Furillo. Jorgenson flew out to right.

The Dodgers were down to their last out when Shotton once more looked down the bench and called Lavagetto's name. The day before, Lavagetto had felt no nervousness against Bevens. But now, having tasted success, having celebrated his stardom with his wife by long-distance telephone, and having distributed cigars in the press box this afternoon, the butterflies were kicking up a storm in his stomach as he walked to the plate. "You got one yesterday," he told himself. "Get one today."

Shea threw a slider. Lavagetto was looking for a slider but swung and missed anyway. The next three pitches were balls, and then came another slider, down and away. He fouled it off to run the count full. The final pitch from Shea to Lavagetto was eminently hittable, a slow curve over the heart of the plate. Lavagetto leaped from his slouched

493

crouch and took a mean hack, gritting his teeth just as he had a day ago. This time, though, he whiffed. For years, every time he would so fondly recall the double that won game four, he would also remember the strikeout that ended game five.

Robinson, aggressive all year, played more aggressively than ever throughout the World Series, always looking for trouble, and finding it with great frequency. Though he was too shrewd to say so, he had established himself at the season's climax as a leader, perhaps even *the* leader of this overachieving and ever-surprising team. Though Reese was often described as the unofficial captain of the Dodgers, Walker as the club's best hitter, and Stanky its toughest thug, Robinson could see that none of those players — and certainly none of the team's pitchers — was in a position to upset the natural order of the Yankee hegemony the way he could.

In a long playoff series like this one, with two teams squaring off perhaps seven times in seven days, personalities matter more than in the regular season. Certain players start to get on the opposition's nerves. A pitcher who has one dominating performance can so thoroughly worry opponents that the mound on which he stands seems to grow taller each time he throws. A slugger who gets hot can discombobulate an entire staff of pitchers, forcing them to hand out walks or make bad pitches even when lesser men are at bat. Robinson through five games was tied with Walker for the team lead in hits with five. He had two walks, two stolen bases, two runs scored, and two driven in. Given how little the Dodgers were hitting, he was arguably the most important offensive force they had. But the things that hadn't shown up in box scores were the things rankling the Yankees most. There was the balk by Shea, the extra base earned by Reiser during the rundown, and the damage done to Berra's self-confidence.

Robinson was making his presence felt among his teammates, as well. He shouted encouragement to Dodger pitchers. He slapped his teammates' backs and rubbed their heads when they made good plays. Most important perhaps, given the general state of insecurity among the Dodgers, he refused to show fear. Among teammates who had wondered before meeting Robinson whether black players had the mental toughness for the game, all doubt had been removed this October. "He was our best player," Bobby Bragan said years later. The question faced now by his teammates was whether they could match his determination and ferocity.

The Yankees always managed to emit an image of refinement, but up close they could be nasty, and during the Series they'd been hurling some of the foulest racial epithets Robinson had heard all year. "They got no class," Robinson told one black reporter. "They hide in the dugout and shout at me. If they weren't yellow, they'd come out in the open and say something. What are they hollering? All kinds of filth, and race remarks. I wish I knew who they are. Nobody says anything when they get on base or out on the field. If they think they can upset my playing, they're crazy." The white press made no mention of the Yankee bench jockeys, but Wendell Smith wrote that the Yankees were indeed cruel. Only Ben Chapman and the Phillies had been crueler, he reported. Robinson never responded verbally to the catcalls. Once again, he channeled his anger.

Beginning with game four, Shotton had dropped Robinson from second to third in the batting order, the spot usually reserved for the team's best all-around hitter. The move had something to do with Reiser's injury but also with Robinson's performance thus far in the Series. In the first inning of game six, Stanky singled to left, Reese singled to center, and Robinson singled to left, loading the bases. The next batter, Walker, hit a routine double-play ball. Rizzuto fielded it, stepped on second, and got out of the way of the charging Robinson as he threw to first. On a close play, the man going from first to second is supposed to slide in hard to break up the double play, but this one wasn't close. The ball was out of Rizzuto's hands long before Robinson arrived, Walker out by a mile. But Robinson barreled in anyway. In fact, he veered from the base path, crouched low, and threw a nasty body block on the Yankee shortstop, who was one of the game's smallest men. Rizzuto flew like he'd been hit by a speeding truck. As he lay writhing on the infield dirt, Robinson picked himself up and ran off the field, never looking back. After DiMaggio, Rizzuto was the Yankees' most important player, a quick and nimble infielder whose elegant defensive play saved countless games for the Yanks. He was the team mascot, too, the butt of the best pranks, everybody's little brother. Because he was so small and vulnerable, Rizzuto's teammates made a habit of retaliating when a runner tried to take him out. The next batter would get beaned, or the opposing team's shortstop would get torpedoed on a close play at second base. Rizzuto wasn't badly hurt. He only had the wind knocked out of him. A couple of innings later, Robinson apologized to the shortstop. The Yankees never retaliated.

The Dodgers got two runs in the first inning of game six and two more in the third when Reese, Robinson, and Walker all doubled, knocking Allie Reynolds from the game and bringing on Karl Drews, a rookie who had appeared in only thirty-four games in the majors to that point. In the bottom half of the inning, the Dodgers' starter, Vic Lombardi, also got in trouble, allowing two runs on a double, three singles, and an error before Ralph Branca came on in relief. Again, Branca failed, giving up two more hits and adding two more runs to Lombardi's ledger, as the Yankees tied the score, 4–4.

In the sixth inning, Edwards singled, Furillo doubled, and Lavagetto, pinch hitting yet again, this time for Jorgensen, hit a fly ball to Berra in right field, deep enough to drive in a run. Then Shotton called for another unlikely pinch hitter — Bragan, the backup catcher, who had played in only twenty-five games and scratched a mere seven hits all season. No one was more surprised than Bragan himself. As he sprinted in from the bullpen and grabbed a bat, he could barely calm his nerves. He felt as if his knees were knocking as he walked toward the plate. He settled down when he reached the batter's box, and on a two-two pitch, the great Joe Page threw a curveball that didn't curve. Bragan blasted it to left for a double, scoring Furillo. When Shotton sent Dan Bankhead in to run for Bragan, Bankhead became the second black man ever to play in a World Series. In the grandstand, Bragan's father didn't notice that his son had been lifted for a pinch runner, and when he saw the long-legged Bankhead rounding third on the next play, he was astonished at how fast Bobby ran. When the inning ended, the Dodgers led, 8–5.

All the pinch hitting and pinch running forced Shotton to improvise. In the bottom of the sixth he sent Hatten out to pitch, Lavagetto to third, and Al Gionfriddo to left. "What's that little Italian's name?" he'd been asking all year long of Gionfriddo. But even after asking, he would go right on ignoring him, and only the most adoring of Dodger fans would have recognized him — in or out of uniform. Over the course of a season, a full-time outfielder might haul in 300 or 350 fly balls. Gionfriddo had seen only about thirty. Why he hadn't been sent to the minors no one knew. Now, as he trotted across the Yankee Stadium outfield, Gionfriddo took in its dimensions. The fence was short in the left-field corner, but it stretched far and deep toward center field, "a good drive in a Buick," as he put it years later. He was fast, but, still, it was an awful lot of ground to cover.

Hatten got into trouble right away. Allie Clark lined to short, Stirnweiss walked, Henrich fouled out, and Berra lined a single. Up stepped DiMaggio representing the tying run. The Yankee slugger had already hit two homers in the Series. He'd also been walked five times, a statistic speaking to the great fear he instilled in Brooklyn's pitchers. From the dugout, coaches waved Gionfriddo toward the left-field line, figuring that DiMaggio would probably pull the ball. The outfielder did what he was told, but he felt uneasy about it. Between Gionfriddo in left and Furillo in center lay a swath of grass large enough to graze a herd of cattle.

With a graceful swing and a sharp crack, DiMaggio sent the ball flying precisely where Gionfriddo had feared, deep into the gap between left and center, toward the Dodger bullpen 415 feet from home plate. Gionfriddo put his head down and began to run. As he approached the fence, he glanced over his right shoulder to locate the ball. It wasn't where he thought it would be. He had almost overrun it. Suddenly, he was unsure where he needed to go and how to get there. He altered course, spinning his body from right to left and thrusting his gloved right hand out wide of his body. His hat flew off his head. The ball was fast approaching the low chain-link fence that separated the Dodger bullpen from the outfield when Gionfriddo's glove intercepted it. Nothing in his life had ever felt so good as that thwack of horsehide on leather. As DiMaggio, galloping around the infield, saw extra bases turned into an out, he reacted as no one had ever seen him react before. In frustration, he kicked at the dirt near second base. "I guess I hit a few harder in my career as a ballplayer," he said after the game, "but right now I can't remember when."

It was a stumbling, bumbling play. Even Gionfriddo admitted he'd been lucky. But it was witnessed by three million or so on television; DiMaggio punctuated it with a long-legged kick; and it set up a decisive seventh game. Also, in the days before instant replay, it was widely assumed that Gionfriddo had robbed DiMaggio of a home run. Photographs and newsreel footage show the ball probably would not have cleared the fence. Even so, if it wasn't the greatest of all World Series grabs, it would at least be remembered that way for a long time. In many ways, it captured perfectly the spirit of this herky-jerky, ugly-beautiful competition. As the Yankees and Dodgers prepared for the season's final game, the men in the press box were still calling this one of the worst — if not *the* worst — World Series ever played. Of course, they were also calling it one of the most — if not *the* most — entertaining. There were long, lousy games filled with endless dropped balls and bad throws, and yet there were moments of pure magic, too. Most magical of all were the Dodgers, a crazy-quilt outfit of underachievers, a bunch of misfits who when the season began didn't even want to play together, now one game from becoming champions of the world. As such, noted an editorial in the *Times,* "They are more uniquely American than any other sports team we can think of at this moment."

As he awaited the seventh and final game, Wendell Smith filed a report with the dateline "PRESS BOX, YANKEE STADIUM, NEW YORK." It was his way of letting black readers know that he was now a fully accredited member of the traveling press, no longer relegated to the grandstands, and entitled to all the same privileges as his white counterparts. Just as Smith had helped Robinson get ahead, Robinson had returned the favor. Smith's coverage of Robinson's rookie year helped him secure a job with the *Chicago American,* making him the first of the prominent black sportswriters to leap from the black press to the white. Though he was on the brink of a new career, he continued filing stories for the *Courier* during the World Series. Just now, click-clacking proudly in the press box, he reminded his readers that Robinson was hitting .304 in the Series, tied for the team lead in hits, and playing errorless — at times even glittering — defense at first base. "Whether the Dodgers win or lose now," he wrote, "this much is certain, they couldn't have done it without Jack Roosevelt Robinson."

Twenty-Two: "And the World Series Is Over!"

After much uncertainty, Shotton settled on Hal Gregg to pitch the seventh game, hoping the pitcher could repeat the success he had had in game four. For the Yankees, Spec Shea took the ball for the third time. Neither pitcher lasted long. In the top of the second, after hits by Hermanski, Edwards, and Furillo, Shea was done, replaced by Bill Bevens, who allowed a double to Jorgensen before pitching out of the jam. The Dodgers jumped to a 2–0 lead.

The Yankees got one run in the bottom of the second when Gregg allowed two walks followed by a single to Rizzuto. In the fourth, Gregg got in trouble again and gave away the Dodger lead. With the score tied at 2–2, Hank Behrman climbed to the mound. He walked Stirnweiss and gave up a run-scoring single to Henrich. The Yankees still had the bases loaded with two outs when Berra came to the plate. His team leading by a run, Berra had a chance to make everyone forget his lousy defense and his .167 batting average. He took a mean swing and hit a bullet to the right side of the infield. The ball looked like it would get through for a two-run single, but Robinson stabbed at it and made a terrific stop, flipping to Behrman at first for the out. After four innings, the score was 3–2 in favor of the Yanks.

Harris by now must have been tired of the pesky Dodgers and their relentless attack on his middling pitchers, so he summoned the only reliable man he had in the bullpen: Joe Page. Nearly given up as a hopeless case back in the spring, Page had emerged in 1947, under the influence of DiMaggio, as a star. From 1946 to 1947, while pitching roughly the same number of innings, he had increased his strikeouts by 50 percent. More important, he had reduced the number of earned runs allowed all season from fifty-four to thirty-nine. Without Page, the Yankees might still have won the pennant, but they probably would have lacked the dominant aura. He had helped a bunch of green starting pitchers escape disaster all season long. Now he was being asked to do it one last time.

It was not unusual in the 1940s for a

manager to bring in his best reliever in the middle of a game and to ask him to go four or five innings. The matter was complicated somewhat in this instance, though, by the fact that Page had already pitched eight innings in three games during the Series. A day earlier, he had been hit hard. Still, the sight of the big lefty climbing onto the mound soothed the rest of the Yankees.

The Dodgers, and Bragan in particular, had hammered Page's curveball in game six, so Page made up his mind to throw no curves at all this time. His fastball was his best pitch, even with a tired arm, and that's what he intended to use. Stanky was the first to face him, grounding out to short. Reese followed with a fly-out to Berra, and Robinson hit one hard but right at Henrich in left. And so it went, fastball after fastball, inning after inning. Page did throw a curve to Dixie Walker and a slider to the pinch-hitter Gil Hodges, but those were the only exceptions. His fastball wasn't exactly humming, but he was hitting his spots, throwing strikes, and the Dodgers were managing nothing but weak swings. With each pitch, Page became more convinced that he was on the verge of something special, that this was a game he would remember all his life.

Headed into the ninth inning, the Yankees

led 5–2. They stood three outs away from the championship. Yankee Stadium was awash in sunshine, the grandstand glowing, fans warm and happy. A rumble of appreciation rose from the crowd as the inning began. A spectacular season and a World Series of fantastic thrills were nearing their end. The crowd thundered again as Page threw his first pitch and Walker tapped it to second base for an easy out.

Miksis came up next and hit a single to center, the first hit all day against Page. In the Brooklyn dugout, players stood on the steps, praying for one more miracle.

At three-forty-nine, Page threw one last fastball. Bruce Edwards swung and hit a sharp ground ball to Rizzuto. Rizzuto flipped the ball to Stirnweiss, and Stirnweiss threw it across the diamond to McQuinn in plenty of time.

"It's a double play!" Yankee announcer Mel Allen told his radio audience. "And the World Series is over!"

As the Yankees burst onto the field to celebrate, the Dodgers slipped quietly off. Branch Rickey put his arm around Shotton's shoulder and walked him to the clubhouse. Robinson, coming down the ramp from the dugout to the locker room, took a baseball out of his glove and bounced it gently against the ceiling, a neat trick to avoid making eye contact. After the players were all inside, Rickey closed the door and spoke to the team for about fifteen minutes. He said he was proud. He said the men had accomplished a great deal. He said he expected the Dodgers to be even better in 1948. But he made no mention of their greater triumph, their acceptance of Jackie Robinson. This wasn't the time or place to speak of moral victories. "We got beat by a darn good ball club," he said.

When Rickey finished, the men began moving about quietly, shuffling slowly in and out of the shower, popping open cans of beer, lighting cigarettes, and packing their gear. Happy Chandler entered the locker room and asked Robinson and Bankhead to pose with him for a picture. Red Barber walked in, too. The broadcaster shook hands with Shotton, then Reese, Robinson, Walker, and Casey, wishing them each a good winter.

A few minutes later, the doors opened and the newspapermen rushed in. They found Robinson sitting on the stool in front of his locker, shirt off and pants still on, a scuffed-up baseball in his right hand.

"We lost," he said. "We got no alibis. We'll get them next year."

The players put on their street clothes, collected their wallets and watches, and said their last good-byes. Their lives had changed from April to October. Outside, the nation was changing, too. A great movement was on its way, glimpsed in 1947 like the morning's first shaft of sunlight. It started in Brooklyn, but it didn't end there.

As Robinson prepared to leave, something happened that eased the pain he felt over losing the World Series. One by one, his teammates approached his locker. They shook his hand and congratulated him on a great season. They told him he played a fine game of ball.

EPILOGUE

On a warm October day, the Robinsons packed their bags and stepped out of their cramped apartment on MacDonough Street. Yet this was no time to rest or rejoice. Jackie had received countless invitations for appearances — at fundraisers, testimonial dinners, athletic events — and he had accepted as many of them as he thought he could handle. His biggest commitment was a four-city vaudeville tour, beginning with a week at the Apollo in Harlem, followed by a week at the Howard Theatre in Washington, D.C., another week at the Regal in Chicago, and, finally, a week at the Million Dollar Theater in Los Angeles.

Robinson neither sang nor danced. His sense of humor, like the alien space ship spotted over the desert in New Mexico earlier that summer, remained wholly unconfirmed. He had no business in vaudeville, but the money was too good to resist:

three thousand dollars a week plus a percentage of the gate. He was twenty-eight, almost twenty-nine, and knew that professional athletes enjoyed short careers. He also knew that Branch Rickey never paid players a nickel more than he had to. So he dedicated himself to a dizzying whirl of money-making schemes. Wendell Smith went to work writing Robinson's autobiography. Producers in Hollywood began plotting scripts for a B movie with the athlete in a starring role. And, to fill in the gaps, Robinson agreed to play a few exhibition baseball games.

The star of the show stepped hesitantly to the stage for his theatrical debut. The show in Harlem attracted big crowds, but the critics hated it. Robinson stood before the audience in suit and tie for about eight minutes, answering prearranged questions from the famous black actor Monte Hawley. Every night, the questions and answers were virtually the same. "Everyone on the team treated me swell," he said at one point. It was like his column for the *Pittsburgh Courier,* only duller. Some musical numbers and comedy sketches rounded out the show, but they didn't help. One critic said the main attraction seemed "disgusted and ashamed." The dignified image Robinson had worked so hard all season to establish, another newspaper writer commented, crumbled before the audience's eyes. In Chicago, where Robinson played to less-than-packed houses, Fay Young of the *Defender* watched the act and, afterward, counseled Robinson to stick to baseball.

On tour, Robinson attended one honorary banquet after another. He would eat a big dinner, receive a trophy, say a few words, then sit down for dessert. He never refused dessert. Before the season began, Rickey had warned that the black community would ruin Robinson by smothering him with praise, and now they were proving the Mahatma once again prescient. The off-season had barely begun, and Robinson's waistline was already expanding.

The four-city tour did not include Jack Jr., who had gone back to Los Angeles with Rachel's mother after the World Series. Jack and Rachel enjoyed the peace of the open road, the luxury of uninterrupted sleep, the thrill of undivided attention. But by November, as they wrapped up their engagements in Chicago, they phoned Rachel's mother and heard that the baby was on the verge of walking. They raced home. "We'd pull off the road," Rachel said, "and Jack would tell me, 'We'll sleep a few hours.' Then I'd feel the car moving." Jack Jr. didn't wait, taking his first steps the day before his parents arrived.

Jackie and Rachel moved in for the winter with Rachel's older brother. Robinson filled his days with golf and his nights with more award banquets while waiting for his movie to start filming. Once again, critics in the black press jumped on him, questioning why the nation's leading symbol of integration would agree to appear in an all-black film. But the answer was obvious: a $14,500 payday. The movie never got off the ground, however, leaving Robinson with enough time for one more business venture. Early in 1948, he took his vaudeville act on the road again, this time through the South, where he stayed in private homes, and where his hosts tried to impress their honored guests by serving up their finest dishes. For breakfast, he usually ate big plates full of eggs, potatoes, and grits. For lunch and dinner, there was pork, fried chicken, biscuits — and more desserts. "We ate like pigs," Robinson recalled. By the time he joined the Dodgers for spring training in March, he weighed about 230 pounds, at least thirty pounds heavier than his playing weight at the start of the 1947 season.

Durocher, back in charge of the team after

his suspension, was livid. "What in the world happened to you?" he screamed, a quotation no doubt scrubbed of foul language in Robinson's account. "You look like an old woman. . . . Why, you can't even bend over!" He was right. Robinson took off much of the weight during training camp, but not all of it, and as the season began, sportswriters said he looked like he was running with a goldfish bowl in his arms. The preseason brought one more bit of unpleasantness: When it came time to settle Robinson's contract for the season, Rickey proved just how firmly he believed in equal rights by treating Robinson as harshly as the rest of the Dodgers. For all his great play and his success as a box-office attraction, baseball's black pioneer was still just a second-year man in Rickey's mind, and second-year men did not get big money. Rickey offered $12,500 and refused to go higher. Robinson was angry. Rachel was angrier. They had both been reading the newspapers and knew that Pete Reiser was getting $20,000, Reese about $17,000, and Branca $14,000. Joe DiMaggio, the only player in Robinson's league in terms of celebrity, would make $70,000 for the season. Yet Robinson, beholden and grateful to Rickey, accepted the offer and told reporters he was satisfied.

Rickey could have paid more, especially given that he was in the process of dumping two of his highest-priced players. He traded Stanky to the Boston Braves, thereby permitting Robinson to move back to second base, his more natural position. And, finally, after several aborted attempts, he sent Dixie Walker to the Pittsburgh Pirates for Preacher Roe, Billy Cox, and Gene Mauch.

Walker had spent a quiet winter back in Leeds, Alabama. Business was fine at his hardware store, his reputation unharmed by his association with baseball's first black player. In the legend of Jackie Robinson, told over and over in books, movies, and documentaries, Walker's trade to Pittsburgh came as punishment for narrow-mindedness. But Rickey probably gets more credit than he deserves in these accounts. Had he traded Walker in 1947, or dumped him entirely, for that matter, the Dodger president could have sent the strongest possible signal: No bigots allowed. But to Rickey, RBIs counted for more than ideology at the time. Rickey also recognized that Walker, despite his nickname, had turned out not to be much of a rebel. In fact, after spring training, he put up no resistance at all. He did nothing to disrupt or distract the team as far as anyone could tell. He did

515

nothing to offend Robinson. He never failed to play hard. When it counted, he put the team first.

By 1948, however, Rickey wanted to unload Walker for all the usual reasons. The right-fielder was old, banged up, and overpaid. He was no longer a good value. What's more, the Dodgers had a surplus of outfielders. And yet even after Rickey decided that he wanted Walker gone, the boss still didn't make a clean break. One day in November 1947, he picked up the phone and placed a call to Walker in Alabama. If Walker was ready to retire, said Rickey, the Dodgers had a place for him in their organization as the new manager of their minor-league team in St. Paul. Rather than being punished, Walker was offered a chance to help develop the club's future stars — including a growing number of black players. Rickey had believed back in the spring of 1946 that players such as Walker would come around once they grew accustomed to playing and living with black men, and the offer to Walker suggested Rickey believed it still. When Walker said he preferred to play another year or two, he understood that it would prompt a trade. A few weeks later, Rickey dealt him.

"Naturally, I regret leaving Brooklyn . . . ," the right-fielder said. "In nine years with the Dodgers I've made many close friends. I love those Brooklyn people." He played two seasons in Pittsburgh before beginning a long career as a coach in the minor leagues. As the years went by, Walker occasionally spoke of his relationship with Robinson. He complained to friends back in Alabama that Rickey, in telling the story of Robinson's breakthrough, found it convenient to add a southern villain to the narrative. He admitted that he felt pressure from his friends and neighbors in Alabama not to play on an integrated team, and admitted taking part in the spring-training protest against Robinson. Yet he continued to insist he was never the leader of the uprising.

"I grew up in the South," he recalled in a 1981 interview, a year before his death, "and in those days you grew up in a different manner than you do today. We thought that blacks didn't have ice water in their veins and so couldn't take the pressure of playing big league baseball. Well, we know now that's as big a farce as ever was. A person learns, and you begin to change with the times. I'll say one thing for Robinson, he was as outstanding an athlete as I ever saw. He had the instinct to always do the right thing on the field. He was a stemwinder of a ballplayer. But, you know, we never hit it off real well. I've gotten along with a lot of blacks since then — I managed 'em in the minor leagues and there's many I came to respect and like — but Jackie was a very antagonistic person in many ways, at least I feel he was. Maybe he had to be to survive. The curses, the threats on his life. I don't know if I could have gone through what he did. I doubt it. But we just didn't gee and haw, like they say down here. Over the years, though, Robinson and I would meet at Old-Timer's Day games and we sat and chatted some. The other night I watched a television program and heard mention of a number of people who were important in the blacks gaining advantages in America. And the name of Jackie Robinson never came up. It surprised me. I mean, how soon people can forget."

The Dodgers started slowly in 1948. They missed Stanky's great gift for getting on base, and they surely could have used Walker, who proved he had one more great season in his rattled old body, hitting .316 in Pittsburgh. Dan Bankhead spent the season in the minor leagues, and while he pitched well there, he never met with much success in the majors. Roy Campanella made his debut on April 20 and in July replaced Bruce Edwards as the starting catcher, making the Dodgers the first team with two black players in the everyday lineup. Campanella, more easygoing in nature than Robinson, soon became one of the most widely liked men on the team and one of the finest catchers in the game. Shortly after Campanella's elevation, Bill Veeck signed the legendary Satchel Paige — reportedly forty-two years old — to pitch for the Cleveland Indians. Paige became a huge attraction in ballparks around the American League and helped carry the Indians to the pennant.

The Dodgers finished third in the National League. Once he burned off the extra weight that slowed him much of the spring, Robinson went on to have another fine season, hitting .296 with twelve homers, eighty-five runs batted in, and twenty-two stolen bases. By 1949, only three teams in the major leagues had black players on their roster: the Dodgers, the Indians, and the Giants. Robinson had broken through, but no great wave followed him. Some teams thought their supply of talent so great that they didn't need black players. Other organizations simply didn't want them. Robinson had his finest season in 1949, hitting a league-leading .342 with sixteen home runs,

124 RBIs, and thirty-seven stolen bases. He won the Most Valuable Player award and led the Dodgers to their second pennant in three years (as well as their second loss to the Yankees in the World Series). Freed from his promise of pacifism, he became one of the game's most vicious bench jockeys, letting the world see some of the hostility that fueled his competitive spirit. He became a mentor to younger black players, pushing them in ways that earned their respect, if not in all instances their friendship. The angrier he got, the better he played. Once, warming up before a game in Milwaukee, he turned suddenly and fired a ball into the Braves dugout, trying to strike the pitcher Lew Burdette. "I wanted to hit him right between the eyes," he said later, explaining that Burdette had been baiting him. A similar incident today would certainly bring a fine and probably a suspension, but Robinson didn't even apologize.

"This guy didn't just come to play," Leo Durocher said. "He came to beat you. He came to cram the goddamn bat right up your ass."

But the biggest fight for Robinson in 1949 came off the field, when he received an invitation to testify before the House Committee on Un-American Activities. At a peace conference, the singer and activist Paul Robeson had said that black Americans, given their country's racist history, could never be expected to fight against a communist enemy. HUAC, as it was known, asked Robinson to appear in order to present a more patriotic view from one of the nation's most widely respected black men. Robinson, urged on by Rickey, agreed to testify. He criticized America's segregationist policies and vowed to fight racism wherever he found it. He said black Americans were stirred up before the Communist Party started making noise and would be stirred up after the party vanished — "unless Jim Crow disappeared by then as well." While he refrained from making a blatant attack on Robeson, he said he and his family had too much invested in the future of the country to throw it away "for a siren song sung in bass," a clear reference to Robeson. The media praised Robinson for his stance ("Jackie Bats 1.000 in Probe of Reds," read the headline in the *New York Age*), and his popularity soared. Robeson, meanwhile, had his passport revoked and his career destroyed. Many years later, Robinson would express some regret for having criticized Robeson.

After 1949, Robinson went on to play five

more splendid seasons and two less-than-splendid ones. From 1949 through 1954, he hit .320 with an average season total of sixteen homers, ninety-three RBIs, and 23.4 stolen bases. In 1955, at the age of thirty-six, he began to slip, his batting average dropping. He sat out games with an assortment of mild injuries. His body thickened, his hair grayed, and his speed, always the key to his game, left him. The Dodgers tried him in the outfield and at third base, in part because he was no longer nimble enough for second base, and, in part, because a younger black player, Jim Gilliam, had come along to stake a claim to second base. Robinson remained a tough player. He seldom struck out, he bunted beautifully, and he still ran the bases boldly, if more slowly than in his prime. In 1955, he suffered a lackluster season but played well down the stretch, helping the Dodgers reach the World Series, giving them yet another shot at the Yankees. In the first game, to the surprise and delight of fans, Robinson stole home, sliding in under the tag of his old rival Yogi Berra, who, to this day, still believes Robinson was out (although rare film footage at the Baseball Hall of Fame appears to show that Berra missed the tag). The Dodgers, to the even greater surprise and delight of their fans, went on to win their first championship, beating the Yankees in seven games. But Robinson did not play in that seventh and decisive game, manager Walter Alston deciding that his team had a better chance to win with Gilliam at second and Don Hoak at third.

Branch Rickey had left the Dodgers after the 1950 season, no longer able to work with his fellow owner, Walter O'Malley. "A psalm-singing faker," O'Malley called Rickey. Rickey soon landed with the Pittsburgh Pirates, which seemed like a natural fit, since he had already traded half of his former team there. But, for the first time in his great career, he failed to build a winner. He lasted a mere five years with the Pirates. He retired from big-league baseball in 1955 and died ten years later.

By the time the 1955 season ended, Robinson was thinking about retirement, too. He and Rachel had three children now, and they had just moved to an expensive new home in Connecticut. That winter, on the evening of December 1, a black woman named Rosa Parks was arrested in Alabama for refusing to relinquish her bus seat to a white passenger. News of the incident must have reminded Robinson of his own bus protest and ensuing court-martial eleven years earlier. Rosa Parks's action sparked a massive boycott of the Montgomery bus system, a protest that riveted the nation's attention and launched a new, more confrontational phase in the fight for civil rights. From Florida the following spring, Robinson wrote to Rachel, "The more I read about the Montgomery situation, the more respect I have for the job they are doing." Eight years earlier, Robinson had been the most prominent symbol of change for the black community, but much had happened since then. Martin Luther King, Jr., only eighteen years old at the time of Robinson's rookie season, emerged now as a powerful leader of a more provocative brand of activism. Later, King would call Robinson "a sit-inner before sit-ins, a freedom rider before freedom rides." Yet Robinson stayed mostly on the sidelines in the early years of King's movement.

Robinson the ballplayer had difficulty fitting in among his peers during the last years of his career. He showed energy on the field and in the dugout, but in the clubhouse he was perceived by some as a grouch. He played better in 1956 than he had in 1955, but not well enough to change the trajectory of his career. His knees and ankles hurt all the time. His throwing arm grew tired.

His weight continued to balloon. He suffered from diabetes. He knew time was running out, but he did not yet know what he would do with his life after baseball, nor how he would replace the lost income. He had a clothing store in Harlem, but business there was not good, and his new construction business had so far not constructed a thing. He thought about managing and believed he would be good at it, but almost any managing job would require a move from the New York area, and he wasn't sure he wanted to spend an entire season away from his family.

Bobby Bragan, his former teammate, had just become the manager of the Pittsburgh Pirates. In 1947, Bragan had bucked at the notion of playing with a black man. But as a coach in the minors he had developed a reputation as an equal-opportunity employer, and he was said to be especially good at working with black ballplayers. That reputation no doubt impressed the man who hired him in Pittsburgh: Branch Rickey. Robinson knew that Bragan, Walker, and several other former teammates had made the transition to coaching. If he did decide to pursue such a job, he wondered if his color would hold him back. In an article called "Why Can't I Manage in the Majors?" he explored some possible answers to the question. "Because I am a Negro? Because I am emotional? Because I can't get along with people, no matter what the pigmentation of their skin? Because white players would resent me and would be reluctant to take orders from me? Because baseball isn't ready now or never will be ready to accept a Negro as a manager at the major league level? Because I'm not qualified by experience or ability?" He concluded that none of those were legitimate reasons.

After the 1956 season, the Dodgers did not ask Robinson to coach. Instead, they traded him to the Giants for the pitcher Dick Littlefield and thirty thousand dollars in cash. Robinson, already leaning toward retirement, refused the trade and formally announced his departure from the game. He ended his ten-year career with a .311 batting average, 137 home runs, 734 runs batted in, and 197 stolen bases. When he was voted to the Hall of Fame five years later, his plaque cited his batting average, his fielding percentage, even his record at turning double plays, but not his race or the impact he had made on baseball and America. In his ten years with them, the Dodgers won the pennant six times. Teams that followed the Dodgers' lead and accepted integration (the Indians and Giants, most notably) became consistent winners, while teams that dawdled or stalled for time (the Cardinals, for one) struggled for years to keep up with the competition. Robinson showed black Americans what was possible. He showed white Americans what was inevitable. At the simplest level, it is the athlete's job to win, which Robinson did during his career in almost every way imaginable.

After baseball, success became more difficult to measure. He went to work for Chock Full o'Nuts, a popular chain of coffee shops, as vice president in charge of personnel relations. The job paid thirty thousand dollars and provided a company car and stock options. The president of the company was worried at the time that his workers, many of them black, might soon unionize. He thought Robinson could help prevent such action. Though he had never expressed any interest in this sort of work, Robinson leaped at the offer. In January 1957, he went to Ebbets Field to clear out his locker.

From his desk at Chock Full o'Nuts, Robinson became a passionate letter writer — one of the nation's most outspoken advocates for civil rights, or, as some saw it, a professional scold. He had opinions on almost everything. He played a lot of golf, attended a lot of banquets, raised money for civil rights groups, campaigned on behalf of a few politicians, dabbled in businesses ranging from banks to fast-food restaurants, and published a weekly column in the *Amsterdam News.* But as the fifties turned to the sixties and the civil rights movement grew more radical, many in the black community began to perceive Robinson, whose politics skewed Republican, as out of step. Malcolm X, once a great fan, ridiculed Robinson now for kowtowing to a series of white masters, from Branch Rickey to Richard Nixon to Nelson Rockefeller. Robinson's brand of integration, characterized by patient suffering and a zipped lip, seemed out of date.

In 1961, Rachel earned a master's degree in psychiatric nursing from New York University and went to work at the First Day Hospital in the Bronx. Before long, she became head of psychiatric nursing at the Albert Einstein College of Medicine. Though she still woke early every day to make breakfast and get the three children ready for school, it was her mother, Zellee Isum, who saw the children out the door and greeted them again when they got home. Rachel loved the work and became widely respected in her field. Sometimes, when asked if she was Mrs. Jackie Robinson, she denied it, preferring to be judged on her own qualifications. Jackie had mixed feelings about his wife's work. He sounded jealous at times, but he confided to one friend that he had never seen his wife happier.

Jack Jr., meanwhile, suffered in the shadow of his father's fame. Robinson had always been disappointed by his son's lack of interest in athletics and his poor performance in school. At the same time, he admitted that he hadn't paid enough attention to his son. Still, he struggled to understand why his other children, daughter Sharon and younger son David, were determined to make the most of their talents, while Jackie Jr. consistently foundered. The relationship between father and son grew chilly. In 1964, Jack Jr. joined the army, and in 1965 he shipped off to Vietnam, leaving behind his pregnant girlfriend. He returned a junkie and went through rehab. In 1971, at the age of twenty-four, he died in an automobile accident.

The following year, while writing the preface for yet another autobiography, Robinson looked back one last time on the summer of 1947, and in particular to the first game of the World Series. He remained unsatisfied.

"There I was the black grandson of a slave, the son of a black sharecropper, part of a historic occasion, a symbolic hero to my people. The air was sparkling. The sunlight was warm. The band struck up the national anthem. The flag billowed in the wind. It should have been a glorious moment for me as the stirring words of the national anthem poured from the stands. Perhaps it was, but then again perhaps the anthem could be called the theme song for a drama called *The Noble Experiment.* Today as I look back on the opening game of my first World Series, I must tell you that it was Mr. Rickey's drama and that I was only a principal actor. As I write this twenty years later, I cannot stand and sing the anthem. I cannot salute the flag. I know that I am a black man in a white world. In 1972, in 1947, at my birth in 1919, I know that I never had it made."

Robinson was bitter over his son's death and in poor health when he wrote those words. The turmoil of the 1960s had been hard on him. He suddenly felt uncertain of his place in the world. He worried that his son David would suffer for having grown up in a mostly white, affluent part of Connecticut. He wrote to Rachel saying that it was important for his son to learn to "talk like he's colored," and to dance the way black men and women danced.

In the summer of 1972, Robinson flew to Los Angeles to celebrate the twenty-fifth anniversary of the 1947 team. He was fifty-three years old and looked older, heavy around the middle, his hair shockingly white, nearly blind from diabetes, survivor of a heart attack. He had long been estranged from the Dodgers, avoiding old-timers' games and banquets. All over the country, honors were pouring in, in part because of the anniversary and in part because it was clear Robinson was seriously ill. This time, he agreed to attend.

The day before the ceremony, on a whim, *Los Angeles Times* reporter Ron Rapoport called the hotel where Robinson was staying. Robinson answered the phone in his room and invited the reporter to drop by for an interview. Rapoport hurried over. He found the former ballplayer lying in his bed, under the covers, the room around him dark. Robinson turned on a table lamp as the reporter pulled up a chair. "The light hurts my eyes," he said. Doctors expected he would soon need his legs amputated.

531

Robinson and the reporter spoke for more than an hour, until Rapoport sensed it was time to go, time to let Robinson turn out the light. He asked one more question:

"Have you ever thought about your place in history?"

"I honestly believe that baseball did set the stage for many things that are happening today," he said, "and I'm proud to have played a part in it."

At Dodgers Stadium the next day, a fan called Robinson's name, waited for him to turn around, and then gently lobbed a baseball his way. Robinson never saw it. The ball struck him painfully in the head. A few months later, before the second game of the 1972 World Series, baseball honored Robinson once again. And once again, he refused to go quietly. By 1972, roughly one in four players were black. A year earlier, the Pirates had won the World Series with a starting lineup consisting almost entirely of black and Hispanic players. Yet Robinson said he would not be satisfied until black men got the chance to manage in the majors, too. "I wish Branch Rickey could be here," he said, as he accepted a plaque in honor of his rookie season. He continued: "I am extremely proud and pleased, but I am going to be more pleased the day I . . . see a black man as manager."

Nine days later he was dead of a heart attack.

"His courage, his sense of brotherhood and his brilliance on the playing field brought a new human dimension not only to the game of baseball but to every area of American life where black and white people work side by side," President Nixon said. Civil rights leader Vernon Jordan called Robinson "a trailblazer for all black people and a great spokesman for justice." The sportswriter Red Smith remembered him as "the unconquerable doing the impossible."

"I'm as sad as could possibly be," Dixie Walker told a reporter.

Sixty years after his debut in major-league baseball, Robinson's stature as an American hero has never been greater. His story has been told countless times — in poems, movies, songs, short stories, sermons, novels, comic books, term papers, plays, and children's books. Ballparks, baseball fields, streets, schools, playgrounds, and scholarships have been named in his honor. His image adorns postage stamps, collectible dolls, T-shirts, coins, and at least four statues. His name is attached to a nonprofit foundation, overseen by his wife, which provides college scholarships and mentoring for minority youths. Robinson is the only player in the history of major-league baseball to have had his uniform number, 42, retired by every team in both leagues. Each year on April 15, in memory of his first game, fans celebrate Jackie Robinson Day wherever big-league ball is played, and the story of his rookie season is told again, handed down like folklore.

Occasionally, some have questioned his legacy. A handful of historians and sociologists have blamed Robinson, along with Branch Rickey, for killing off Negro-league baseball. Others, noting the declining number of American black players in the game today, not to mention the low number of black spectators at big-league ballparks, have suggested that Robinson's impact may have been fleeting. But the Negro leagues were doomed with or without Robinson, like the black-owned hospitals and taxi companies that prospered in the heyday of Jim Crow. And no one could have foreseen the way professional football and basketball have drawn young black athletes away from baseball.

In 1947, when integration was new and the barriers to democracy for black Americans were concrete, Robinson presented a solution that would soon become a template

534

in the fight for racial equality. Over one spectacular summer, he proved that black Americans had been held back not by their inferiority but by systematic discrimination. And he proved it not with printed words or arguments declaimed before a judge. He proved it with deeds.

That was Jackie Robinson's true legacy. Given a chance to change the world, he never hesitated. He played hard and won. After that, it was a whole new ballgame.

ACKNOWLEDGMENTS

In telling the story of Jackie Robinson's first season, I was fortunate to talk to many of the participants and observers who figured in these events sixty years ago. With a few exceptions, all of them agreed to be interviewed, giving generously of their time and recollections. I am especially grateful to Rachel Robinson, who met with me three times and answered additional questions by telephone and email. She's a hero in her own right, and Jackie was a lucky man to have had her by his side.

I am grateful for interviews to Marty Adler, Jack Banta, Dottie Banta, Buzzie Bavasi, Bobby Bragan, Ralph Branca, Bobby Brown, Roy Campanella, Jr., Hilton Clark, William P. Coleman, Mimi Connelly, Jack Courson, George Crowe, Bob Dillinger, Chris Durocher, Eddie Erautt, Carl Erskine, William "Benny" Felder, Henry Foner, Bernard Fradkin, Joe Frazier, Lonny Frey,

Joe Garagiola, Margot Hayward, Ernie Harwell, Gene Hermanski, Tot Holmes, Ralph Houk, George Houser, Dan Hurley, Monte Irvin, Clarence L. Irving, Gilbert Jonas, Ralph Kiner, Clyde King, Norma King, Clem Labine, Jack Lang, Joe Laurice, Buddy Lively, Don Lund, Bill Mallory, Edwina Gaiser-Marchev, Marty Marion, Len Merullo, John Miley, Ox Miller, Orestes "Minnie" Minoso, Les Moss, Juanita Nelson, Bill Nunn, Jr., Buck O'Neil, Andy Pafko, Freddie Palmisano, Dave Parker, Sidney Poitier, Colin Powell, Charles Rich, Branch Rickey III, Phil Rizzuto, Eddie Robinson, Sharon Robinson, Will Robinson, Lester Rodney, Al Rosen, Esther Roth, Michael Roth, Mary Ann Sain, Freddy Schmidt, Johnny Schmitz, Howie Schultz, Joe B. Scott, Bud Selig, George "Shotgun" Shuba, Seymour Siwoff, Wyonella Smith, Marian and Donald Spencer, Delores Squires, Gerry Staley, Jerry Stern, Ed Stevens, Stan Strull, William Taylor, Bobby Thomson, Bob Usher, Johnny Van Cuyk, Jimmy Wilkes, and Leonard Zegans.

Thanks to the friends and research assistants who helped pan for gold in libraries and archives around the country: Lori Azim, Andrew Bentley, Joe DeMartino, Dalia Naamani-Goldman, Sam Goldsmith, Steve

Johnson, Bob Kazel, David King, Irving Matus, Clarissa del Pilar, Scott Schleifer, and Diane Wright.

Thanks to the writers who shared their memories and expertise: Kevin Baker, Martha Biondi, Jimmy Breslin, Paul Dickson, Eric Foner, Harvey Frommer, Pete Golenbock, Jerome Holtzman, Jane Leavy, Michael G. Long, Leonard Lopate, Bill Madden, William Marshall, Jeffrey Marx, Leigh Montville, Michael Penn, Joshua Prager, Ron Rapoport, Christopher Renino, Jeremy Schaap, and Studs Terkel. Special thanks to the writer Jules Tygiel, who shared notes and hundreds of pages of transcribed interviews collected in preparing his marvelous book *Baseball's Great Experiment*. In donating his research materials to the National Baseball Hall of Fame, he has done a service to all the writers who follow in his footsteps. I was also fortunate to have access to the papers of Carl T. Rowan, who worked with Robinson on the book *Wait Till Next Year*. Rowan's papers, at the Library of Congress and Oberlin College, contained transcripts of taped interviews with Robinson, his mother, and many other characters central to this story.

Thanks to the librarians and archivists who helped me along the way: at the National Baseball Hall of Fame, Claudette Burke, Jim Gates, Pat Kelly, Sue MacKay, Tim Weil, and everyone else who pitched in; at the *Birmingham News,* Amber Long; at the New York Public Library, David Smith; at the *Pittsburgh Courier* archives, E. Gaines; at the Cincinnati Reds Hall of Fame, Greg Rhodes; at the Library of Congress, David Kelly and Jeff Flannery; at the Dwight D. Eisenhower Presidential Library, Dwight Strandberg; at the Harry S. Truman Presidential Library, Randy Sowell; at the National Archives, John Vernon; at the Virginia Historical Society, Katherine Wilkins; at Oberlin College, Ken Grossi; at the Carnegie Museum of Art, Kerin Shellenbarger.

Also, thanks to Dave Smith of Retrosheet; Barbara Sawyer at the Jackie Robinson Foundation; Bill Guilfoile, formerly of the Hall of Fame; and the invisible forces who maintain www.baseball-reference.com, www.sabr.org, www.baseballlibrary.com, www.paperofrecord.com, and www.baseball almanac.com. Thanks to Eric Enders and Joseph Dorinson for their expert fact-checking. The mistakes in the book are all mine, but some of the great, Gionfriddo-esque catches are theirs.

I am also grateful to my brother, Matt Eig, and to my friends Richard Babcock, Joseph

Epstein, and Ron Jackson, who all read the manuscript with care. I owe a tremendous debt to Robert Kurson, a great writer and friend, who helped with the idea for the book, and to my friend and *Wall Street Journal* editor Bryan Gruley, for reading many drafts of many chapters along the way and making every one of them better.

Thanks to my editor at Simon & Schuster, Bob Bender, who shepherded this book with a steady hand, good humor, and great intelligence. Also at Simon & Schuster, thanks to Brianne Halverson, Johanna Li, Victoria Meyer, David Rosenthal, Kelly Welsh, and everyone else who helped. Thanks to David Black, a fantastic agent and friend, who brings a Robinson-like zeal to his work. At Black Inc., thanks also to David Larabell.

To all my family, and especially to Ben, Jake, Matt, Penny, Hayden, Lewis, Judy, Gail, Don, SuAnn, and Jonathan, I offer my thanks and love. My paternal grandparents, Louis Eig and Ida Eig, were regulars at Ebbets Field back in the 1940s and 1950s. My maternal grandparents, Frank and Betty Weiner, were regulars at Joe's Restaurant, which also happened to be Branch Rickey's favorite spot. To this day, my parents, Phyllis and David Eig, remain devoted to the Dodgers — the *Brooklyn* Dodgers, that is.

For a long time growing up, I don't think it dawned on me that the team had moved to L.A., such was their commitment. My parents taught me a lot about loyalty in those days. They're still teaching me — about loyalty and a whole lot more. Their enthusiasm and support is a source of constant joy. This book is dedicated to them. Thanks, Mom and Dad.

Finally, I owe far more than I can ever recount to my children, Jeffery and Lillian, and to my wife, Jennifer Tescher, who talked with me about this book for untold hours, read countless revisions of the manuscript, and gave me infinite support, always with a beautiful smile. She's certainly the hero of my own story.

NOTES

I can't imagine what Jackie Robinson went through in 1947. By the time of my birth in Brooklyn, the Dodgers were in L.A., Ebbets Field had been replaced by a public housing project, and Robinson was a blurry image in my father's home movies. That's one good reason why I have tried in these pages *not* to imagine what Robinson went through in 1947. I have worked at every turn to present verifiable facts. Nothing here is imagined or invented. No dialogue has been re-created for dramatic effect. The facts speak for themselves, and I think they speak much more powerfully than the myths that have come to cloud Robinson's story. This book relies on primary materials: interviews, newspaper articles, oral histories, and, for a few games, movie reel footage. I have tried whenever possible to confirm details with multiple sources. When conflicts arose, I tended to put my trust in reports written or recorded in and around 1947, before most of the mythmaking began. Robinson's first autobiography, for example, published immediately after his rookie season, strikes me as more reliable than his later published accounts. As I researched this book, I was fortunate to have access to several private scrapbooks, including the one belonging to Rachel Robinson. As a result, some of the articles cited in the notes below lack headlines, while others lack dates, and one or two come from unnamed newspapers. I was also fortunate to find transcripts of unpublished interviews conducted by the writers Jerome Holtzman, Carl Rowan, and Jules Tygiel. Their contributions are cited in the notes below. All other interviews are my own.

Prologue

deep sleep: Jackie Robinson and Wendell Smith, *Jackie Robinson: My Own Story* (New York: Greenberg, 1948), 123.

room 1169: "Debut 'Just Another Game' to Jackie," *Sporting News,* April 23, 1947.

stomach in knots: "Dodgers Buy Jackie Robinson; 'You Can Win Pennant' — Durocher," *New York Post,* April 10, 1947.

Come to Brooklyn: Robinson and Smith, *Jackie Robinson,* 123.

"I'm sorry, but": "Negro's Jailer Warned Too Late to Stop Mob," *Brooklyn Eagle,* May 24, 1947.

One prominent black journalist: "Looking 'Em Over," *Baltimore Afro-American,* May 11, 1946.

felt the weight on his shoulders: Sam Lacy story with no headline, *Baltimore Afro-American,* November 3, 1945.

A cold wind: Weather reports, *New York Times, Brooklyn Eagle, New York Post,* April 11, 1947.

"Simple, wasn't it?": Robinson and Smith, *Jackie Robinson,* 124.

rough Italian kids: David Halberstam, *Summer of '49* (New York: Avon Books, 1990), 248.

"I want a ballplayer with guts": Carl Rowan and Jackie Robinson, *Wait Till Next Year* (New York: Random House, 1960), 117.

second most famous: "Jackie Robinson Is Second Most Popular American in Air Poll," *Chicago Defender,* November 22, 1947.

Black parents named: Letters to Robinson, Library of Congress.

White kids from small towns: Interviews with John Miley, Tot Holmes.

Passover Seders: Interview with Henry Foner.

White business owners: Letter from George Marchev to Rachel Robinson, Library of Congress.

Chapter One: Jack Roosevelt Robinson

could neither read nor write: Arnold Rampersad, *Jackie Robinson* (New York: Random House, 1997), 11.

"You're about the sassiest": Carl Rowan notes from interview with Mallie Robinson, Library of Congress.

"I always lived so close to God": Ibid.

"If you want to get closer to heaven": Ibid.

brighter and more beautiful: Ibid.

"She was hands caressing us": Jackie Robinson, *Baseball Has Done It* (Brooklyn: Ig Publishing, 2005), 41.

One exasperated Pepper Street homeowner: Rowan notes from interview with Mallie Robinson, Library of Congress.

"Nigger! Nigger! Nigger!": Ibid.

Jack never forgave: Ibid.

magical things happened: Robinson and Smith, *Jackie Robinson,* 8.

"If I was good enough, I played": "Jackie Robinson Says," *Pittsburgh Courier,* April 5, 1947.

Mack wore his Olympic jacket: Rampersad, *Jackie Robinson,* 31.

He remained Jack: "Wilson Captures Prep

Title With 27 1–2 Points," *Los Angeles Times,* May 17, 1936.

influence of the Reverend Karl Downs: Jackie Robinson with Alfred Duckett, *I Never Had It Made* (Hopewell, NJ: Ecco Press, 1995), 7.

"All Jackie did at Pasadena": "Jackie Robinson Big Threat on U.C.L.A. Football Eleven," *Los Angeles Times,* August 27, 1939.

"I was aggressive": Robinson, *I Never Had It Made,* 9.

"The Gold Dust Trio": Rampersad, *Jackie Robinson,* 68.

"steely hard eyes": Ibid., 71.

neither drank nor smoked: Interview with Rachel Robinson.

the fashion choice as a token: Rampersad, *Jackie Robinson,* 78.

she preferred to call him Jack: Interview with Rachel Robinson.

blue suit, the only one he owned: Ibid.

disappointing peck on the cheek: Rampersad, *Jackie Robinson,* 80.

"sitting next to a nigger": Robinson, *I Never Had It Made,* 14.

The provost marshal hung up: Transcript of Rowan interview of Robinson, Library of Congress.

"What did you say you were going to do?": Ibid.

"I didn't even stop talking": Robinson, *I Never Had It Made*, 18.

"I put my finger": Ibid., 19.

"Captain, tell me": Ibid., 20.

"I looked it up": Rampersad, *Jackie Robinson*, 108.

"He liked to play around the basket": "Jackie Robinson, College Basketball Coach," *Austin American-Statesman*, April 15, 1997.

four hundred dollars a month: Rampersad, *Jackie Robinson*, 113.

"pretty miserable way to make a buck": Robinson, *I Never Had It Made*, 23.

"We . . . pulled up": Jules Tygiel, *Baseball's Great Experiment* (New York: Vintage Books, 1984), 63.

Robinson ordered the driver: Interview with Buck O'Neil.

"nip frosting off a cake": Leroy "Satchel" Paige, as told to David Lipman, *Maybe I'll Pitch Forever* (Lincoln and London: University of Nebraska Press, 1993), 41.

"I use my single windup": David Sterry and Arielle Eckstut, *Satchel Sez: The Wit, Wisdom, and World of Leroy "Satchel" Paige* (New York: Three Rivers Press, 2001), 22.

"You keep on blowing off": Neil Lanctot, *Negro League Baseball* (Philadelphia: University of Philadelphia Press, 2004), 242.

In those fourteen outings: Lawrence D. Hogan, *Shades of Glory* (Washington, D.C.: National Geographic, 2006), 381.

"I never expected the walls": Robinson, *I Never Had It Made,* 24.

Chapter Two: "Some Good Colored Players"

Fay Young sensed it: "We Won't Stand for Any Bunk," *Chicago Defender,* September 1, 1945.

"Just rumors": Ibid.

they warned Rickey: Robinson, *Baseball Has Done It,* 52.

"First, to win a pennant": Ibid.

"the most liberal city in America": Martha Biondi, *To Stand and Fight: The Struggle for Civil Rights in Postwar New York City* (Cambridge: Harvard University Press, 2003), 45.

"If baseball belonged to all the people": Robinson and Smith, *Jackie Robinson,* 58.

"There is no good reason": Ibid.

"I know Southern ballplayers": Ibid., 63.

"It's too bad those colored boys": Tygiel, *Baseball's Great Experiment,* 33.

asked Dodson for his help: Ibid., 57.

Dodson, thoroughly charmed: Dan Dodson, "The Integration of Negroes in Baseball," *Journal of Educational Sociology,* vol. 28, no. 2, October 1954, 73–82.

"Things worthwhile generally": Branch Rickey, *Branch Rickey's Little Blue Book* (New York: Macmillan, 1995), 11.

The other epigram: "When All Heaven Rejoiced: Branch Rickey and the Origins of the Breaking of the Color Line," *Nine: A Journal of Baseball History and Culture,* Fall 2002.

"massive, benign, and bucolic": "Thoughts on Baseball," *New Yorker,* May 27, 1950.

"Who wants to sleep anyhow?": "Man of Empire," *Newsweek,* August 8, 1949.

summoned his secretary to join him: Jules Tygiel notes from interview with Red Smith, Baseball Hall of Fame archives.

"Dear Ones at Home": Rickey letter, Library of Congress.

"the finest man ever brought to the game": "Wesley Branch Rickey," *New York Post,* November 16, 1965.

"A man of many facets": Ibid.

the careful notes he made: Rickey Papers, Library of Congress.

"not a single Negro player": "Negro Player Issue Heads for Showdown," *Sporting News,* November 1, 1945.

"He stared and stared": Donald Honig, *Baseball When the Grass Was Real* (Lincoln and London: University of Nebraska Press, 1993), 189.

interrupted more than once: Notes from Christopher Renino interview with Clyde Sukeforth.

"What will you do?": Rickey, *Branch Rickey's Little Blue Book,* 82.

hands were clenched: "The Most Unforgettable Character I've Met," *Readers Digest,* October 1961.

asked to return a questionnaire: Sotheby's catalogue, *The Barry Halper Collection of Baseball Memorabilia,* 1999, 33.

"If I had not been so black": Tygiel, *Baseball's Great Experiment,* 12.

no written rule: Ibid., 30.

"He is not now major league stuff": "Negro Player Issue Heads for Showdown," *Sporting News,* November 1, 1945.

a shoebox full of fried chicken: Rampersad, *Jackie Robinson,* 136.

his best blue suit: Interview with Rachel Robinson.

"certificate of respectability": Rampersad, *Jackie Robinson,* 136.

a defining moment of their lives: Interview with Rachel Robinson.

embarrassed to be toting the food: Rachel Robinson, *Jackie Robinson: An Intimate Portrait* (New York: Harry N. Abrams, Inc., 1996), 46.

The Robinsons and a Mexican man: "I Live With a Hero," *McCalls,* January 1951.

a big suitcase wrapped with heavy cord: Interview with Rachel Robinson and photographs.

The family offered: "I Live With a Hero," *McCalls,* January 1951.

Rachel couldn't sleep: Rampersad, *Jackie Robinson,* 138.

"WE WASH WHITE FOLKS' CLOTHES ONLY": Rowan and Robinson, *Wait Till Next Year,* 135.

"hot feeling close to sickness": Ibid.

"My man had become": Rachel Robinson, *Jackie Robinson: An Intimate Portrait,* 48.

Some two hundred baseball players: Robinson and Smith, *Jackie Robinson,* 67.

nothing but his shoes and glove: Ibid., 66.

"Duck!": Ibid., 68.

Robinson found himself wishing: Ibid., 72.

"Suddenly I hated everybody": Ibid.

consulted some of his lieutenants: Interview with Buzzie Bavasi.

"Those who had no prejudices": "This is My Story," *Baltimore Afro-American,* March

22, 1947.

One wag, Sam Maltin: Robinson and Smith, *Jackie Robinson,* 109.

leaped into the car of a stranger: Ibid.

Chapter Three: The Uprising

spoke openly of his belief: Interview with Bobby Bragan.

They had their own dialects and customs: Halberstam, *Summer of '49,* 248.

twenty dollars per player per day: "Dodgers Win, Head for States," *Daily Mirror,* April 7, 1947.

"near the slum district": Photograph caption, *Chicago Defender,* March 15, 1947.

with whom Robinson roomed: "From A to Z," *New Jersey Afro-American,* March 22, 1947.

only a cockroach could love: Tygiel, *Baseball's Great Experiment,* 166.

Campanella decided not to complain: Roy Campanella, *It's Good to Be Alive* (New York: Signet, 1974), 127.

some doubt crept in: Robinson and Smith, *Jackie Robinson,* 118.

"Jimcro" food: "Stomach Ailment Benches Jackie; Victim of Havana Housing Jimcro," *People's Voice,* April 5, 1947; "Havana Diet Slows Robinson," *New York Post,* March 27, 1947.

"For what it's worth": "Robinson's Status Puzzles Scribes," *Los Angeles Times*, March 6, 1947.

Arroz con pollo: "From A to Z," *New Jersey Afro-American*, March 22, 1947.

he was beginning to wonder: Robinson and Smith, *Jackie Robinson: My Own Story*, 121.

First base is a busy place: Robinson and Smith, *Jackie Robinson*, 119.

"I was a disgruntled ballplayer": Ibid.

Howie Schultz, one: Interview with Howie Schultz.

"You couldn't possibly dislike him": Ibid.

probably had colitis: "Durocher Tests Robinson Again as Dodgers Beat Montreal, 7–0," *Herald Tribune*, March 30, 1947.

"the experience is a nerve-wracking one": "Jackie Reveals Reactions to Living in Baseball Showcase," *New Jersey Afro-American*, March 15, 1947.

"I wouldn't want to feel": "Robinson Refuses to Join Dodgers if Resentment Exists," *Sporting News*, April 2, 1947.

"Stick it in his fucking ear!": Joshua Prager, *The Echoing Green: The Untold Story of Bobby Thomson, Ralph Branca and the Shot Heard Round the World* (New York: Pantheon, 2006), 11.

"He can't hit": Rickey, *Branch Rickey's Little*

Blue Book, 52.

a bit of a loner: Tygiel interview with Johnny Jorgensen, Baseball Hall of Fame archives.

taken a Dale Carnegie course: "The Artful Dodger," article from unnamed publication, Baseball Hall of Fame archives.

Higbe always maintained: Kirby Higbe, *The High Hard One* (Lincoln and London: University of Nebraska Press, 1998), 103.

he could relate to Walker's feelings: Tygiel interview with Pee Wee Reese, Baseball Hall of Fame archives.

assumed Robinson wouldn't last: Ibid.

"Dixie Walker was my roommate": Interview with Bobby Bragan.

Bragan liked the nickname: Ibid.

"We just grew up segregated": Ibid.

"Back then," he recalled: Higbe, *The High Hard One,* 3.

"The Bottoms was a colored neighborhood": Ibid., 10–11.

"Throwing rocks at Negroes": Ibid., 11.

Durocher wore a yellow bathrobe: Harold Parrott, *The Lords of Baseball* (Atlanta: Long Street Press, 2001), 260.

"I don't care if a guy is yellow or black": Ibid.

recalled the advice of Dan Dodson: "The Integration of Negroes in Baseball," *Journal of Educational Sociology,* October 1954.

He also said Robinson was quiet: Tygiel

interview with Higbe, Baseball Hall of Fame archives.

an acute attack of indigestion": "Dodgers Vanquish Browns, 3–1, Higbe Winning in Short Stint," *Herald Tribune,* March 24, 1947.

"Recently the thought": Letter from Dixie Walker to Rickey, Library of Congress.

insisted he had never seen a petition: "52 years on the road," *Birmingham Post,* April 1, 1982.

"I didn't know if they would spit": "Dixie Walker Remembers," *New York Times,* December 10, 1981.

Dixie Walker Hardware: Interviews and emails with Geri Worley and Kay Huey; photographs from Hueytown, Alabama.

sensed that Walker was under great stress: Arthur Mann, *The Jackie Robinson Story* (New York: F.J. Low Co., 1950), 97.

include the young slugger Ralph Kiner: Ibid.

put him out of action: William Marshall, *Baseball's Pivotal Era, 1945–1951* (Lexington: The University Press of Kentucky, 1999), 114.

"The Brooklyn Dodgers today": "Jackie Robinson Becomes Dodger," *Los Angeles Times,* April 11, 1947.

Chapter Four: Opening Day

The room was a mess: Interview with Rachel Robinson.

"Just in case you have trouble": Rowan and Robinson, *Wait Till Next Year,* 179.

He took the subway to work: Interview with Rachel Robinson and photographs.

"the first colored boy": "Dodgers Play Braves, Eye Cards," *New York Post,* April 15, 1947.

Robinson grinned but didn't say anything: "Looking 'Em Over," *Richmond Afro-American,* April 19, 1947.

He decided not to call a special meeting: Ibid.

Robinson was relieved: Ibid.

"It fit me": Robinson and Smith, *Jackie Robinson,* 126–27.

"This is my first ballgame": "The Powerhouse," *Daily News,* April 16, 1947.

nearly three-fifths of the fans were black: Tygiel, *Baseball's Great Experiment,* 178.

smallpox scare: " 'Old' Reiser, 'New' Hermanski Stars Of Dodgers' Opening Day Triumph," *Brooklyn Eagle,* April 16, 1947.

"The biggest threat to his success": Tygiel, *Baseball's Great Experiment,* 162.

"The conduct of 'SOME' ": "Sports Beat," *Pittsburgh Courier,* April 26, 1964.

Rachel and Jack Jr. waited: Interview with Rachel Robinson.

sick with diarrhea: Ibid.

the absence of roof lights: "City Orders Taxicabs to Show Roof Lights when Unoccupied and Cruising the Streets," *New York Times,* May 29, 1947.

Her first order of business: Interview with Rachel Robinson.

The men in the section wore jackets: News photographs, April 15, 1947.

light-blue suit and matching cap: News photographs; "History, Not Hysteria," *Newsday,* April 13, 1997.

Fussing over the baby: Interview with Rachel Robinson.

the Dodgers for the most part left Robinson alone: Interviews with Gene Hermanski, Bobby Bragan, Ralph Branca, et al.

"Jackie is very definitely brunette": Email interview with Robert B. Parker.

"My mother worried": Ibid.

"Looking at a ball game": Robert B. Parker, *Mortal Stakes* (New York: Dell Publishing, 1975), 11.

they empathized with him: Interviews with Hermanski, Bragan, Branca, et al.

painfully slow rendition: "The Powerhouse," *Daily News,* April 16, 1947.

"Blacks lived right next door": Interview with Ralph Branca.

"the Dodgers are inept and helpless": ". . .

Cardinals and Red Sox Again — Who Else?" *New York Post,* April 15, 1947.

"C'mon, Jackie!": "Jackie Sparks Dodgers," *Richmond Afro-American,* April 19, 1947.

thirty-three ounces and thirty-five inches: Interview with Anne Jewell, Louisville Slugger Museum.

"Too bad about that double-play": "Powerhouse," *Daily News,* April 16, 1947.

"George Washington and Abraham Lincoln": Interview with Gene Hermanski.

a mob of 250 people: "Looking 'Em Over," *Richmond Afro-American,* April 19, 1947.

he released a heavy sigh: Ibid.

"It was all right": "Debut 'Just Another Game' to Jackie," *Sporting News,* April 23, 1947.

Chapter Five: Up in Harlem

"on that Triple-Borough Bridge": Arthur Mann, *Baseball Confidential* (New York: David McKay Co., 1951), 130.

"I don't even have a hotel room": Ibid., 131.

Stevens had grown up in poverty: Interview with Ed Stevens.

"I was considered one of the best-fielding": Ibid.

his Dodger days were numbered: Interview with Howie Schultz.

sprain an ankle and miss a few games: Par-

559

rott, *The Lords of Baseball,* 250.

458,000 black people: Biondi, *To Stand and Fight,* 3.

"The Negro people": Ibid., 1.

"I consider it a great honor": "Jackie Robinson Chairman of UNAVA," *People's Voice,* June 1, 1946.

"Branch Rickey was not favorably inclined": Interview with Lester Rodney.

go slowly and avoid unnecessary risk: Parrott, *The Lords of Baseball,* 250.

"Jackie's greatest danger is social": "Meddling of Well-Wishers Hurts Jackie," *Amsterdam News,* April 19, 1947.

"The Negroes have the legs": Roger Kahn, *The Era* (New York: Ticknor & Fields, 1993), 43.

Jackie Robinson Booster Club: "Jackie Robinson Boosters Ready to Support Star," *Amsterdam News,* April 19, 1947.

a high, inside curve: Allan Roth scorecard, Retrosheet, Inc.

"That's because their heels are longer": Kahn, *The Era,* 44.

736 servicemen: "Giants Defeat Dodgers, 4–3, As 53,000 Jam Polo Grounds," *Daily Mirror,* April 20, 1947.

dining at Lawson Bowman's: Photograph, *Chicago Defender,* May 3, 1947.

Filtered light and the sound of traffic: Interview with Stan Strull, former batboy.

the worst locker in the clubhouse: Sketches of clubhouse made by Stan Strull for author Christopher Renino.

Players were supposed to mark a chalkboard: Interview with Stan Strull.

a woman named Mabel C. Brown: Interview with Rachel Robinson.

Without having seen the place: Ibid.

Robinson gave an interview: Interview with Gil Jonas.

"When my father had some money": Ibid.

"Would you prefer another infield position": "Robinson Confident of Brooklyn Pennant Success This Campaign," Lafayette High School newspaper, undated article from Gil Jonas scrapbook.

he snapped a picture of the athlete: Gil Jonas scrapbook.

"All hands agree now": "Robinson May Oust Stanky at Second Base," *New York Post,* April 22, 1947.

a few snippets of the invective: Robinson and Smith, *Jackie Robinson,* 128.

"Figuratively, he was still fighting the Civil War": Interview with Howie Schultz.

"For one wild and rage-crazed minute": Robinson, *I Never Had It Made,* 60.

"Listen, you yellow-bellied cowards": Ibid., 61.

561

Even Dixie Walker: Rowan and Robinson, *Wait Till Next Year,* 183.

The Sporting News *noted that all ballplayers:* "Jockeys Ride Every Rookie," *Sporting News,* May 21, 1947.

"We will treat Robinson the same": Tygiel, *Baseball's Great Experiment,* 183.

"Ballplayers who don't want to be in the same ball park": "Name Guilty in Robinson Plot," *Chicago Defender,* May 17, 1947.

"I didn't know people could be that cruel": Interview with Gil Jonas.

"I watched people who were hard-hearted": Ibid.

Chapter Six: praying for base hits

"Hiya, Babe": "... The 'Big Guy' of Baseball Comes Home," *New York Post,* April 28, 1947.

Bobby Thomson, a rookie: Interview with Bobby Thomson.

Nor was he interested in Robinson's color: Ibid.

"We knew he was pretty good": Ibid.

Louis waved to Robinson: "Stanky Bunt Beats Ottmen in 9th, 9–8," *New York Times,* April 28, 1947.

still in debt by about $200,000: Donald McRae, *Heroes Without a Country* (New York: Ecco, 2002), 242.

impressed by the sharpness of his mind: Rampersad, *Jackie Robinson,* 92.

presenting him with an autographed baseball: "From A to Z," *Richmond Afro-American,* May 3, 1947.

Photographers sprang from the dugout: Red Barber, *1947: When All Hell Broke Loose* (New York: Da Capo Press, 1982), 162.

tiny bedroom, eight-feet-by-twelve: Interview with Rachel Robinson; visit to 526 Mac-Donough.

Brown spent most of her waking hours: Interview with Rachel Robinson.

Finian's Rainbow *and* Brigadoon: Untitled, undated newspaper article from Rachel Robinson's scrapbook.

"I think sometimes people miss that part": Interview with Rachel Robinson.

Rachel would ask the sorts of questions: Ibid.

"like an elevator in the Empire State Building": Robinson and Smith, *Jackie Robinson,* 145.

gnashed his teeth: Interview with Rachel Robinson.

the only thing he ever admitted being worried about: Ibid.

Robinson wondered if he would see Schultz's name: Robinson and Smith, *Jackie Robinson,* 145–46.

Robinson worried: Ibid.

563

His biggest fear: Interview with Rachel Robinson.

Not one of them invited Jackie and Rachel: Ibid.

Norma King, the wife: Interview with Norma King.

Rachel had dreamed of the day: Interview with Rachel Robinson.

kneel by the side of their bed and pray: Ibid.

"Our approach was almost humorous": Interview with Colin Powell.

stopped taping it: "Dodgers Stay With Robinson," *New York Post,* May 1, 1947.

"that blacks weren't ready for the majors": Robinson, *I Never Had It Made,* 59.

"There were times": Ibid., 63.

"There were things some people take for granted": Interview with Rachel Robinson.

"Before I play with you": Leo Durocher, *Nice Guys Finish Last* (New York: Simon & Schuster, 1975), 206.

"Stanky, although he was from the South": Transcript of Rowan interview of Robinson, Library of Congress.

"That's a hit in my book": Barber, *1947,* 213.

"There's no reason to get all excited": "Dodgers Stay With Robinson," *New York Post,* May 1, 1947.

Chapter Seven: Cardinal Sins

two weeks to cut nine players: "Durocher to Help Rickey Cut 9 Dodgers Adrift by May 19," *Brooklyn Eagle,* May 3, 1947.

considerable sum of $250,000: "Pirates Purchase Higbe for Quarter of Million," *Daily News,* May 4, 1947.

"poverty and distress, want and sickness": "Boro Opens $650,000 Drive for N.Y. Fund," *Brooklyn Eagle,* May 2, 1947.

"I remember when I was a young boy": Peter Golenbock, *Bums* (New York: G.P. Putnam Sons, 1984), 149.

"That there's dissension on the club": "Cards' Poor Showing No. 1 Puzzle to Fans," *Daily News,* May 3, 1947.

"Sure, we're down in the dumps": "Cards Resolute Despite Slump," *Daily News,* May 4, 1947.

A milk-chugging, vitamin-popping: Interview with Marty Marion.

"I heard talk": Kahn, *The Era,* 56.

carving and smoothing the handles: Interview with Marty Marion.

"For me at the time": Kahn, *The Era,* 56.

"beat his gums": Notes from Tygiel interview with Bob Broeg.

"Tell them this is America": Ford Frick, *Games, Asterisks, and People* (New York: Crown Publishing, 1973), 97.

"I don't know how Sam delivered the message": Ibid.

"You know baseball players": Transcript of Jerome Holtzman interview of Frick.

Stanley Woodward broke the story: "Frick, Breadon Together Quash Anti-Negro Action," *Herald Tribune,* May 9, 1947.

"If you do this you will be suspended": Ibid.

a race riot had left one prisoner dead: "Race Riot Rages in Army Prison," *Brooklyn Eagle,* May 3, 1947.

school officials in Albany were battling: "Judge Voids School Ban on Robeson in Albany," *Brooklyn Eagle,* May 6, 1947.

Burt Shotton didn't believe it: "Check NL 'Robinson Strike,' " *Daily Mirror,* May 9, 1947.

"essentially right and factual": "Views of Baseball," *Herald Tribune,* May 10, 1947.

playing golf and chopping down trees: Durocher, *Nice Guys Finish Last,* 261.

"writers have been studiously trying to avoid": "Robinson Issue Must Be Faced and Settled," *Daily Mirror,* May 10, 1947.

"the presence of Negroes": "The First Negro Player Steps on the Scales," *Sporting News,* May 21, 1947.

"a big leaguer of ordinary ability": ". . . Lynch Mobs Don't Always Wear Hoods," *New York Post,* May 10, 1947.

"Man, they just don't pitch Jackie": "Dan Burley's Confidentially Yours," *Amsterdam News,* May 10, 1947.

He checked the lineup card: Robinson, *Jackie Robinson,* 145.

"the loneliest man": ". . . Lynch Mobs Don't Always Wear Hoods," *New York Post,* May 10, 1947.

Chapter Eight: The Great Road Trip

players read and discussed: Barber, *1947,* 176.

It hadn't occurred to Branca to ask: Interview with Branca.

"just can't bring the Nigger here": Parrott, *The Lords of Baseball,* 242.

Chandler had already been on the phone: "Report Robinson Asked Cops' Aid After Threats," *Daily News,* May 10, 1947.

"Jackie has been accepted in baseball": Ibid.

Freddy Schmidt, a pitcher: Interview with Schmidt.

"We voted not to play": David Falkner, *Great Time Coming* (New York: Touchstone, 1995), 165.

"Well, that's the end of Williams": Burt Solomon, *Baseball Timeline* (London: DK Publishing, 2001), 445.

"And don't bring your team back here": Parrott, *The Lords of Baseball,* 243.

he let the rest of the team check into: "Hotel 'Bars' Jackie in Philly," *Pittsburgh Courier,* May 17, 1947.

"At least two letters of a nature": "Robinson Reveals Written Threats," *New York Times,* May 10, 1947.

hearing rumors of threatening letters: "Report Robinson Asked Cops' Aid After Threats," *Daily News,* May 10, 1947.

"Mr. Rickey thought": Interview with Buzzie Bavasi.

"Some of the fellows may be riding Jackie": "Opposing Players Attempting to Avoid Taking Rap for Any Mishap to Jackie," *Sporting News,* May 21, 1947.

Chapman told his players: Interview with Schmidt.

"Jackie, you know": Ibid.

"I know what you are going thru": Library of Congress archives.

"I happen to be a white Southerner": Ibid.

"Saw you play in Wichita": Ibid.

"We are members": Ibid.

"Your decision to break": Ibid.

"I can't take it anymore": Tygiel, *Baseball's Great Experiment,* 169.

His mood darkened: Interview with Rachel Robinson.

He made little or no effort: "Jackie Will Get Equal Chance, Rest Up to Him," *Sporting*

News, May 21, 1947.

"He was the kind of person": Interview with Rachel Robinson.

"a loving send-off": Rampersad, *Jackie Robinson,* 180.

an R-17 instead of a G-7: Hillerich & Bradsby archives.

"He was under such pressure": Interview with Branca.

They appreciated the way he kept to himself: Interviews with Bragan, et al.

just so long as they respected him: Transcript of Rowan interview of Robinson, Library of Congress.

"I wasn't much in favor": Interview with Jack Banta.

"To be a Negro was to live": Sinclair Lewis, *Kingsblood Royal* (New York: Popular Library, 1947), 62.

Robinson preferred newspapers: Interview with Rachel Robinson.

"I happen to be a bit proud": Transcript of Rowan interview with Robinson, Library of Congress.

Chapter Nine: Tearing Up the Pea Patch

Some apartment buildings banned: "Apartment Houses Barring Video Sets," *New York Times,* February 13, 1947.

ten beers at ten cents a beer: "Game Challenged by Television's Growth," *Sporting News,* May 21, 1947.

manufacturers produced 20 million radios: Monthly reports, Radio-Electronics-Television Manufacturers, *TV Factbook #18,* January 15, 1954.

"Certain Aspects of Bovine Obstetrics": Bob Edwards, *Fridays With Red* (New York: Simon & Schuster, 1993), 35.

"one foot and five toes in the pickle bag": "Allen and Barber Give Fans Crisp, Colorful W.S. Airing," *Sporting News,* January 8, 1947.

"Well, I'll be a suck-egg mule": " 'Suck-Egg-Mule' Kicks Up Fuss, So Barber Explains," *Sporting News,* October 22, 1947.

a late lunch one afternoon: Barber, *1947,* 49.

"a fine young man": Ibid., 50.

"I'm going to bring a Negro": Ibid.

He dabbed some butter: Ibid.

"He had shaken me to my heels": Tygiel, *Baseball's Great Experiment,* 54.

"I'm going to quit": Jules Tygiel, editor, *The Jackie Robinson Reader* (New York: Dutton, 1997), 58.

"It tortured me": Ibid.

"Well, I said, I'm Southern": Ibid., 59.

"If I did do anything constructive": Ibid., 63.

Margot Hayward and her cousin: Interview with Margot Hayward.

"I always thought their lives": Ibid.

Little would sit next to his radio: Malcolm X, as told to Alex Haley, *The Autobiography of Malcolm X* (New York: Ballantine Books, 1965), 169.

"become something in life": Ibid., 35.

"It didn't bother my teammates": Ibid.

Glenn Miller's "Moonlight Serenade": Ibid., 36.

"Well, yes, sir, I've been thinking": Ibid., 43.

"Jackie Robinson had, then": Ibid., 179.

Chapter Ten: Pee Wee's Embrace

"If tens of thousands of black Southerners": Nicholas Lemann, *The Promised Land* (New York: Alfred A. Knopf, 1991), 51.

"Perhaps never in history": Ibid., 52.

"Police rookies patrol the streets": The WPA Guide to Cincinnati (The Cincinnati Historical Society, 1987), 224.

Robinson played cards: "Chandler Praises Jackie, Wishes Him Luck," *Richmond Afro-American,* May 17, 1947.

They played for no more than twenty-five cents: "Dugout Doings," *Pittsburgh Courier,* June 7, 1947.

William Mallory bussed tables: Interview with William Mallory.

many carried shoeboxes: Interviews with

571

Mallory, Donald Spencer, et al.

skies started to clear two hours before the game: "Dodgers Bow to Reds, 7–5," *Daily Mirror,* May 14, 1947.

"It was like a picnic, like a holiday": Interviews with Marian and Donald Spencer.

"The place was packed — all blacks": Interview with Eddie Erautt.

"I was warming up on the mound": Golenbock, *Bums,* 161.

"I saw the incident in Cincinnati": Interview with Lester Rodney.

"the toast of the town": "Dodgers' Pitchers in the Groove — Bullpen to Mound to Showers," *New York Post,* May 14, 1947.

"applauded every time he stepped": "Blackwell to Face Hatten Today; Tatum Goes Well in Debut Here," *Cincinnati Enquirer,* May 14, 1947.

"My father had done his own soul searching": "In Brooklyn, Honoring Men Who Did the Right Thing," *New York Times,* November 2, 2005.

"You know, I didn't particularly": "What Jackie Robinson Meant to an Old Friend," *New York Times,* July 17, 1977.

warm-up pitches sailed high: "Dodgers Glad to Escape Reds' Lair as Road Setbacks Increase," *Brooklyn Eagle,* May 15, 1947.

"Our team, baseballically speaking": "Rickey

Lauds Shotton, Team at Rotary Lunch," *Brooklyn Eagle,* June 5, 1947.

"It is true that I had stored": Robinson, *I Never Had It Made,* 80.

Chapter Eleven: The Glorious Crusade

not even to the beautiful young secretary: Interview with Wyonella Smith.

"a glorious crusade": W.E.B. DuBois, *Dusk of Dawn* (New York: Schocken Books, 1971), 130.

"Everybody was great to me": Transcript of Jerome Holtzman interview of Wendell Smith.

he was so affable: Interviews with Wyonella Smith and Will Robinson.

"I wish I could sign you, too, kid": "Wendell Smith — A Pioneer for Black Athletes," *Sporting News,* June 22, 1974.

He simply went home and cried: Interview with Wyonella Smith.

seventeen-dollar-a-week job: "Wendell Smith — A Pioneer for Black Athletes," *Sporting News,* June 22, 1974.

"While Hitler cripples the Jews": Hogan, *Shades of Glory,* 327.

"Have you seen any Negro ballplayers": Transcript of Holtzman interview of Wendell Smith.

the owners stared in silence: Ibid.

Smith would say he had phoned Muchnick: Ibid.

"wasn't necessarily the best player": Ibid.

"And when I said 'Jackie Robinson'": Ibid.

" 'Yes, he's a bad guy to get along with' ": Ibid.

"Now, Mr. Rickey": Letter from Smith to Rickey, Library of Congress.

"Through all of this": Transcript of Holtzman interview of Wendell Smith.

"Sure there was added pressure being Jewish": Hank Greenberg, *Hank Greenberg: The Story of My Life* (Chicago: Triumph Books, 2001), 110.

"That particular play": "The Sports Beat," *Pittsburgh Courier,* May 24, 1947.

"Hope I didn't hurt you": Ibid.

"Perhaps I do look bad on a curve": "Higbe Tackles Former Flock Mates Tonight," *Brooklyn Eagle,* May 16, 1947.

"The guys on the team are all for him": "The Sports Beat," *Pittsburgh Courier,* May 24, 1947.

Chapter Twelve: "A Smile of Almost Painful Joy"

"I Am an American Day": "Edw. G. Robinson in American Day Rally," *Chicago Herald American,* May 17, 1947.

Not since 1930: "Record 46,572 See Dodgers Beat Cubs, 4–2," *Chicago Tribune,*

May 19, 1947.

"Its Negro district is immense": St. Clair Drake and Horace R. Clayton, *Black Metropolis* (Chicago: University of Chicago Press, 1993), xxxv.

feeling as if he and his companions: "The Racial Gap in the Grandstands," *BusinessWeek,* October 2, 2006.

"It was so exciting": Interview with Bud Selig.

"The telephone booths are not men's wash rooms": "Through the Years," *Chicago Defender,* May 17, 1947.

143 *"As big as it was":* "Jackie's Debut a Unique Day," *Chicago Sun-Times,* October 25, 1972.

Afterward, thousands of black fans: Parrott, *The Lords of Baseball,* 266.

"as much depth as a shot of whiskey": "Dodgers' Hurling Woes Blamed on Rickey," *Daily News,* May 21, 1947.

spent the night at the home of: "The Sports Beat," *Pittsburgh Courier,* May 31, 1947.

"We didn't see much of him on the road": Interview with Gene Hermanski.

Almost every black celebrity: "Jesse Johnson, St. Louis Business Promoter, Dies," *Chicago Defender,* February 23, 1946.

about six thousand of them black: "Cardinal

575

'Health Resort' Makes Rivals Feel Better, Fans Worse," *St. Louis Post-Dispatch,* May 22, 1947.

"Robinson was cheered each time": Ibid.

"Watch this guy!": "The Sports Beat," *Pittsburgh Courier,* May 31, 1947.

Ralph Branca noticed: Interview with Branca.

Bobby Bragan, one of the opponents: Interview with Bragan.

Chapter Thirteen: Up and Down MacDonough Street

took their meals at a small table: Interview with Rachel Robinson.

their full-size bed neatly made: Ibid.

She felt important: Ibid.

Over on Ralph Avenue: City telephone directories; interviews with Rachel Robinson, Clarence L. Irving, et al.

She felt isolated at times: Interview with Rachel Robinson.

Rachel also noticed that her husband didn't like: Ibid.

turned to Thurgood Marshall of the NAACP: Letter from Robinson to Marshall, Library of Congress.

he would brag about how much of the twenty-five dollars remained: Interview with Rachel Robinson.

In Montreal, Jack and Rachel had each been: Rampersad, *Jackie Robinson,* 155.

He had made up his mind: Interview with Rachel Robinson.

she would offer a game of honeymoon bridge: Ibid.

"active listener": Ibid.

once he got going, he found: Ibid.

An old friend who was studying piano: "Mrs. Jackie Robinson," *Sports Illustrated,* May 1949.

Sometimes as a child she had felt: Interview with Rachel Robinson.

"The excitement, the joy": Ibid.

"We were very, very much in love": Ibid.

"a battle was underway for Harlem's patronage": "Robinson Pulls Fans From Negro Loop Game," *Daily Mirror,* May 29, 1947.

"if Booker T. Washington himself was playing": Ibid.

Sidney Poitier, twenty years old: Interview with Sidney Poitier.

on his feet, screaming: Interview with Hilton Clark.

The Covingtons were one of those families: Interviews with Rachel Robinson, Sharon Robinson, Clarence L. Irving, et al.

George Marchev, owner of the: Letter from Marchev to Rachel Robinson, Library of Congress.

Brown, the black man Marchev decided: Interviews with Freddie Palmisano and Edwina Gaiser-Marchev.

"Jackie Robinson opened the door of baseball": Copy of Marchev's prepared eulogy, Edwina Gaiser-Marchev.

Jewish workers filed 43 percent: Biondi, *To Stand and Fight,* 16.

"Why is this night different": Interview with Henry Foner.

"When Robinson came among us": "The Year of Years," *Daily News,* October 9, 2005.

The Orange Blossom was a new restaurant: Interviews with Clarence L. Irving, Delores Squires, et al.

"You have to remember something": Interview with Clarence L. Irving.

Chapter Fourteen: A Real Gone Guy

fans started screaming: "Reiser Hurt Crashing Wall; Flock Wins, 9–4," *Daily News,* June 5, 1947.

"Hell, fellas": "Flock Loses Reiser Services for Week," *Brooklyn Eagle,* June 5, 1947.

felt well enough to ask for a cigarette: "Reiser Hurt Crashing Wall; Flock Wins, 9–4," *Daily News,* June 5, 1947.

"What happened?": Ibid.

Rickey had been working out a deal: Mann, *The Jackie Robinson Story,* 104.

"How 'ya doin', Pete?": Interview with Bobby Bragan.

"Jackie's nimble": "Jackie Helps Dodgers Near Record Gate," *Pittsburgh Courier,* May 31, 1947.

the crowd rose to give Rachel and Jack Jr.: "Branca Wins in Relief Role, 6–5, After Losing, 3–1, to Cincinnati," *New York Times,* June 11, 1947.

2,000 Ladies Day "fanettes": "Robinson Bat Blazes as Flock Plays Dead," *Brooklyn Eagle,* June 12, 1947.

"in the charmed circle to stay": Ibid.

Bond Bread, which used: "Diamond Confetti," *Pittsburgh Courier,* May 31, 1947.

"The St. Louis Cardinals aren't only": "St. Louis Pilot, Players Friendly, Helpful to Jackie," *Pittsburgh Courier,* June 21, 1947.

"Boy, if you'd hit a home run today": Ibid.

"Did I spike you, Jackie?": Ibid.

"Listen, Robinson": Ibid.

collapse of the Roman empire: "Dodgers Collapse Result of Casualties," *Brooklyn Eagle,* June 16, 1947.

"Shotton's team as now constituted": Ibid.

"just a boy who doesn't know what a curveball is": "Dodgers Stop Cubs, 2–1, With Unearned Runs," *Daily News,* May 17, 1947.

when Snider complained about being made to bunt: Barber, *1947,* 156.

"I ache all over and now": "Reiser Passing Up Hospital to Aid Desperate Dodgers," *New York Post,* June 16, 1947.

knocked himself silly again: "Reiser — The Kid They Can't Miss," *Daily News,* June 17, 1947.

threatening to break his neck in a fair fight: "Three Cubs Fined After 2d Dodger Brawl," *Chicago Tribune,* May 24, 1946.

"I was on the bag, but I kind of leaned forward": Interview with Lennie Merullo.

Branch Rickey removed his coat: "Speed on Basepaths Gives Dodgers Well-Earned Verdict Over Bucs," *Brooklyn Eagle,* June 25, 1947.

Robinson's foot was wedged: Ibid.

Roth, too, was a rookie and an outsider: Interviews with Esther and Michael Roth.

Shotton became a believer: Prager, *The Echoing Green,* 183.

"I think that the other clubs": "Reiser's Dizzy Spells Worry Boss Rickey," *Brooklyn Eagle,* June 24, 1947.

"who would not fit into our plans": "Reiser Nerves Examined; Star Has Dizzy Spells," *Daily Mirror,* June 25, 1947.

"In all my years in baseball": "Reiser Flies to Johns Hopkins," *New York Post,* June 24, 1947.

"He is a major leaguer in every respect":

"Chapman Says Jackie Keeping Brooklyn in Race by Brilliant Playing," *Pittsburgh Courier,* June 28, 1947.

"He is 'one of the boys' ": Ibid.

"It is my deep conviction": "Truman Demands We Fight Harder to Spur Equality," *New York Times,* June 30, 1947.

"the presence of a Negro player": To Secure These Rights: The Report of the President's Committee on Civil Rights (Washington: U.S. Government Printing Office, 1947), 18.

"Say, Jackie": "Jackie Robinson: The Great Experiment," *Sport,* October 1948.

"joked and kidded with Jackie": "The Sports Beat," *Pittsburgh Courier,* June 28, 1947.

they never approached the story: Transcript of Jerome Holtzman interview of Wendell Smith.

"Bo Jangles of the Diamond": "Bo Jangles of the Diamond," *St. Louis Post-Dispatch,* June 29, 1947.

"The time has come": "Jackie Robinson Takes Lead Role as Dodgers Walk into the Lead," *St. Louis Post-Dispatch,* June 27, 1947.

Chapter Fifteen: A Good Thing for Everybody

Ben Chapman had been thoroughly cured: "Report Pirates, Phillies Seek Colored Stars," *New Jersey Afro-American,* July 5, 1947.

"We were delighted that Jackie had gotten": Interview with Monte Irvin.

"We were like janitors": Ibid.

He didn't feel like getting back to baseball: Ibid.

he felt a spark: Ibid.

"They pay our boy good": Roy Campanella, *It's Good to Be Alive* (Boston: Signet, 1974), 71.

"Mr. Rickey certainly was": Ibid., 106.

"I hear you went over": Ibid., 109.

Campanella sat dumbstruck: Ibid., 110.

"I had not the slightest doubt": Bill Veeck and Ed Linn, *Veeck as in Wreck* (Chicago: University of Chicago Press, 2001), 171.

"Judge Landis wasn't exactly shocked": Ibid.

"I moved slowly and carefully": Ibid., 175.

"I am operating under the belief": "Cleveland Buys Doby, 1st Negro in AL," *Daily News,* July 4, 1947.

"more surprised than excited": "Doby Helps Team Win Second Game," *New Jersey Afro-American,* July 12, 1947.

The team's two first basemen: Joseph Thomas

Moore, *Pride Against Prejudice* (New York: Praeger Publishers, 1988), 48.

two black men in jackets and ties: "Protection Unnecessary for Doby's Debut," *Sporting News,* July 16, 1947.

Pete Norton of the Tampa Tribune *warned:* "Dixie Action on Negroes Urged," *Sporting News,* July 16, 1947.

No one was buying it: "Two Negroes Play Tonight With Browns," *St. Louis Post-Dispatch,* July 17, 1947.

"A bunch of bums": Interview with Bob Dillinger.

Tom Baird, a white man: Lanctot, *Negro League Baseball,* 315.

Heath grabbed the piece of lumber: James A. Riley, *The Biographical Encyclopedia of the Negro Baseball Leagues* (New York: Carroll & Graf Publishers, 1994), 128.

"The Browns couldn't beat the Monarchs": Larry Moffi and Jonathan Kronstadt, *Crossing the Line* (Iowa City: University of Iowa Press, 1994), 14.

"We were apprehensive": Interview with Eddie Robinson.

"Doby wasn't prepared": Interview with Al Rosen.

"a complete bust": Veeck and Linn, *Veeck as in Wreck,* 177.

583

"There is considerable apprehension": "Sports Beat," *Pittsburgh Courier,* August 9, 1947.

white baseball had "no right to destroy": *New York Age,* November 17, 1945.

a $2-million-a-year business: Hogan, *Shades of Glory,* 343.

At Yankee Stadium, attendance: Lanctot, *Negro League Baseball,* 317.

a mere thirty-eight hundred fans: "Eagles Twice Lick Elites in Baltimore," *New Jersey Afro-American,* July 26, 1947.

"We'll hire any Negro player": "Big Leagues Scout 10 Negro Players," *Chicago Defender,* August 9, 1947.

"You doubled your ambition": Interview with Minnie Minoso.

Chapter Sixteen: The Poison Pen

he still wasn't even sure: "Between Two Put-outs," *New York Times,* January 8, 1957.

"You'd have thought the Dodgers": "Branca 1-Hitter Blanks Cards, 7–0, for Flock," *Daily News,* July 19, 1947.

Thirteen radio stations around the country: "14 Hits Trip Brooks," *New York Times,* July 20, 1947.

"I live in a small all negro town": Letter to Robinson, Library of Congress.

On occasion, a writer and his wife: Interviews

584

with Jack Lang and Lester Rodney.

2.4 million on weekdays: "Captain Bob's Amazing Eleventh-Hour Rescue," *Time,* March 25, 1991.

a city kid, born in Washington Heights: Golenbock, *Bums,* 299.

"the asshole of the Depression": Ibid.

On his fourth try, he was offered: Ibid., 300.

Powers ran it word for word: Ibid.

Labine challenged the writer: Ibid., 302.

"The ballplayers called him Poison Pen": Interview with Jack Lang.

"This story belongs on page three": "Giants Massacre Flock, 19–2, On 15-Hit Barrage; Gain 2d," *Daily News,* July 4, 1947.

"Wally Westlake, which is a baseball player": "Bucks Top Flock in 2, Westlake Drives in 7 Runs in First," *Daily News,* July 16, 1947.

The headline in the Daily News *went:* "Dodgers Rout Lively, 12–1; 16th for Branca," *Daily News,* July 23, 1947.

"His legs are agile, his hands sure": "Dodgers Beat Cards — In Raising Rookies," *Daily News,* July 27, 1947.

"Eef I have my good arm": David Maraniss, *Clemente* (New York: Simon & Schuster, 2006), 248.

"I am positive": Transcript of Rowan interview of Robinson, Library of Congress.

585

Chapter Seventeen: The Unbeatable Yankees

offered DiMaggio to the woeful: Richard Ben Cramer, *Joe DiMaggio: The Hero's Life* (New York: Simon & Schuster, 2000), 223.

the heel injury jolted Joe in the worst way: Ibid., 227.

"Greatest left-handed hitter I've ever seen": Halberstam, *Summer of '49,* 45.

he told manager Bucky Harris: Cramer, *Joe DiMaggio,* 228.

"political and social-minded drum beaters": Tygiel, *Baseball's Great Experiment,* 83.

Not until they found a black man worthy: Ibid., 224–25.

Some began skipping the flights: "Yanks in Player Revolts; DiMaggio Reported Fined," *Brooklyn Eagle,* May 22, 1947.

MacPhail sent a newsreel crew on the field: "Six Yanks Balk at Publicity Stunts, Fined by M'Phail," *New York Post,* May 22, 1947.

Butler-Mitchell Boys Club collected $1.03: "Buffalo Boys' Pennies Reduce DiMaggio's Fine," *New York Times,* May 24, 1947.

"It would be goin' over the shortstop's head": Cramer, *Joe DiMaggio,* 230.

certain that his teammates distrusted: Ibid., 230–31.

586

Suddenly, Page found a focus: Ibid., 231.

dressing like his roommate: Ibid., 230–31.

Had Page failed that day: "Page's Pitching Major Surprise of Campaign," *New York Post,* July 11, 1947.

Chapter Eighteen: Dixie Walker's Dilemma

was on the training table: "Robinson Wins in Uphill Battle for Teammates' OK," *Boston Daily,* June 28, 1947.

"You're improving a lot": Ibid.

"best friend and chief adviser": Vincent X. Flaherty column, *Los Angeles Examiner,* July 12, 1947.

"Some sports writers fall for anything": Rachel Robinson scrapbook.

Robinson said that Walker was the only man: Transcript of Rowan interview of Robinson, Library of Congress.

There was a faint sense: Interviews with Branca, King, et al.

What was the point of playing: Golenbock, *Bums,* 216.

"You fellas can win the pennant": Ibid., 169.

"Put Burt on a bench": "About a 2d Stringer Named Burt Shotton," *Brooklyn Eagle,* July 30, 1947.

Myron Uhlberg received two tickets: Interview with Myron Uhlberg.

"It's not even baseball": Ibid.

a smattering of racist cries: "Sidelights on the Dodger-Cardinal Series," *Pittsburgh Courier,* August 9, 1947.

white men with standing-room-only tickets: Ibid.

"this summer of our Lord 1947": "Here to Yonder," *Chicago Defender,* August 9, 1947.

Chapter Nineteen: The Footsteps of Enos "Country" Slaughter

Wilder lived in Richmond: Margaret Edds, *Claiming the Dream* (Chapel Hill: Algonquin Books, 1990), 21.

the St. Louis Cardinals were his biggest worry: Interview with Douglas Wilder.

"the arguingest little man": Edds, *Claiming the Dream,* 29.

middle seat in the back: Interview with Wilder.

Yet Doug had not given much thought: Ibid.

"Wow!" said the kid: Ibid.

"They have to beat us": "Showdown Series at Hand as Cardinals Face Dodgers," *New York Post,* August 18, 1947.

one curve for every three fastballs: Alan Roth scorecards, Retrosheet, Inc.

"He just thinks too much": "Bucs Get Quick Chill, 3–1; Branca Wins 18th," *Daily News,* August 25, 1947.

Wilder and the barbershop quartet: Interview with Wilder.

"Hit da ball, Jackie boy! Hit da ball!": Ibid.

"I was shocked": Ibid.

"What else could it have been?": "Slaughter's 'Mis-step' Draw's Robbie's Fire," *New York Post,* August 21, 1947.

"Jackie was lucky he wasn't maimed": Ibid.

Harold Parrott, the team secretary: Ibid.

"It took me the better part": Interview with Wilder.

Only four times: "Rookie of the Year . . . Jackie Robinson," *Sporting News,* September 17, 1947.

"No other player on this club": Ibid.

Bankhead became the inspiration for Troy Maxson: Riley, *The Biographical Encyclopedia of the Negro Baseball Leagues,* 54.

"Call me if I can help": "Heavy Pressure on Bankhead," *New York Post,* August 26, 1947.

"It was as though he had been hit by Joe Gluttz": "Pirates Overwhelm Flock, 16–3; Bankhead Routed, Hits HR," *Daily News,* August 27, 1947.

"It was just one of those days": "Bankhead's Failure in Bow Discounted," *New York Post,* August 27, 1947.

Garagiola called fastball after fastball: Interview with Joe Garagiola.

Robinson said he did: Robinson and Smith, *Jackie Robinson,* 158; interview with Garagiola.

He appeared to laugh: Photograph, *Sporting News,* September 24, 1947.

He grabbed Robinson's hand: "Jackie's Clutch Playing Thaws Flocks' Reserve," *Daily News,* September 16, 1947.

"I bet Robinson just a hit a home run": "Sports Train," *People's Voice,* September 20, 1947.

"Was that you, Papa?": Interview with Garagiola.

As the Dodgers jogged off the field: "Dodgers Win, 8–7, Take Card Series," *New York Times,* September 14, 1947; interview with Branca.

"last bit of passive but ever-apparent": "Jackie's Clutch Playing Thaws Flocks' Reserve," *Daily News,* September 16, 1947.

"In selecting the outstanding rookie of 1947": "Rookie of the Year . . . Jackie Robinson," *Sporting News,* September 17, 1947.

gifts that would include a new Cadillac: "Jackie Robinson Given Auto, Wrist Watch, Money," *Chicago Defender,* October 4, 1947.

a Jackie Robinson movie and a Jackie Robinson vaudeville show: "Jackie Robinson Takes to Radio, Personal Tours," *Chicago*

Defender, September 20, 1947.

ten thousand dollars for Robinson to play: "Globetrotters Make For Jackie Robinson," *Chicago Defender,* October 4, 1947.

"It's been a long time since we've had one man": "Grimm Convinced Robinson is 'Slick' Operator," *St. Louis Argus,* September 12, 1947.

what Robinson really deserved was a bigger payday: "The Powerhouse," *Daily News,* September 23, 1947.

As researcher Henry Fetter has noted: "Robinson in 1947: Measuring an Uncertain Impact," *Jackie Robinson: Race, Sports, and the American Dream* (Armonk, NY: M.E. Sharpe, 1998), 183–92.

"Our Bums will make bums of the Yankees": "Brooks Welcomed By a Happy Crowd," *New York Times,* September 20, 1947.

"There's no use going across the East River": "Brooks Are Champs at Last," *New York Post,* September 23, 1947.

As the Dodgers stepped down: "Reese, Robinson Caught in Jam at N.Y. Station," *Sporting News,* October 1, 1947.

"I'm tickled silly": "Conquering Bums Return as Faithful Go Nertz," *Daily News,* September 20, 1947.

Chapter Twenty: Shadow Dancing

Robinson had no trouble sleeping now: Interview with Rachel Robinson.

only the two most popular men: "Paper Snowstorm Falls on Players," *New York Times,* September 27, 1947.

Mallie Robinson flew in: "Jackie's Wife Busy Calming Jumpy Kin," *New York Post,* September 30, 1947; " 'He's Successful Son, Too,' Jackie's Ma Says of Him," *Chicago Defender,* October 11, 1947.

the mothers stayed with Florence: Interview with Rachel Robinson.

Jack and Rachel felt enough a part: Ibid.

The intensity of the emotions fascinated her: Ibid.

The winners of the Series would get: "Series Swag Misses Record; Yankees' Full Cut Put at $5,800," *Daily Mirror,* October 11, 1947.

134 prominent black out-of-towners: "Sports Fans Swarm Into New York to Watch Jackie Star in Series," *Chicago Defender,* October 11, 1947.

"all to see this great boy Robinson": Ibid.

"Why, we could put on": "Shotton Picks Flock to Capture Series," *Brooklyn Eagle,* September 27, 1947.

He not only predicted victory: "Shotton Set on Starting Hurlers — Lombardi Will Follow Branca," *New York Post,* September 27, 1947.

"The New York Yankees should win": "Experience Gives Yankees Edge Over Dodgers in World Series," *Herald Tribune,* September 28, 1947.

"Only one thing remains": "The Sports Parade," *New York Post,* September 24, 1947.

a called strike from Spec Shea: "Durocher Has His Day, Shakes Hands with Hap," *Daily Mirror,* October 1, 1947.

25,000 or so watching from nearby rooftops: "Cross-Section of U.S. Sees Opener of Classic," *Daily Mirror,* October 1, 1947.

Fifty thousand television sets: "The News of Radio," *New York Times,* October 10, 1947.

One watering hole in Flatbush: "Young Mound Aces Slated for Action," *New York Times,* September 30, 1947.

At the Park Avenue Theatre: "1st Televised World's Series Game Nips Broadway Theatre B.O. by 50%," *Variety,* October 1, 1947.

When Judge Samuel S. Liebowitz heard: "Series Fever Grips Court," *New York Times,* October 1, 1947.

When President Truman was asked: "Truman to Pass Series; Has Too Much to

593

Do," *Chicago Tribune,* September 26, 1947.

Twenty-two men worked the cameras: "In the Wake of the News," *Chicago Tribune,* October 1, 1947.

New, more powerful camera lenses: "Baseball on Video," *New York Times,* October 5, 1947.

"To the individual before a television screen": Ibid.

no problem picking up Robinson: "By the Way," *Los Angeles Times,* October 3, 1947.

Robinson had a smile on his face: "A Mother Looks On," *New York Post,* October 1, 1947.

Mallie Robinson strained: Ibid.

saw her lips form the words: Ibid.

"I know all about Robinson": "Yankees Deride Dodgers' Bunt and Run Attack," *Chicago Tribune,* September 30, 1947.

"If I had an arm like that": "First Game Gossip," *Sporting News,* October 8, 1947.

throwing a ball from home plate into a barrel: "Fourth Game Gossip," *Sporting News,* October 15, 1947.

he bolted for third before he could see: Movie reel footage.

"hithering and thithering": "By the Way," *Los Angeles Times,* October 3, 1947.

Shea, in at least one: "Clinical Notes on

First Game," *Brooklyn Eagle,* October 1, 1947.

Shea picked up the ball and slammed it angrily: Movie reel footage.

"For the first time in my life": "The Other Side," *Chicago Defender,* October 11, 1947.

"You'll go wild!": "Powerhouse," *Daily News,* October 2, 1947.

They bought him a savings bond: Golenbock, *Bums,* 194.

"You don't think I was scared": "Dodgers Unawed by Yankee 'Might,' " *Daily News,* October 1, 1947.

"This is one defeat that gave us confidence": Ibid.

"Yes": "Shotton's New Suit and Bow Tie Fail to Change Dodgers' Style," *Herald Tribune,* October 2, 1947.

Chapter Twenty-One: "We Aren't Afraid"

Ted Williams showed up: "This Morning With Shirley Povich," *Washington Post,* October, 5, 1947.

their team bus pelted with eggs: Interview with Ralph Houk.

"bored and contemptuous": "Views of Sport," *Herald Tribune,* October 2, 1947.

"All right, Pete": "Inside Story of an Inning That Hit the Peak of Drama," *Sporting*

News, October 15, 1947.

Bevens made up his mind: "Lavagetto Mussed Up by Dodgers; Yanks Funereal, Bev Near Tears," *Daily News,* October 4, 1947.

Men edged forward: "Cookie's Rap Turns No-Hit Loss Into Dodger Victory," *Sporting News,* October 15, 1947.

Lavagetto knew that Bevens: Golenbock, *Bums,* 178.

Bevens inhaled, checked the runner: Movie reel footage.

Lavagetto grimaced and swung: Ibid.

"We had it all the way": "Mad Dodgers Maul Cookie; Harris Defends Reiser Walk," *Daily Mirror,* October 4, 1947.

"You got one yesterday": Golenbock, *Bums,* 178.

Lavagetto was looking for a slider: Ibid.

he would also remember the strikeout: Ibid., 179.

"He was our best player": Interview with Bobby Bragan.

"They got no class": "Yank Jockeys Anger Jackie," *People's Voice,* October 11, 1947.

The ball was out of Rizzuto's hands: Movie reel footage.

He felt as if his knees: Interview with Bragan.

Bragan's father didn't notice: Notes from Tygiel interview of Johnny Jorgensen, Baseball Hall of Fame.

"What's that little Italian's name?": Golenbock, *Bums,* 179.

"a good drive in a Buick": Ibid.

he felt uneasy about it: Ibid., 181.

Nothing in his life had ever felt so good: "Gionfriddo Got Thrill of Lifetime Making Catch," *Brooklyn Eagle,* September 6, 1947.

"I guess I hit a few harder": "Just Dropped Into Glove, Explains Al Gionfriddo," *Daily Mirror,* October 6, 1947.

Even Gionfriddo admitted: "Gionfriddo Got Thrill of Lifetime Making Catch," *Brooklyn Eagle,* September 6, 1947.

"They are more uniquely American": "The World Series," *New York Times,* October 7, 1947.

"Whether the Dodgers win or lose now": "Robbie Bats .296, Fields Brilliantly," *Pittsburgh Courier,* October 11, 1947.

Chapter Twenty-Two: "And the World Series Is Over!"

made up his mind to throw no curves: "It's Page, Page, Page for the Jack, Jack, Jack, After the Fray," *Daily Mirror,* October 7, 1947.

With each pitch, Page became more convinced: Ibid.

Yankee Stadium was awash in sunshine: "Yanks Champs! Trim Flock, 5–2; MacPhail Retires From Baseball," *Daily News,* October 7, 1947.

Page threw one last fastball: Ibid.

"It's a double play!": "Dodger Clubhouse Heartbreak Hotel," *Daily Mirror,* October 7, 1947.

took a baseball out of his glove: Ibid.

This wasn't the time or place: Barber, *1947,* 360.

"We got beat": "Dodger Clubhouse Heartbreak Hotel," *Daily Mirror,* October 7, 1947.

The broadcaster shook hands: Barber, *1947,* 357.

scuffed-up baseball in his right hand: Robinson and Smith, *Jackie Robinson,* 141.

"We lost": "Bums Swear Revenge," *People's Voice,* October 11, 1947.

They told him he played a fine game of ball: Robinson and Smith, *Jackie Robinson,* 169.

Epilogue

three thousand dollars a week plus: "GAC Setting Up Dates For Jackie Robinson, Negro Ball Player," *Variety,* September 24, 1947.

knew that professional athletes: "Jackie Asks

for Fans' Advice on '48 Pay, Gets '$20,000' Reply," *Sporting News,* November 12, 1947.

"Everyone on the team treated me swell": "Jackie Playing to Sellouts; May Net 5 Grand a Week," *Sporting News,* October 29, 1947.

"disgusted and ashamed": Baltimore Afro-American, November 1, 1947.

counseled Robinson to stick to baseball: "Through the Years," *Chicago Defender,* November 22, 1947.

"We'd pull off the road": Rampersad, *Jackie Robinson,* 191.

he usually ate big plates: Ibid., 192.

"We ate like pigs": Robinson, *I Never Had It Made,* 71.

"What in the world happened to you?": Pittsburgh Courier, March 13, 1948.

Robinson was angry: Rampersad, *Jackie Robinson,* 192.

Business was fine at his hardware store: Interviews with Geri Worley, Jack Courson, et al.

placed a call to Walker: "Walker Has Few Regrets," *New York Times,* December 9, 1947.

"Naturally, I regret leaving Brooklyn": Ibid.

"I grew up in the South": "Dixie Walker Remembers," *New York Times,* December

10, 1981.

"This guy didn't just come to play": Roger Kahn, *Boys of Summer* (New York: Harper & Row, 1971), 393.

"unless Jim Crow disappeared": Rampersad, *Jackie Robinson,* 214.

"A psalm-singing faker": John C. Chalberg, *Rickey & Robinson: The Preacher, the Player, and America's Game* (Wheeling, Ill.: Harlan Davidson, Inc., 2000), 150.

"The more I read about the Montgomery situation": Rampersad, *Jackie Robinson,* 287.

His knees and ankles hurt all the time: Ibid., 299.

business there was not good: Ibid., 252.

construction business had so far: Ibid., 299.

He thought about managing: Ibid.

"Why Can't I Manage in the Majors?": Ibid., 300.

The job paid thirty thousand dollars: Ibid., 304.

he had never seen his wife happier: Rampersad, *Jackie Robinson,* 361.

"There I was the black grandson": Robinson, *I Never Had It Made,* xxii.

"talk like he's colored": Rampersad, *Jackie Robinson,* 424.

Ron Rapoport called the hotel: Interview with Ron Rapoport.

"The light hurts my eyes": "Jackie Died Hop-

ing MLB Would See the Light," *Chicago Sun-Times,* April 19, 2005.

"I honestly believe that baseball": "Jackie Robinson Seeks and Finds Sensitivity," *Los Angeles Times,* June 5, 1972.

The ball struck him painfully: "Jackie Died Hoping MLB Would See the Light," *Chicago Sun-Times,* April 19, 2005.

"I wish Branch Rickey could be here": "Jackie Wants to See Black Man Managing," *Los Angeles Times,* October 16, 1972.

"His courage, his sense of brotherhood": "Nixon, in Tribute, Cites Robinson's Courage, Brilliance," *New York Times,* October 25, 1972.

"a trailblazer for all black people": Ibid.

"the unconquerable doing the impossible": "Death of an Unconquerable Man," *New York Times,* October 24, 1972.

"I'm as sad as could possibly be": "Nixon, in Tribute, Cites Robinson's Courage, Brilliance," *New York Times,* October 25, 1972.

ABOUT THE AUTHOR

Jonathan Eig is a senior special writer for *The Wall Street Journal* based in Chicago. He was formerly executive editor of *Chicago* magazine. He is the author of *Luckiest Man: The Life and Death of Lou Gehrig.*

The employees of Thorndike Press hope you have enjoyed this Large Print book. All our Thorndike and Wheeler Large Print titles are designed for easy reading, and all our books are made to last. Other Thorndike Press Large Print books are available at your library, through selected bookstores, or directly from us.

For information about titles, please call:
(800) 223-1244

or visit our Web site at:
www.gale.com/thorndike
www.gale.com/wheeler

To share your comments, please write:
Publisher
Thorndike Press
295 Kennedy Memorial Drive
Waterville, ME 04901